Yale French Studies

NUMBERS 118 & 119

Noeuds de mémoire: Multidirectional Memory in Postwar French and Francophone Culture

MICHAEL ROTHBERG, DEBARATI SANYAL, AND MAX SILVERMAN	1	Editors' Note: *Noeuds de mémoire,* Multidirectional Memory in Postwar French and Francophone Culture
MICHAEL ROTHBERG	3	Introduction: Between Memory and Memory, From *Lieux de mémoire* to *Noeuds de mémoire*

I. Tortured Histories

JIM HOUSE	15	Memory and the Creation of Solidarity During the Decolonization of Algeria
ROSS CHAMBERS	39	The Long Howl: Serial Torture
DEBARATI SANYAL	52	Crabwalk History: Torture, Allegory, and Memory in Sartre

II. Entangled Lives

ESTELLE TARICA	75	Jewish Mysticism and the Ethics of Decolonization in André Schwarz-Bart
RONNIE SCHARFMAN	91	Reciprocal Hauntings: Imagining Slavery and the Shoah in Caryl Phillips and André and Simone Schwarz-Bart
FRANÇOISE LIONNET	111	"Dire *exactement*": Remembering the Interwoven Lives of Jewish Deportees and Coolie Descendants in 1940s Mauritius
FRANÇOISE VERGÈS	136	Wandering Souls and Returning Ghosts: Writing the History of the Dispossessed
DAVID CARON	155	Tactful Encounters: AIDS, the Holocaust, and the Problematics of Bearing Witness

III. Visual Traces

ELIZABETH EZRA	177	Cléo's Masks: Regimes of Objectification in the French New Wave
BILL MARSHALL	191	Of Cones and Pyramids: Deleuzian Film Theory and Historical Memory
LIBBY SAXTON	209	Horror by Analogy: Paradigmatic Aesthetics in Nicolas Klotz and Elisabeth Perceval's *La question humaine*
MAX SILVERMAN	225	Memory Traces: Patrick Chamoiseau and Rodolphe Hammadi's *Guyane: Traces-mémoires du bagne*

Yale French Studies

Michael Rothberg, Debarati Sanyal, and Max Silverman,
   Special editors for this issue
Alyson Waters, *Managing editor*
Editorial board: Thomas Kavanagh (Chair), R. Howard
   Bloch, Jessica DeVos, Edwin Duval, Awendela
   Grantham, Alice Kaplan, Christopher L. Miller,
   Jean-Jacques Poucel, Maurice Samuels, Yue Zhuo
Assistant editor: T. Chapman Wing
Editorial office: 82-90 Wall Street, Room 308
Mailing address: P.O. Box 208251, New Haven,
   Connecticut 06520-8251
Sales and subscription office:
Yale University Press, P.O. Box 209040
New Haven, Connecticut 06520-9040
Published twice annually by Yale University Press

Copyright © 2010 by Yale University
All rights reserved.
This book may not be reproduced, in whole or in part,
   in any form (beyond that copying permitted by
   Sections 107 and 108 of the U.S. Copyright Law and
   except by reviewers for the public press), without
   written permission from the publisher.

Designed by James J. Johnson and set in Trump
   Medieval Roman by The Composing Room of
   Michigan, Inc. Printed in the United States of
   America by Sheridan Books, Ann Arbor, Michigan.

ISSN 044-0078
ISBN for this issue 978-0-300-11885-8

MICHAEL ROTHBERG, DEBARATI
SANYAL, AND MAX SILVERMAN

Editors' Note: *Noeuds de mémoire*
Multidirectional Memory in Postwar French and Francophone Culture

This volume considers the emergence of a multidirectional conception of history and memory in modern French and Francophone cultural production and proposes new models and metaphors for the heterogeneity and circulation of histories in contemporary cultures of remembrance. The volume is specifically concerned with postwar approaches to the past that bring disparate histories of violence into relation with one another and, in so doing, illuminate the dynamic and palimpsestic structure of collective memory. Despite the memory boom of the 1990s and the attendant rise of trauma theory in the past decades, there remains a tendency to consider traumatic events—and the Holocaust in particular—as singular, incomparable, and unrepresentable. The radical singularity of the Holocaust remains something of a critical doxa, even though the Nazi genocide continues to generate hermeneutic models that have illuminated other histories such as the Algerian war or the genocide in Rwanda. Thus, although thinkers such as Hannah Arendt, Aimé Césaire, and Frantz Fanon forged links between the Nazi genocide and colonialism in the immediate aftermath of World War II, scholars in French and Francophone Studies have until recently rarely addressed the historical, representational, and commemorative connections between the Holocaust and other legacies of racialized violence. This is in part due to the taboo on invidious comparisons between the Holocaust and other genocides, but also because entrenched disciplinary boundaries between national histories, literatures, and fields (such as the compartmentalization of Holocaust Studies and Postcolonial theory or French and Francophone Studies) have discouraged such research programs.

The articles here seek to move beyond reified structures of discipline and field in order to reopen the question of cultural memory in a transnational age. Without relativizing the singularity of diverse histories of violence, this volume probes the points of contact between the memories and legacies of genocide, colonialism, and slavery in a world defined both by decolonization and the aftermath of the Shoah. The volume thus contributes to the emergence of a pluralized conception of history and memory, one that investigates the points of contact between distinct legacies of historical trauma, and in so doing, illuminates the layered structure and unpredictable energy of collective memory.

MICHAEL ROTHBERG

Introduction: Between Memory and Memory
From *Lieux de mémoire* to *Noeuds de mémoire*

It would be impossible to overstate the influence of Pierre Nora's massive, multi-part *Lieux de mémoire* project, a series of volumes that conjoins rich contributions to an understanding of France and French culture with an innovative methodology for studying collective memory.[1] In the quarter century since the first volume was published in 1984—and in the two decades since Nora's introduction to the project first appeared in English in 1989—the concept of the "lieu de mémoire" or "site of memory" has been at the center not just of considerations of French negotiations with its national past but of studies of remembrance on an international scale. Drawing our attention to the way the past finds articulation in a wide array of "sites"—considered broadly to include not only monuments and museums, but also novels, cities, personages, symbols, and more—Nora's project has inspired reflection and scholarship on national memory in Germany, Italy, the Netherlands, and Spain, among other places.[2] Although emerging from a commitment to the exceptionality of France's relation to its national past, the approach pioneered in *Les lieux de mémoire* has proven highly exportable as a model for the consideration of diverse memory cultures.

 1. *Les lieux de mémoire*, ed. Pierre Nora (Paris: Gallimard, 1984–1992). In English: *Realms of Memory: The Construction of the French Past*, 3 volumes, under the direction of Pierre Nora, English Language edition ed. Lawrence D. Kritzman, trans. Arthur Goldhammer (New York: Columbia UP, 1996–1998); and *Rethinking France*, under the direction of Pierre Nora, trans. Mary Trouille (Chicago: University of Chicago Press, 2001–2006).
 2. On the translation of the *Lieux de mémoire* project into other languages and national contexts, see Pim den Boer, "Loci memoriae—Lieux de mémoire," *Cultural Memory Studies: An International and Interdisciplinary Handbook*, ed. Astrid Erll and Ansgar Nünning in collaboration with Sara B. Young (Berlin and New York: Walter de Gruyter, 2008), 19–25.

YFS 118/119, *Noeuds de mémoire*, ed. Rothberg, Sanyal, and Silverman, © 2010 by Yale University.

Yet, almost from the beginning and despite hailing Nora's project as an unprecedented scholarly achievement, critics have lodged a variety of complaints against both Nora's conceptualization of memory and the scope of the *Lieux de mémoire* volumes. One consistent set of criticisms has targeted Nora's polarization of history and memory and his seemingly progressive narrative of the former's eclipsing of the latter—hence, the central irony that a project that has helped stimulate a boom in the study of memory is premised on the demise of memory! As Nora polemically insisted in the first paragraph of his programmatic general introduction "Between Memory and History," "Memory is constantly on our lips because it no longer exists." In this story of an "accelerati[ng] history" overtaking "[t]he equilibrium between the present and the past," *lieux de mémoire* play a transitional role and serve as the "sites" of a "residual sense of continuity": "*Lieux de mémoire* exist because there are no longer *milieux de mémoire*, settings in which memory is a real part of everyday experience" (*Realms* 1: 1). As this nostalgia-tinged tale of decline indicates, Nora's innovative rewriting of the French past from a nonlinear, "site-specific" perspective remains indebted to a rather traditional teleological view of modernity. What he repeatedly calls "real" or "true" memory appears to give way to the artificial reconstructions of postmodern memory sites divorced from any organic community of remembrance. Without denying the profound transformations in the present's relationship to the past—in its "time-sense" or historical consciousness—it remains worth asking whether binary oppositions between history and memory or the real and the artificial can account for contemporary cultures of memory and new modes of transmission of the past.[3]

A second strand of criticism reveals the stakes of Nora's commitment to a linear and binarized account of history and memory. Notwithstanding Nora's avowed interest in a "polyphonic" approach (*Realms* 1.xxiii), the collection ultimately puts forward a starkly limited conception of the nation purged of many of its imperial adventures and minoritarian inflections—purged, in short, of phenomena that trouble the linear narrative of historical progress and the stark opposition between history and memory. Despite an emphasis on the

---

3. On the time-sense of modernity and postmodernity, see, respectively, Reinhart Koselleck, *Futures Past: On the Semantics of Historical Time* (New York: Columbia University Press, 2004); and Fredric Jameson, *Postmodernism, or, the Cultural Logic of Late Capitalism* (Durham: Duke University Press, 1992). Jameson is, as is well known, dubious about the state of historical consciousness in postmodernity.

local and the heterogeneous—on what volume three of *Les lieux de mémoire* calls "Les France"—the project has surprising absences. Of course, any attempt at an encyclopedic representation of a nation-state will generate an immediate list of overlooked features and will fail to encompass many histories that certain critics will find essential. Yet, the gaps in Nora's sites of memory appear particularly glaring. In a long and largely appreciative review, for instance, Tony Judt observed the "bizarre" fact that "there is no entry in any of the volumes of *Les lieux de mémoire* on either Napoleon Bonaparte or his nephew Louis Napoleon, or even on the political tradition of *bonapartisme* that they bequeathed to the nation." Such an oversight, Judt clarifies, not only ignores the extent to which France remains tied to "the spirit of Napoleon" and the "imperial ambitions" of the Bonapartes, but also suggests that Nora's project cuts itself off from "Europe as a whole," whose sites of memory "could [not] possibly neglect" Napoleon's "battles, his laws, his depredations, his unintended impact on resentful national sensibilities in the Low Countries, Italy, and Germany."[4] Even more sharply—and more relevantly to our project in this volume —Perry Anderson has pointed out that the effect of the project's admitted "Gallocentrism" and its seeming unease with certain social divisions has been that "the entire imperial history of the country, from the Napoleonic conquests through the plunder of Algeria under the July Monarchy, to the seizure of Indochina in the Second Empire, and the vast African booty of the Third Republic, becomes a *non-lieu* at the bar of these bland recollections." As Anderson asks with respect to one of the turning points of the era of decolonization, "What are the *lieux de mémoire* that fail to include Dienbienphu?"[5] In the selected (but still massive) English version of Nora's collective project, the three-volume *Realms of Memory*, the scope of the sites considered narrows even further in its focus on the Hexagon, with the effect that "the contests and conflicts that are so amply documented in the collection are not about France per se but about the nature of its national identity," in the words of Hue-Tam Ho Tai.[6] Despite its debt to

4. Tony Judt, "A la Recherche du Temps Perdu," *New York Review of Books* (December 3, 1998), 54.
5. Perry Anderson, *The New Old World* (New York: Verso, 2009), 161–62.
6. Hue-Tam Ho Tai, "Remembered Realms: Pierre Nora and French National Memory," *American Historical Review* 106/3 (June 2001): 910. Tai's essay provides an excellent review of the project as a whole and also focuses on differences between the French and English versions. Another useful account of *Les lieux de mémoire* can be found in Anne Whitehead, *Memory* (New York: Routledge, 2009), 141–47.

new directions in critical historiography, the project under Nora's direction ends up reproducing a reified and ironically celebratory image of the nation-state it set out to deconstruct, as even he seemed to recognize in his afterword "The Era of Commemoration" (*Realms* 3: 609–37).[7]

This volume of *Yale French Studies* both takes inspiration from Nora's magisterial project of turning critical attention to processes of remembrance in modernity and shares many of the concerns critics have raised about that project's limits—its overly schematic approach to the history/memory couplet, its nostalgic plotting of loss, its reduction of Frenchness to the Hexagon, and, especially, its elision of France's long and complex colonial and postcolonial history.[8] From an Anglo-American perspective, where postcolonial studies and various forms of minority critique have had a significant presence in the academy for more than two decades, *Les lieux de mémoire*'s amnesiac relation to French colonial history and to the impact of decolonization and postcolonial migrations is startling—even more so when we consider Nora's personal engagement during the Algerian War of Independence and his devastating book on French Algerians.[9] But here Nora is probably more symptomatic than unique. French society in general has been slow to respond to the "fracture coloniale" recently

---

7. In that afterword, Nora writes: "the very dynamics of commemoration have been turned around; the memorial model has triumphed over the historical model and ushered in a new, unpredictable, and capricious use of the past—a past that has lost its peremptory and constraining organic character" (*Realms* 3, 618). Here we see a replay of the organic/inauthentic and history/memory binaries from the introduction. We also have a foretaste of the increasingly aggressive position Nora will take through his involvement in the "Liberté pour l'histoire" movement (also discussed by Françoise Vergès in this volume) and in his comments on the "terrorist" nature of the countermemory of minority groups. See Pierre Nora and Françoise Chandernagor, *Liberté pour l'histoire* (Paris: CNRS, 2008); and Jacques Buob and Alain Frachon, "'La France est malade de sa mémoire': Pierre Nora et le métier d'historien," in "Colonies: Un débat français," *Le monde 2* (May–June 2006): 6–9.

8. This volume grows out of conversation and collaboration between the editors over the past two years. Besides taking part in this collective project, each editor has also been at work on his or her own investigation of "knots of memory" within and beyond French and Francophone culture. See Michael Rothberg, *Multidirectional Memory: Remembering the Holocaust in the Age of Decolonization* (Stanford: Stanford University Press, 2009); Debarati Sanyal, "Auschwitz as Allegory in Night and Fog," *Concentrationary Cinema: Aesthetics as Political Resistance in Alain Resnais's "Night and Fog,"* ed. Griselda Pollock and Max Silverman (Berghahn, 2010); and Max Silverman, "Interconnected Histories: Holocaust and Empire in the Cultural Imaginary," *French Studies* 62/4 (2008): 417–28; as well as forthcoming book-length projects by Sanyal and Silverman.

9. See Pierre Nora, *Les Français d'Algérie* (Paris: Julliard, 1961).

diagnosed by progressive French critics, even as—further irony—Anglo-American postcolonial studies marks an enormous debt to anti- and postcolonial Francophone thinkers and writers such as Aimé Césaire, Frantz Fanon, Léopold Sédar Senghor, and, more recently, Maryse Condé and Édouard Glissant.[10]

Inspired by those thinkers and others, we seek to offer a counter-image of memory that does not merely take an "additive" approach. Attempting to fill in the gaps and silences of Nora's volume is not an adequate response to its limits; while such a project is necessary, it is somewhat different from what we have attempted here. Our volume starts from the assumption that more than a quantitative supplement is needed; rather, the limits of *Les lieux de mémoire* suggest the necessity of a new model—or models—of remembrance. In calling for such a new approach under the sign of "noeuds de mémoire"—knots of memory—we hope to stimulate further conceptualization of collective or cultural memory beyond the framework of the imagined community of the nation-state.[11] Nora's project derives in part from Maurice Halbwachs's contention that there are as many memories as there are groups, but that each group possesses a coherent language of remembrance—such a methodological *parti pris* leads to the result that the heterogeneity of "les France" gives way to an implicitly restricted notion of a homogenized France stripped of its colonies and the ongoing legacies of colonialism. A project oriented around *noeuds de mémoire*, on the other hand, makes no assumptions about the content of communities or their memories. Rather, it suggests that "knotted" in all places and acts of memory are rhizomatic networks of temporality and cultural reference that exceed attempts at territorialization (whether at the local or national level) and identitarian reduction. Performances of memory may well have territorializing or identity-forming effects, but those effects will always be contingent and open to resignification.

The project of rethinking French and Francophone sites of memory as *noeuds de mémoire* traces its inspiration to many sources, but, ap-

---

10. The allusion here is to the pathbreaking collection *La fracture coloniale: La société française au prisme de l'héritage colonial*, ed. Pascal Blanchard, Nicolas Bancel, and Sandrine Lemaire (Paris: La Découverte, 2006).

11. As den Boer points out, *Knoten* [knots] is one of the words Nora offers as a possible translation of *lieux* into German in his contribution to a volume on German sites [*Orte*] of memory. Despite this suggestion, however, we would still argue that Nora's practice is more singular than the metaphor of knots as we use it here is meant to imply.

propriately enough for such a non-nationalist project, one of the most important predecessors has been an Anglophone critic, Paul Gilroy. His 1993 book *The Black Atlantic: Modernity and Double Consciousness* helped break the national frame of minority critique by promoting an African diasporic perspective that, crucially, refused any temptation of "ethnic absolutism" and thus concluded by staging an extended dialogue about the overlapping traumatic legacies of Atlantic slavery and the Nazi genocide of European Jews. Without traducing the specificity of either of these complex and painful histories, Gilroy opened up a space in which to explore the mutual imbrication of black and Jewish counter-cultures of remembrance.[12] In his follow-up volume, *Against Race: Imagining Political Culture Beyond the Color Line* (2000), known in the UK by the more suggestive title *Between Camps: Nations, Cultures, and the Allure of Race*, Gilroy continues to develop his cosmopolitan project by considering precisely those Francophone black Atlantic intellectuals, like Césaire and Fanon, who testified both to the ongoing catastrophe of colonialism and to the events—which they saw as related—of the Nazi genocide. "Why," Gilroy asks, "does it remain so difficult for so many people to accept the knotted intersection of histories produced by this fusion of horizons?"[13] In the decade since Gilroy posed this question, much has changed—but much has also stayed the same. Even as critics—including those represented in this volume—have begun to explore the "knotted intersections" of history and memory that cut across categories of national and ethnic identity, institutions of knowledge-production, nation-states, and many embattled communities continue to disavow the evidence of cosmopolitan impurity.

Noeuds de mémoire as we conceive them here are not static conglomerations of heterogeneous elements. As James Young and others have taught us, sites of memory do not remember by themselves—they require the active agency of individuals and publics.[14] Such agency entails recognizing and revealing the production of memory as an ongoing process involving inscription and reinscription, coding and

---

12. Paul Gilroy, *The Black Atlantic: Modernity and Double Consciousness* (Cambridge: Harvard University Press, 1993). See especially the final chapter "'Not a Story to Pass On': Living Memory and the Slave Sublime," 187–223.

13. Gilroy, *Against Race: Imagining Political Culture Beyond the Color Line* (Cambridge: Harvard UP, 2000), 78.

14. James Young, *The Texture of Memory: Holocaust Memorials and Meaning* (New Haven: Yale UP, 1993).

recoding. Max Silverman's discussion of Patrick Chamoiseau and Rodolphe Hamadi's notion of "memory traces" illustrates such a production; in Silverman's intertextual reading, which closes our volume, the poetic means employed by the writer and the photographer reconfigure the ruins of the penal colony in French Guyana as a transnational palimpsest of uncanny associations. Silverman's essay joins those by Ross Chambers, Françoise Lionnet, Libby Saxton, and Debarati Sanyal in looking to prison or camp spaces as particularly resonant knots or nodes of memory—although all are careful not to reproduce a facile notion of the camp as the "nomos" or paradigm of a totalized modernity, as Giorgio Agamben's important and influential work risks doing.[15]

In attempting to conceptualize the knotted nature of collective memory, Halbwachs's notion of the "social frameworks of memory" remains an important starting point because it breaks the commonsense, methodological individualism of much study of memory.[16] However, the metaphor of the framework may fail to capture the dynamism inherent in remembering—what we call memory's multidirectionality. As several of the essays collected here illustrate, memory emerges from unexpected, multidirectional encounters—encounters between diverse pasts and a conflictual present, to be sure, but also between different agents or catalysts of memory. *Noeuds de mémoire* are not particular to the post-1945 period—the primary focus of our volume—but there can be no doubt that the dynamics of decolonization, transnational capital, and globalized media in the twentieth and twenty-first centuries have accelerated the flow of the materials of memory across borders of all kinds and multiplied the possibilities of encountering alterity. Focusing especially on the technologies of modernity in a US context, cultural historian Alison Landsberg has argued that, "in a global cultural economy, the theory of collective memory as articulated by Halbwachs seems inadequate, for the very notion of global flows challenges the idea of stable shared frameworks." Contrary to Nora's lament about the loss of authentic memory cultures, however, Landsberg suggests—and many of our contributors confirm—that the dislocation of cultures in modernity is productive of novel forms of memory, which Landsberg deems "pros-

---

15. See Giorgio Agamben, *Homo Sacer: Sovereign Power and Bare Life*, trans. Daniel Heller-Roazen (Stanford: Stanford UP, 1998).
16. Maurice Halbwachs, *Les cadres sociaux de la mémoire* (Paris: PUF, 1952).

thetic memories": "Mass culture has had the unexpected effect of making group-specific cultural memories available to a diverse and varied populace. In other words, this new form of memory does not, like many forms of memory that preceded it, simply reinforce a particular group's identity by sharing memories. Instead, it opens up those memories and identities to persons from radically different backgrounds."[17] Elizabeth Ezra's account in this volume of masks in the films of the Nouvelle Vague confirms Landsberg's insight about the possibilities of the prosthetic. Ezra shows how masks and other artifacts serve as indexes of intersecting regimes of objectification, which allows her to illustrate how mass cultural commodification does not simply stamp out difference but can also provoke unexpected juxtapositions. As history and modernity "accelerate," in Nora's terms, memory does not recede, but rather pluralizes and blurs the boundaries of identity; such pluralization and blurring need not be coded as loss.

Referring to Nora's introductory account of the replacement of "real" *milieux de mémoire* by "forgetful" *lieux de mémoire*, Dominick LaCapra has argued that Nora's polarized conceptions of memory and history and of authenticity and artificiality as well as his narrative of decline testify to a sense of loss at the same time that they represent a fetishistic "neutralization of trauma": "Nora feels that something essential has been lost, and—whether or not the loss is itself imaginary—the very opposition between history and memory serves to commemorate and assuage it."[18] Neither sites nor knots of memory are necessarily limited to the evocation of trauma, yet as LaCapra suggests in his response to Nora, traumatic histories are often at stake in modern modes of remembrance, even if those modes sometimes disavow rupture.[19] Readers will note the proximity of memory

17. Alison Landsberg, *Prosthetic Memory: The Transformation of American Remembrance in the Age of Mass Culture* (New York: Columbia University Press, 2004), 10–11.

18. Dominick LaCapra, *History and Memory after Auschwitz* (Ithaca: Cornell University Press, 1998), 18–19.

19. In his lucid, nuanced genealogy of the trauma paradigm, Roger Luckhurst takes inspiration from Bruno Latour and considers the concept of trauma as itself a "knot," a "hybrid assemblage" that "tangle[s] up questions of science, law, technology, capitalism, politics, medicine and risk." Focusing, as the contributors to this volume do, on knots of traumatic memory thus facilitates a particularly fruitful approach to central issues in French and Francophone culture, one that can move both horizontally across the social field and vertically through disparate layers of history. See Roger Luckhurst, *The Trauma Question* (London and New York: Routledge, 2008), 14–15.

and trauma in the contemporary French and Francophone—indeed, global—knots of memory explored here, but this proximity also raises a number of difficult and unavoidable methodological problems central to this volume's intervention.

First, it is necessary to acknowledge Kristin Ross's critical observation in her exemplary study *May '68 and Its Afterlives* that the obsession in memory studies with traumatic histories can threaten to displace other kinds of memory—in particular, memories of collective mobilization—with potentially deleterious, depoliticizing results.[20] While Ross is certainly correct that memory studies has skewed toward the study of catastrophe instead of toward alternative political possibilities, her separation of trauma and politics may nonetheless simplify the multidirectional dynamics of collective memory. The case of André Schwarz-Bart, for instance—considered here, via different critical lenses, by Ronnie Scharfman and Estelle Tarica—provides one telling example of how a deep investment in confronting trauma opens up a space for new imaginations of relation across difference, in this case for an imagination that links the Shoah with the legacies of slavery and colonialism in the Caribbean (which makes Schwarz-Bart another predecessor for Gilroy's cosmopolitan project). Solidarity, in other words, is a frequent—if not guaranteed—outcome of the remembrance of suffering, as Jim House's survey of imaginative and biographical links between French and Algerian antiracist and anticolonial activists illustrates powerfully.[21]

Ross adds a second, legitimate concern to her critique of the contemporary configuration of memory studies, a concern shared by the scholar and memory activist Françoise Vergès in her reflections for this volume: not only has trauma predominated over politics, but memory of the Holocaust has predominated over that of all other traumatic histories. According to some hypothetical quantitative criterion, it is certainly arguable that the Nazi genocide of Jews has—at least since the late 1970s—been the object of some of the most developed cultures of memory both in the French-speaking world and elsewhere in Europe and North America. But again, the evidence considered here complicates the picture. From the early response of French intellectuals such as Alain Resnais, Henri Alleg, and Jean-Paul Sartre

    20. Kristin Ross, *May '68 and Its Afterlives* (Chicago: University of Chicago Press, 2004).
    21. See also Jenny Edkins, *Trauma and the Memory of Politics* (New York: Cambridge University Press, 2003).

(the subjects of essays in this volume by Ross Chambers and Debarati Sanyal), which merged opposition to the French war in Algeria to a nascent memory of Nazi genocide, to more recent transnational links such as those found in *Le dernier frère*, Nathacha Appanah's 2007 novel of almost forgotten Mauritian Holocaust memory, considered here by Françoise Lionnet, memory of the Holocaust has emerged in dialogue with—has grown out of and contributed to—memory of slavery, colonialism, and other human-made catastrophes. The contributions to this volume confirm that memory does not obey the restricted economy of the zero-sum game, but emerges in a general, productive economy of relays and ricochets, as Bill Marshall's Deleuze-inspired considerations of cinematic remembrance suggestively illustrate. Some of these multidirectional interventions may be more ethical than strictly political insofar as they focus on the reconceptualization of contact with alterity, as David Caron does here under the sign of "tact" in juxtaposing an AIDS memoir with a journal of the Nazi Occupation. Other examples, however, come even closer to the model of politics Ross has in mind: Libby Saxton, for example, considers an explicitly politicized invocation of the Holocaust at the multidirectional confluence of neoliberal globalization and anti-immigrant policy in her detailed account of Nicolas Klotz and Elisabeth Perceval's controversial film *La question humaine* (*Heartbeat Detector*, 2007).

No singular model of *noeuds de mémoire* emerges from this volume—nor was it intended to. Rather, in issuing a call to leading scholars of contemporary French and Francophone literature and culture to contribute to a multidirectional approach to memory, we have sought to open up new, yet-to-be created avenues for the study of the times and places of remembrance. New modes of associative reading and—as some of the contributions suggest—new modes of writing will be required that do not so much abandon as transgress the norms of disciplinary knowledge production. The transnational approach to collective memory requires a collaborative methodology, for once remembrance is freed from the (never actually) homogenous space-time of the nation-state, potential links and references multiply beyond the grasp of any one scholar. Although this volume ranges from metropolitan France across the Atlantic to the Caribbean and back toward Africa and the Indian Ocean, it makes no attempts at comprehensiveness: future knots of memory remain to be untied.

I. Tortured Histories

JIM HOUSE

Memory and the Creation of Solidarity During the Decolonization of Algeria[1]

In November 1960, Armand Dymenstajn, a senior-ranking member of the French antiracist association the MRAP—the Movement against Racism, Anti-Semitism and for Peace—wrote the following in his organization's newspaper:

> In more than one respect the situation of Algerians in France recalls that of Jews during the Occupation. No special sign exists for Algerians like the yellow star—there is no need, the police round-ups show that. But as for the rest: there is a curfew for Algerians, they come under a special police force, and can be certain neither of the permanency of their homes, nor of their jobs due to being banned from different parts of France, and due to internment.[2]

The MRAP established a series of connections between the treatment of Jews during the Occupation and that of Algerians by successive French regimes. This article examines some of these links made by individuals and antiracist and anticolonial groups between anti-Semitism, the Holocaust, and fascism on the one hand, and forms of colonial racism and domination on the other, with particular reference to the drawn-out process of decolonization in Algeria and its impact in "metropolitan" France.

In so doing, I seek to examine the "space" that exists between events, processes, and forms of domination that are certainly similar, but that are not identical. This "similarity in difference" is nonetheless sufficient to encourage people—whether from groups suffering

---

1. I would like to thank Neil MacMaster, Neelam Srivastava, Anne Whitehead, and the editors for their comments on earlier versions of this essay.
2. "La condition des Algériens en France," *Droit et liberté* 194 (November 1960): 6. All translations are my own.

racial domination or otherwise—to engage in various forms of political or humanitarian identification and solidarity with (other) groups who are experiencing such domination, as a powerful mechanism to build and reinforce practices of resistance.

This essay first examines why, how, and in what context the connections such as those by Dymenstajn in the above quotation were made in the period before the October 1961 anti-Algerian police violence in Paris.[3] However, Algerian resistance, colonial state violence, and anti-Semitism are all key components of Franco-Algerian colonial history going back many decades before World War II. So in fact, the experiences of World War II inflect, rather than create *ex nihilo*, the conditions of possibility within which some metropolitan French people would make such parallels, and elaborate discourses and practices of political and ethical solidarity with Algerians. Nonetheless, we will see that the rhetorical idiom of protest immediately prior and subsequent to the October 1961 events was very much grounded in themes that were often specific to the post-1945 context before being further shaped by the evolving Algerian war-time situation. This longer-term approach is also designed to bring out the multidirectional memories[4] that often form the backdrop to a political engagement by some French people "with Algerians" and that I examine in the final section. Throughout, this article examines how particular historical events, and the subsequent personal, semi-public and public memories that these events generate, are articulated and intertwined.

ANTIRACISM BEFORE 1945

While elements of French Republican antiracism evolved after 1945 toward a wider conception of what racism was, where racism came from, and how it should be fought, we need to go back to the 1930s to better understand both the innovations and the continuities after 1945.

Republican antiracism emerged during the Dreyfus Affair to defend Republican values against challenges from the anti-Semitic forces mostly situated on the anti-Republican Right. One of the key legacies of the Dreyfus Affair in the 1920s and 1930s was therefore a defini-

---

3. See Jim House and Neil MacMaster, *Paris 1961: Algerians, State Terror, and Memory* (Oxford: Oxford University Press, 2006).
4. See Michael Rothberg, *Multidirectional Memory: Remembering the Holocaust in The Age of Decolonization* (Stanford: Stanford University Press, 2009).

tion of racism that centered upon anti-Semitism: in the 1930s, anti-Semitism was the key form of racism against which groups such as the LICA (International League Against Anti-Semitism)—founded in 1928—and the French Human Rights League (LDH, created in 1898 during the Dreyfus Affair itself), both operated.

In the 1930s, for these groups, as for many others, anti-Semitism derived from fascism: fighting racism and fighting fascism were considered to belong to the same process, hence these groups supported the Popular Front. However, beyond fleeting collaborative enterprises immediately prior to and during the Popular Front, this "Republican antifascism" existed in a tense relationship with Algerian nationalism and other radical anticolonial groups more generally, as it would do after 1945:[5] after 1935, the united antifascist front led the French Communist Party (PCF) away from its initially radical anticolonialism, since the PCF—like the LICA—believed that keeping Algeria French would strengthen the fight against Nazism.[6] In brief, for many French left-wing organizations that denounced racism in the 1930s, antifascism and anticolonialism were therefore far from going hand-in-hand. There was thus a tension between the espousal of universal themes such as opposition to racism, and the problem that France's colonial enterprise was structurally discriminatory against particular groups.

Furthermore, in the 1930s, the idea of there being a plurality of racisms that all needed combating made little headway, just as the idea of there being a French "colonial racism" had little success within Republican antiracism. Indeed, both the LICA and the LDH talked openly of France's "civilizing mission." The LICA, for example, only included consideration of colonial racism in the context of widespread anti-Semitism among the European settlers in colonial Algeria, Morocco, and Tunisia.[7] In effect, a further complicating factor was that Algerian nationalism, despite its denunciation of all forms of racism, at times had recourse to anti-Semitism.[8] Such examples show that the

5. See Catherine Lloyd, *Discourses of Antiracism in France* (Aldershot: Ashgate, 1998), 106–107.
6. Jonathan Derrick, *Africa's "Agitators": Militant Anticolonialism in Africa and the West, 1918–1939* (London: Hurst, 2008), 326, 350–55.
7. See House, "Antiracism in France, 1898–1962. Modernity and Beyond," *Rethinking Antiracisms. From Theory to Practice*, ed. Floya Anthias and Cathie Lloyd (London: Routledge, 2002), 111–27.
8. Rabah Aissaoui, *Immigration and National Identity: North African Political Movements in Colonial and Postcolonial France* (London: I.B. Tauris, 2009), 107–109.

"Jewish" and "colonial" histories are not separate experiences: as in Morocco and Tunisia, Jews in colonial Algeria existed in a complex political "space," caught between opportunistic European far-right politics and popular anti-Semitism within elements of the Muslim Arab-Berber communities.

If Republican antiracism before 1945 therefore presupposed a certain mode of thinking about what racism was (principally anti-Semitism), it also had a restrictive and restricting definition of where it mostly came from: anti-Republican political movements. Such groups thus refrained from criticizing the Republican state. There was considerable difference between this position and that of many radical anticolonial groups formed by the colonized themselves: such groups stressed that racism was all pervasive, and an intrinsic component of the colonial system and hence of the colonial state and society. Such groups espoused a more transversal fight against colonial racism, based on a trans-imperial, often diasporic imaginary that was often articulated within the idiom of Marxism.[9] However, for such groups, fighting anti-Semitism was rarely a priority. Before 1939, beyond very general antiracist declarations formulated within a Republican register, the number of links made between colonial racism and anti-Semitism was therefore limited, restricting the possibilities for a more transversal antiracism.

NEW FORMS OF ANTIRACISM AFTER 1945 AND THE EMERGENCE OF A RADICAL COMPARATIVISM

In the immediate postwar period, antiracist activists in France realized that the defeat of Nazism and the Occupation would not signal the end of an anti-Semitism that was widespread throughout French society. This feeling was reinforced by the inadequacies of the postwar judicial purges, followed by amnesties in the early 1950s.[10] Antiracist activists therefore promoted the well-established antifascist logic of vigilance against a return of fascism, just as the postwar period saw a re-affirmation of Republican values: at the time, the institutionalized racism practiced by Vichy was not considered to have been the work of Republican institutions, but of their very antithesis, the Nazi occu-

---

9. See Philippe Dewitte, *Les mouvements nègres en France 1919–1939* (Paris: L'Harmattan, 1985).
10. See Stéphane Gacon, *L'Amnistie: de la Commune à la guerre d'Algérie* (Paris: Seuil, 2002), 211–51.

pier. Importantly, the late 1940s also saw the re-affirmation of French imperialism.

Yet in many other respects, the experiences of the Holocaust (as it would later come to be called), of anti-Nazi Resistance, and the considerable increase in Algerian migration and Algerian nationalist organization in France, each in their own way, began to transform some sectors of Republican antiracism: the result was a broader, and more complex, antiracist landscape, as can be seen by an analysis of the pro-Communist antiracist association the MRAP that both reflected and promoted this change.

In 1947, the Antiracist Alliance had been created, aiming for a more inclusive antiracism both in terms of the ideological belonging of activists and the broader definitional approach to racism. As the Alliance's Gérard Rosenthal declared in 1948: "antiracism must extend its realm of action to include all manifestations of racism."[11] However, the Alliance could not survive the new Cold War dynamic within French politics of the late 1940s. Formed in 1949, the MRAP emerged from the break-up of this short-lived Alliance and was made up of mostly Jewish former Resistance activists from the National Movement Against Racism that had underlined the need for solidarity between Jews and non-Jews to oppose Nazism. MRAP activists were generally from working-class and/or immigrant backgrounds, and they often defined themselves in relation to the re-formed, anti-Communist LICA.[12] Bernard Lecache, the leader of the LICA, would try, unsuccessfully, to open out his re-formed association to accept a similarly more pluralistic definition of racism.

The MRAP thus emerged in a context of division within the antiracist movement. It immediately sought to be ethnically inclusive, and, while initially the vast majority of the MRAP's members were Jewish, Aimé Césaire was also involved.[13] The MRAP's innovative campaigning stemmed from the specific context of a rise in anti-Algerian hostility in the late 1940s, and the forms taken by the French police's repression of the popular MTLD (Movement for the Triumph of Democratic Freedoms) organization, the forerunner of the FLN.

---

11. *Rapport sur la question noire* (Paris: Congrès national de l'alliance antiraciste, 1948), 1.

12. Albert Lévy, *Mémoire du MRAP*, speech given on October 16, 1993, 3.

13. African American musicians, singers, and entertainers figured prominently in MRAP events: Babe Wallace sang in Yiddish at one fund-raiser in October 1950. See *Droit et Liberté* 45 (October 13–19, 1950): 1, 3.

From its inception, the MRAP started to use the theme "colonial racism," accepting that there was a plurality of racisms and, importantly for what will follow, that colonialism bred racism. This was a significant departure from the pre-1939 period, as we have seen. The MRAP's Marxist-inspired analysis of the exploitation of colonial immigrant labor certainly helped this identification.

Notwithstanding this plurality and diversity of forms of racism, the MRAP argued that, for the means of mobilization, all racisms had to be considered as inseparable. Albert Lévy, one of the MRAP's founders, refers to the MRAP's conception of the "unity in diversity" of racism.[14] It followed from this that Jews should support other racialized groups and help anticolonial movements. If forms of racism were inseparable, the MRAP argued, there was also the latent possibility that one form of racism would come to target other groups. Such arguments therefore encouraged "collective solidarity for persecuted groups."[15] The MRAP's predictions soon appeared accurate, since the anti-Semitic Poujadist movement, which gained strength from 1953 onward, increasingly adopted an anti-Algerian stance in this key transitional decade during which "Vichy" and "Algerian War" generations on the far-right would come to co-exist.[16]

The MRAP's antiracist definitions and conceptualizations called for new solidarities between Jews and Arab-Berber Algerians, as mass police round-ups of Algerians became common-place at MTLD street protests: 1,127 Algerian demonstrators were arrested on September 17, 1950, for example. In its press release, the MRAP judged that "the most terrible racism governed these operations. These methods recall the arrests based on facial appearance undertaken by the corps of police 'specialists' set up by the traitors PUCHEU and Xavier-VALLAT to look for Jews [during Vichy]."[17] The MRAP also produced posters, one saying: "Like in the dark days of the Occupation / Racist round-ups in Paris / . . . the police picked out their victims according to their facial appearance."[18] Another MRAP poster made even more explicit the analogy with Nazi Occupation and the Holocaust:

14. Author's interview with Albert Lévy, Paris, September 18, 1995.
15. Lloyd, *Discourses of Antiracism*, 113. As Lloyd shows (*Ibid.*, 137, 143), the MRAP combined reference "back" to the Holocaust with references to other on-going forms of oppression, such as anti-black racism in the USA (and the struggles against it).
16. See Romain Souillac, *Le mouvement Poujade: de la défense professionnelle au populisme nationaliste (1953–1962)* (Paris: Presses de Sciences Po, 2007).
17. MRAP Archives, Paris, resolution dated September 19, 1950.
18. *Droit et liberté* 42 (September 22–28, 1950): 3.

This spectacular deployment of repressive forces, these arbitrary arrests, this awful racism are all directly inspired by the means used by the Nazi occupier and its agents. The cries of "dirty wog" that were heard during the police operations are like those of "dirty Jew" that the Vichy police came out with when they were handing over the thousands of innocent people into Deportation and the gas chambers.[19]

However, the MRAP's calls for an end to such policing methods fell on deaf ears: some 10,000 Algerians were stopped in Paris on December 8, 1951, for example. The MRAP's Albert Lévy then popularized the term *chasse au faciès* to describe the way in which the security forces picked out potential "suspects" on the basis of supposed facial characteristics. In a speech given in 1993, Lévy explained how he had seen thousands of Algerians prevented from attending the December 8, 1951 rally at the Vél' d'Hiv' stadium where the MTLD was to be joined by the United Nations ambassadors from Arab countries: the Vél' d'Hiv' was used during the infamous July 16, 1942 Vichy round-up of "foreign" Jews, and thus invested with particular memorial symbolism within antiracist communities. Lévy had first come across the use of the term *chasse au faciès* by defendants during the trial he had followed in 1949 of those having worked for the dedicated anti-Jewish section of the police (*Police aux Questions Juives*) of the Vichy regime, to explain how they sought to identify "Jews" during the police round-ups. This "administrative and pseudo-scientific expression" struck Lévy, and henceforth the MRAP newspaper (for which Lévy wrote) adopted it in its campaigning. As he explained: "this was how the terms invented under the Nazis to describe anti-Jewish operations were used after the war to characterize those targeting Arabs."[20]

It should be noted that the MRAP's position asserted that the means used by the State to detain and "police" Algerians were similar to those used against Jews during the Occupation, and that the same police personnel was often implicated. The MRAP was not saying that the ends pursued by these arrests were the same, nor that Vichy was the Republic: indeed MRAP calls the Vichy police "traitors."[21] However, while the MRAP was therefore hoping to play on the memory of forms of solidarity resulting from anti-Nazi Resistance,

19. MRAP Archives, Paris.
20. Lévy, *Mémoire du MRAP*, 7.
21. See Rothberg, *Multidirectional Memory*, 243.

this aim was often thwarted by the existence of a deep-seated anti-Algerian racism, exacerbated by the repression of Algerian nationalism both before[22] and after 1954.

Indeed, in January 1958, the MRAP's newspaper gave the following, sarcastic example: "one of our friends, a Jewish primary school teacher, told us the other day that he'd been stopped coming out of the metro station during a police round-up of Algerians. The shape of his face had made him a 'suspect': the detective was probably acting a few years too late."[23]

In fact, there were many cases of "mistaken identity" of this type during the war, including the writer Gabriel García Marquez, and other foreign nationals (as opposed to Algerians and those from the French Antilles, who were French citizens), who were arrested and then brutalized by police, creating concern within many "non-white" groups across France and a trans-ethnic memory of suffering that has yet to be studied. Such repression drew Moroccans, Algerians, Tunisians, and Antilleans[24] in France closer together, and also affected African Americans and South Americans.

On August 28, 1958, as the FLN started violent attacks on targets in metropolitan France for the first time, the Vél' d'Hiv' and Japy gymnasium were requisitioned for use after a series of police round-ups of Algerians, thus providing opponents of this policy with a further symbolic link with the Vichy use of the sites to detain Jews prior to deportation.[25]

The solidarity that the MRAP expressed with Algerians was largely a result of the direct experiences of racism suffered under the Nazi occupation by the MRAP activists and their families, notably those who had lived in central Paris and who had been victims of, or witnessed, the police round-ups and the everyday fear these induced. We can also see an example of Paul Gilroy's suggestion to set histories of racism in relation to each other.[26] Such a radical comparative and solidaristic

---

22. On July 14, 1953, the Paris police fatally shot six Algerian nationalists (and one French trade unionist) at a demonstration at Place de la Nation. See Maurice Rajsfus, *1953: un 14 juillet sanglant* (Paris: Agnès Viénot Editions, 2003).
23. "Au faciès, " *Droit et liberté* 169 (January 1958): 2.
24. See Raoul Capitant, "Après l'Algérie, les Antilles," *Matouba (Revue des étudiants antillais de la Guadeloupe et de la Martinique)* 2 (April 1962): 1–2.
25. See Jean-Luc Einaudi, *La bataille de Paris* (Paris: Seuil, 1991), 52–53.
26. See Paul Gilroy, *The Black Atlantic: Modernity and Double Consciousness* (London: Verso, 1993), 213–17 and Gilroy, *Between Camps: Race, Identity and Nationalism at the End of the Colour Line* (London: Allen Lane, 2000).

antiracism might come from staying in the same place (Paris). It might also stem from geographical displacement, as we can see with Frantz Fanon: his early trajectory from the Caribbean to Paris and Lyon via North Africa as a soldier and then student is perhaps emblematic in this respect.[27]

Through the MRAP's discourse of the need for solidarity between different groups targeted by racism, we can see the development of what Pnina Werbner describes as "antiracists as a community of suffering [who] can, potentially, evolve their own counter-discourses and self-identifications in the political arena," as a means of transcending their different ethnicities.[28] Gilroy has also commented on Fredric Jameson's judgment on the need not to collapse different experiences of racism into each other, but rather to consider parallels on the level of "a more primary experience, namely that of fear and vulnerability."[29] The above quotations from the MRAP arguably echo these experiential similarities between Jews and Arab-Berber Algerians (and other groups) in France, and highlight the way in which exclusionary practices of the State come to affect different groups.

Connections established between Nazi Occupation and the repression of Algerians were therefore commonplace within at least one prominent association well before the outbreak of the Algerian war in 1954, suggesting the existence of an established rhetorical idiom within sectors of the French left from which various groups would subsequently draw in their critique of anti-Algerian policies, a syncretic rhetoric in which antifascism would also play an important role.

However, such campaigning by the MRAP was not devoid of tensions that we will see resurfacing across the French left after the October 1961 violence. Firstly, while the MRAP could identify with Algerians as victims of racism, the question of Algerian independence proved a very thorny issue both for the association and the French Communist Party (PCF). Demanding equality for Algerians as fellow citizens, as the MRAP did, was a much less radical stance than demanding independence for Algeria.

27. Jim House, "Colonial Racisms in the 'Métropole': Reading *Peau noire, masques blancs* in Context," in *Frantz Fanon's* Black Skin, White Masks. *New Interdisciplnary Essays*, ed. Max Silverman (Manchester: Manchester University Press, 2005), 46–73.

28. "Essentializing Essentialism, Essentializing Silence: Ambivalence and Multiplicity in the Constructions of Racism and Ethnicity," in *Debating Cultural Hybridity*, ed. Pnina Werbner and Tariq Modood (London: Zed Books, 1997), 242.

29. Gilroy, *The Black Atlantic*, 206.

Secondly, while it is easy to understand the painful reminders of repressive state *savoir-faire* that post-1945 police round-ups would have provoked in those having suffered Vichy persecution (the MRAP commemorated Vichy, the Holocaust, and anti-Nazi resistance with great vigor), such campaigning registers usually served as a substitute for explicit reference to previous colonial repression. As Pierre Vidal-Naquet pointed out, before the late 1950s there was little awareness in metropolitan France of French anticolonialism or of colonial violence. Hence in the 1950s, the only way of approaching the racialized colonial power relations affecting Algerians in France was often through an analogy with apparently "noncolonial" forms of racism practiced during the Occupation.[30] Of course, using the analogy with Vichy was a rhetorical strategy by the MRAP and other activists, given the moral opprobrium that anti-Semitism attracted at this point: "cross-referencing" in this way, as we have seen, might attract transversal support, by stressing how the persecution of one group could pave the way for the oppression of others. But such antiracist and antifascist discourses were also arguably based on a shared unawareness of methods of colonial governance in Algeria, since before 1957, the MRAP activists, like virtually all other metropolitan French people, were often reliant on radio and print media heavily censored by the State. We are therefore perhaps dealing not only with the selectivity of memory understood as a repertoire of possible events from which campaigners might deliberately and reflexively draw to mobilize the past, with the MRAP here "translating" individual and collective experiences of anti-Semitism into a broader oppositional political discourse. What also emerges is the difference between collective memories of Nazi occupation on the one hand, and the impact of social silence regarding colonial repression *in the colonies* on the other.

OCTOBER 1961 AND BEYOND

From 1957, the French Federation of the FLN set about putting in place an extremely efficient money-raising apparatus that supplied the Algerian armed struggle with 80% of its finances, hence the French authorities' desire to crush the FLN through the return of Maurice Papon from Algeria to be Chief of Police in Paris in March 1958.[31]

---

30. Pierre Vidal-Naquet, *Les assassins de la mémoire* (Paris: La Découverte, 1987), 170.

31. See House and MacMaster, *Paris 1961*, Part One.

The decision to impose a curfew on Algerians in October 1961 came as Papon's response to FLN attacks on the police in Paris. Given that the Constitution of the Fifth Republic forbade any distinction between different categories of French citizens on the grounds of "race" or "origin," the curfew could only "advise" Algerians—officially termed "French Muslims from Algeria"—"in the most insistent way" not to be out between 8:30 pm and 5:30 am.

The contradictions between the constitutional equality afforded Algerians and their actual treatment by the police gave campaigners considerable scope for parallels with practices under the Occupation. While Jewish-based organizations and individuals figured prominently among those making such links, they were far from the only ones. For example, a text written by Paris university professors, and read out in lectures in late October 1961, described the curfew as a "racist measure," one for which "the only precedent in France since 1789 has been the measures taken by the Nazis during the Occupation."[32]

The curfew gave the police the opportunity for further arbitrary detention and brutality, hence the FLN's response in the guise of the 17 October demonstrations that were by definition also a boycott of the curfew. After the frenzy of police violence of October 17 and the following days, we see a continuation of the parallels made by campaigners between the persecution of Jews and the treatment of Algerians. However, we can also detect signs of a slight shift in emphasis toward a growing awareness of colonial-based forms of anti-Algerian violence. As Michael Rothberg has argued, the late-Algerian War period saw an increasing recognition that racialized state violence could work against different groups.[33]

Reactions from Jewish or majority-Jewish organizations immediately after October 17 showed the differences separating many Jews in metropolitan France from those in Algeria, where some Jews were being tempted by a pragmatic, tense, and ultimately short-lasting alliance with far-right extremists in a last bid to keep Algeria "French." On the contrary, many left-wing Jews in France were generally more favorable to Algerian independence, and likely to empathize with Algerians and draw upon analogies with the recent atrocities against Jews in France and continental Europe more generally (as opposed to Algeria) to better denounce the violence of October 17.[34]

32. Paulette Péju, *Ratonnades à Paris* précédé de *Les harkis à Paris* (Paris: La Découverte, 2000), 169 (first published 1961).
33. See Rothberg, *Multidirectional Memory*, 195; 236–45.
34. On the history of Jews in Algeria during this period, see Benjamin Stora, *Les*

The governing council of the Auschwitz Deportees Association had a letter published in *Le monde* on November 4, 1961 that expressed its "profound emotion at the massive round-ups and the transfer of thousands of human beings to the *Palais des Sports*, the police brutality, and the splitting up of families that reminded its members in a cruel way of what they had experienced and suffered."[35] At the MRAP's small-scale meeting held on November 8 to protest the events, Rabbi Sirat ironically declared: "the only possible memory this can bring back is twenty years ago, when any Jew could be taken to the centers of civilization that were the Vél' d'Hiv' and Drancy. Something needs to be done so that that cannot start again."[36] Daniel Mayer, the President of the LDH, talked of October 17 as an "evening reminiscent of the Berlin *Kristallnacht*. Once we accept that in front of us, people are called 'wog' or 'nigger' instead of Arab, we accept Auschwitz and the furnaces."[37] We can see evidence here of the continuity in the sort of parallels made between Vichy and anti-Algerian violence that I analyzed in the previous section. Most famously, perhaps, the respected former Resistance activist, parliamentarian Eugène Claudius-Petit, asked Interior Minister Roger Frey in the National Assembly on October 30: "Must we expect to see soon, because there is a slippery slope here, the shame of the yellow crescent after having experienced that of the yellow star? We are living through what we didn't grasp that Germans were experiencing when Hitler came to power."[38]

While for the moderate left, which included the MRAP, Algerians could be presented as the victims of racism, such Republican discourses had more difficulty in figuring Algerians as political actors: the Communist and Socialist-inspired left was generally happier in its denunciation of repression since this involved a critique of the Gaullist state.[39]

---

trois exils. Juifs d'Algérie (Paris: Hachette, 2006), 139–65. The MRAP's newspaper published an open letter from a group of Algerian self-named "Jewish Patriots" in Constantine who refused any association with pro-French Algeria extremists. See *Droit et liberté* 200 (May 1961): 5.

35. *Le monde*, November 4, 1961.
36. Quoted in Einaudi, *La Bataille de Paris*, 241.
37. *Ibid.*, 242–43.
38. National Assembly, second session of October 30, 1961, in *Journal officiel de la République française, débats parlementaires*, October 31, 1961: 3605.
39. Writing in the MRAP's newspaper, Robert Misrahi refused what he called the "abstract humanism" involved in discourses that, according to him, figured Algerians

Yet how to talk about the massacre of October 17 split the moderate from the radical anticolonial left: the influential social Catholic monthly *Esprit* criticized the position set out in an appeal published by the more radical *Les temps modernes* that stated: "we refuse to differentiate between the Algerians crammed into the *Palais des Sports* waiting to be 'deported' and the Jews locked up at Drancy before Deportation."[40] *Les temps modernes*, while stating that Papon was keen to be viewed as General Massu, the "victor" of the "Battle of Algiers," had also drawn many parallels between the action of Papon's police and Vichy anti-Semitism.[41] For *Esprit*, in contrast, it was "useless to collapse one historical event into another."[42] Some within the MRAP, such as the historian Madeleine Rebérioux, also warned against overplaying any analogy between Hitler's Germany and de Gaulle's Paris.[43]

But was the police violence a massacre, a pogrom, or a *ratonnade*, the latter a recent term referring to the hunting down of Algerians by European settlers or the parachutists? *Ratonnade*, rather than pogrom, eventually became the term most commonly used, and showed recognition of the colonial dynamic at play in the violence. As *Les temps modernes* put it: "born in Algiers, the 'ratonnade' is becoming established in Paris."[44] Such is the legacy of October 1961 to have firmly established the term *ratonnade* in the vocabulary of metropolitan France. However, the co-existence and, at times, rhetorical interchangeability of the terms pogrom and *ratonnade* showed the connections many in France made between registers of anti-Jewish and anti-Algerian violence,[45] although tensions remained regarding the most suitable term to use.

---

as victims of racism without supporting the political struggle for Algerian independence. Misrahi, "Les Juifs contre le racisme anti-musulman," *Droit et liberté* 204 (15 December 1961–15 January 1962): 7–8.

40. "Appel," *Les temps modernes* 186 (November 1961): 624.

41. "The Jews packed into the Vel' d'Hiv' during the Occupation were treated less brutally by the German police than the Algerians were by the Gaullist police in the *Palais des Sports*" ("La 'Bataille de Paris'," *Les temps modernes* 186 (November 1961): 618.

42. "Contre la barbarie," *Esprit* (November 1961): 668. The *Esprit* editorial nonetheless termed the holding centers for detained Algerians after October 17 "concentration camps" (667), and argued that the French could not claim in 1961, as some Germans had after 1945, that they had been unaware of what the State was doing in their name (note 1, 669).

43. "Réminiscences," *Droit et liberté* 204 (December 15–January 15, 1962): 7–8.

44. "La 'Bataille de Paris,'" 618.

45. See, for example, Albert Lévy, "Pas de ça chez nous," *Droit et liberté* 203 (November 15–December 15, 1961): 1. Lévy's article underlines both the parallels between

ALGERIAN RESPONSES

Through the presence on the streets of the imperial capital of tens of thousands of determined but peaceful Algerians, the FLN had hoped to "force" the French left into supporting its hand in the negotiations with the French state. While the FLN leadership in France was very angry at what it considered to be the PCF's long-term betrayal of the Party's internationalist obligations to help oppressed peoples, the FLN knew that it had to find a range of themes capable of "speaking" to both Communists and Socialists. Throughout the war, the FLN was very skilful in addressing the French public and world opinion more generally. The francophone Algerian elite that ran the French FLN Federation from Cologne knew metropolitan French society intimately well, and always stressed transversal themes such as antifascism, antiracism, and the right to human dignity, for example, to better "build bridges" with French people that it knew were otherwise often hostile. The FLN therefore tended to imitate and appropriate the dominant, often Republican-based themes used by the French left that we have already analyzed. The Provisional Algerian Government's brochure of December 1961 denouncing the violence of October 17 stated that: "to apply these measures that are just as shameful as those experienced by Jews at a given moment, discrimination was undertaken based on the physical appearance of the passers-by."[46]

The FLN highlighted that the curfew was a discriminatory measure establishing an unwarranted distinction between a category of French citizens and that ran counter to France's Republican principles. Ali Haroun, the FLN cadre responsible for much of the FLN's campaigning literature in France, has stated that, by concentrating on "the racist curfew," as he termed it, "it was straightforward to recall the measures taken by the Nazis toward a certain category of the French population in the very recent past."[47] The idea here was also to embarrass France on the international stage by drawing such parallels.

Vichy anti-Jewish repression and racism against Algerians (a common objectification and bestialization of the victims), while also recognizing the difference in circumstances.

46. *Les manifestations algériennes d'octobre 1961 et la répression colonialiste en France* (Gouvernement provisoire de la République algérienne: Tunis, 1961), quoted in Amiri, *Les fantômes du 17 octobre 1961*, 183.

47. *La 7è Wilaya. La guerre du FLN en France, 1954–1962* (Paris: Seuil, 1986), 365. Haroun confirmed the purposes of this rhetorical strategy during an interview that I conducted with him in Algiers on March 21, 2009.

This is certainly not to suggest that many Muslim Algerians did not genuinely empathize with the sufferings of Jews (as we shall see later), but arguably shows once more the particular shared idiom in which the racialized physical and symbolic violence of anti-Semitism and the persecution of Arab-Berber Algerians were being configured within some political discourses of this period.

However, the FLN contained not just a francophone elite engaging in highly-charged rhetorical tactics in the public sphere linking two different forms of persecution (links that might have been facilitated by the FLN leadership's first-hand experience of World War II while in France or Algeria). The Federation's core membership in Paris was essentially made up of the 125,000 Algerian migrant workers, some 11,400 of whom found themselves arrested en masse on October 17. Algerians were bussed in requisitioned vehicles to holding centers such as the *Palais des Sports* (a similar means of transport had been used during the anti-Jewish round-ups under Vichy, providing further links for oppositional campaigners), and then held in terrible conditions. For several days in detention, many Algerians suffered further violence and/or a lack of proper medical care and nutrition. It was during this detention that some Algerians became convinced that the French police were trying to "gas" them.[48]

There is certainly no evidence that the Paris police deliberately tried to "gas" Algerians. The most likely explanation is that the stench of urine and excrement, combined with the use of strong cleaning detergent, created this impression among the Algerian detainees. But for the impression of an attempt at "gassing" to have emerged more or less simultaneously from several distinct holding centers, suggests a shared and multidirectional memory among Algerians. In the nineteenth century, during the conquest of rural Algeria, the term *enfumade* had come to refer to a method of "smoking out" entire villages that had taken refuge from the French army in caves. Furthermore, there existed a popular memory of being gassed by the Spanish in the Rif mountains of northern Morocco during the Rif War in the 1920s (there were many exchanges between Northern Morocco and Western Algeria); after the May 1945 Sétif uprisings, the Algerians murdered in reprisal by the French had their bodies incinerated in lime kilns;

---

48. I am very grateful to Neil MacMaster for allowing me to use material here from his unpublished paper, "Rumours of Genocide: Police Repression of Algerian Nationalists and the Paris 'gas chambers' of October 17, 1961" (2008).

French army units would pour toxic gas into caves in which Algerian guerrilla fighters had taken refuge. Finally, in a highly publicized case in March 1957, other Algerians had died of asphyxiation during detention in wine vats.

The memories of this colonial violence overlapped, at least partially, with that of the Holocaust: many Algerians had been in France for a considerable amount of time, and some would have witnessed the mass round-ups of Jews in Paris, and others, or the same, would have known of the persecution of Jews in Vichy Algeria. One Algerian described in a written report to his FLN superiors what he saw when he was taken to the *Palais des Sports*: "There we made a macabre discovery. The [Algerian] brothers were lying on the ground, their heads split open and limbs dislocated. All these horrors were comparable to those endured by the Jews in the Nazi concentration camps."[49]

The Paris police regularly threatened Algerians not just with being thrown into the Seine, but also with sending them to "the gas chambers" and with "incineration." There were many Jews in the working-class districts where Algerians lived, and the French police would insult and brutalize them upon looking at their identity papers, often in the presence of their Muslim Algerian co-detainees. The case of Moïse S. illustrates this point. Having already been assaulted and physically abused by the police in September 1961, he was arrested on October 19, 1961 after having been mistaken for a (Muslim) Algerian, and taken from one police station to the next where he was assaulted. However, the police were made aware that Moïse S. was Jewish and insulted him on that basis: he heard one officer say, "all that's to be done with him is to put him in an oven."[50]

Memories of colonial atrocity, Nazi genocide, and anti-Semitism were therefore interconnected in the shared representations that informed some Algerians' perceptions of what was happening to them in detention, and the Eichmann trial, that had started in April 1961, had arguably added a further layer to such historical sensibility. Alongside the sedimented, syncretic racism of the Paris police, we can also see, on the contrary, a clear example of the linked Franco-Algerian (and wider) encounters producing a multidirectional memory that testified

---

49. Police Prefecture Archives, Paris, H1B35, anonymous FLN report number 122142 (October 30, 1961).

50. Police Prefecture Archives, Paris, Ha110, report from the internal police investigation into the Sebbah case, quoted in Linda Amiri, *La bataille de France. La guerre d'Algérie en métropole* (Paris: Robert Laffont, 2004),162–63.

to the hybrid social and political historical consciousness of Algerians in both France and Algeria.

UNDERSTANDING MOTIVATIONS FOR SOLIDARITY

An analysis of personal histories and trajectories further underlines the complex interplay of reasons explaining how and why some people during the Algerian War elaborated comparative, interconnected perspectives on racial domination and the resistance to this. Oral history and written testimony provide examples of how experiences of or relating to the Holocaust, and/or anti-Nazi resistance, and World War II more generally, motivated French people of a variety of left-wing opinions to become actively involved in different ways in the Algerian War.

Martin Evans has shown the extent to which the legacy of radical anti-Nazi Resistance—if not active participation in that Resistance—often provided an inspiration for illegal participation in the FLN's many support networks in France.[51] In trying to understand what it was that led French people to identify with Algerians whether on a political or humanitarian basis, we often need to think about what makes them "exceptional": what personal, professional, or political event(s) in their lives had led them to side "with Algerians"? The variety of ideological motivations for such involvement has been famously described by Pierre Vidal-Naquet as extending across, and sometimes combining—in differing proportions—Dreyfusard, revolutionary, and Third-Worldist identifications.[52]

No matter what an individual's ideological identification(s), direct personal experience and/or transmitted memory often played a key role. Given that French people were socialized into hostility against Algerians, and educated to believe that Algeria constituted an integral part of France, the counter-knowledge that preceded such a decision to help the FLN, or indeed to denounce torture and other abuses,[53] had to come from somewhere.

---

51. *The Memory of Resistance* (Oxford: Berg, 1997).
52. "Une fidélité têtue. La Résistance française à la guerre d'Algérie," *Vingtième siècle. Revue d'histoire* 10 (1986): 3–19.
53. Mention should also be made here of ethnographer Germaine Tillion, a former Resistance activist (deported to Ravensbrück) who became a prominent figure of the War of Independence and fierce critic of torture: her writings on Algeria were profoundly influenced by her experiences during 1940–1945. However, during the first part of the war Tillion adopted an essentially liberal-reformist agenda, arguing that social-economic

The life history of photographer Elie Kagan well illustrates such themes. Kagan took some of the few images portraying the aftermath of the violence on October 17, 1961. A reporter with the left-wing newspaper *Libération*, Kagan moved around central and suburban Paris on his Vespa, and his images figured in many of the publications denouncing the violence in the weeks following October 17, and have ever since constituted probably the most important iconographical trace of the violence. Shortly after Kagan's death in 1999, a book of his photos was published, and this gives more biographical detail. As a child, Kagan, the son of Jewish migrant parents (mother Polish, father Russian), had had to wear the Jewish star.[54] A laconic *curriculum vitæ* of Kagan's, dated November 18, 1961, reproduced from his personal archives in this book, states the following: "I was born in 1928, and was therefore too young in 1940 to have taken part in any combat (which I regret, however) and, because of this, had no activity in the Resistance. Only the fact that I hid in March 1943 in the *Haute Savoie* region stopped me from being deported" (Einaudi and Kagan, 62).

Another, but only partially legible, document reproduced in this book, and that resembles an *aide-mémoire* for a future autobiography, says that Kagan's mother was arrested on July 16, 1942—a day of mass police round-ups of Jews in Paris—and then escaped from the police station where she was taken (Einaudi and Kagan, 70) But under the entry "October 17, 1961," this document says: "October 17, 1961: *Ratonnades* in Paris hundreds of deaths, some Jews that have suffered so much remain indifferent, as do the Communists in Nanterre (what's happened to the internationalism of the proletariat?)" (Einaudi and Kagan, 71). Kagan is therefore angered by the lack of reaction of some in France—the majority—and especially Jewish people and Communists, and this anger with the PCF co-exists for many on the radical left with their opposition to the Gaullist state: the meanings evoked by their "17 October," are therefore at least dual, anti-Gaullist and anti-PCF.

---

improvements might enable Algerians to identify with a less structurally unequal French Algeria, and she worked closely with the French administration under the Fourth Republic to achieve this end. Tillion had, in fact, gained detailed knowledge of rural Algerian society through fieldwork undertaken in the Aurès region between 1934 and 1940: her personal trajectory thus shows a return to Algeria in 1954, rather than a post-1945 "discovery" of Algeria. See Nancy Wood, *Germaine Tillion, une femme-mémoire. D'une Algérie à l'autre* (Paris: Autrement, 2003).

54. Jean-Luc Einaudi, "Élie Kagan, le témoin," in Jean-Luc Einaudi and Elie Kagan, *17 octobre 1961* (Paris: Actes Sud, 2001), 8.

In an unpublished manuscript, part of which is also reproduced in this book, Kagan, in a poem or free prose, alternates "October 1961" and "July 1942" twice consecutively, and says that his experience of October 17, 1961, notably that of finding Algerians injured in the metro, brings back memories that attack him (*m'assaillent*), and mentions those "indifferent French" who did not intervene when Jews were being arrested under the Vichy regime: Kagan thus denounces both the active agency involved in the repression and the complicity of many Parisians in this violence, and these for 1942 and 1961. This last reflection is stimulated by a metro transport employee who approaches Kagan and remonstrates: "Don't you know that taking pictures in the metro is not allowed?" Kagan asks her, in turn, if she doesn't know that killing people in the metro is not allowed (Einaudi and Kagan, 74–75). Kagan's personal trajectory clearly—and understandably—figures July 1942 and October 17, 1961 together as key events.

Monique Hervo's case is rather different. On October 17, 1961 she was one of the few metropolitan French women in the FLN demonstrations. Hervo worked for the International Civil Service (ICS) humanitarian organization in La Folie, one of the Nanterre shanty-towns in the north-western suburbs where many thousands of Algerians lived. She had identified so closely with the Algerian cause that she had taken up residence there, whereas these spaces had become so feared by most other French people that even doctors refused to enter them. Hervo's diary of the years 1959–1962 constitutes one of the most extraordinary chronicles of the war of liberation in metropolitan France, describing the police repression in the shanty-towns in the form of sieges, helicopters hovering overhead, raids by the feared *harki* units (the Algerian police auxiliaries brought over from Algeria to repress the emigrant community), beatings, and assassinations. Hervo also shows the resilience of the Algerian population, most of whom in her shanty-town came from the militant pro-nationalist area of the Aurès mountains and had fled the repression in Algeria for Paris.[55]

In the spring of 1945, Monique Hervo as a sixteen-year old girl guide, had helped stretcher the survivors of Buchenwald camp as they arrived in Paris. She explains that, due to this experience: "I discovered

---

55. Monique Hervo, *Chroniques du bidonville : Nanterre en guerre d'Algérie, 1959–1962* (Paris : Le Seuil, 2001).

how far hatred of the Other can lead. Since then, my existence has not had the same color to it" (Hervo, 25). Indeed, she was clearly marked by this experience, and by the fact that: "subsequently, the Occupation often made me think of the colonial occupier in Algeria." And then, after 1954: "war was here again, with all its trappings, including deportation to the regroupment camps in Algeria . . . and which made me think back to the concentration camps but in another way, of course." Monique Hervo added that she recognized that making such links (*rapprochements*) was a sensitive subject. Additionally, she could empathize with those who needed to flee wars because, like the Algerians whose lives she had chosen to share in the shanty-town, she, as a child, had had to escape war in the form of the German invasion of northern France. In the 1950s, she then met colleagues within the ICS who influenced her nascent anticolonialist thought.[56]

The biography of Adolfo Kaminsky is little-known, although he was an important figure within the FLN in France, since he falsified key identity papers, as he had done in the French Resistance. Born in 1925 to Russian Jewish parents, Kaminsky arrived in France as a child from Argentina, and had been arrested with his family in Normandy by the Gestapo. The Argentinian Consulate managed to intervene to get them out of the Drancy camp, and Kaminsky then joined the Resistance. He explained that his main motivation in helping the FLN was an opposition to colonialism.[57] Kaminsky had discovered colonial racism on a tourist visit to Algeria in 1953–54, and the reality of war in Paris became evident to him from 1957 onward:

> *chasse au faciès*, endless police checks. I didn't know any Algerians personally, but my South American friends told me that they were often stopped because of their Mediterranean appearance. In my mind, it was totally intolerable that the French authorities should be chasing after non-white people (*basanés*), like the Nazis had been after Jews several years earlier.

Kaminsky was also shocked by the use of torture, since many of his Resistance comrades had suffered the same fate: "The victims had changed, but the methods [*against Algerians*] were the same."[58]

---

56. Interview with the author, Albertville, April 29, 2002.
57. Interview in Jacques Charby, *Les porteurs d'espoir. Les réseaux de soutien au FLN pendant la guerre d'Algérie : les acteurs parlent* (Paris: La Découverte, 2003), 98–100.
58. Sarah Kaminsky, *Adolfo Kaminsky, une vie de faussaire* (Paris: Calmann-Lévy, 2009), 151–52.

Kaminsky's case raises the question of the presence of a sizeable number of Jewish people within the FLN support networks: Egyptian Jews, recruited by Henri Curiel, were particularly numerous, as were those from Paris. The FLN always advertised itself to the outside world as a multi-ethnic organization: after all, the fight for independence was a political battle, it constantly argued, and the number of non Arab-Berbers who defended its cause, from Fanon to Sartre to Kaminsky, provides support for this position. Nonetheless, the FLN also viewed the indigenous Jews of Algeria as having "collaborated" with the colonial regime once Jewish men were assigned full French citizenship in 1870, and the FLN subsequently elaborated a vision of Algeria nationhood as Arab-Muslim, one that runs against the religious and cultural pluralism of the country.[59] Gilbert Meynier's description of the FLN's attitude toward the Jews of Algeria in particular as one of "ambivalence" therefore appears justified.[60] At the trial of the Jeanson FLN support network in September 1960, the government commissioner famously accused the FLN of "Nazism" because of its alleged ambivalence toward Algerian Jews, no doubt as a retort to the many analogies the pro-FLN defense counsels, led by Jacques Vergès, had made at the trial between Nazism and the torture of Algerians and the regroupment camps, both sides sharing a rhetoric of denunciation.[61]

Finally, the case of Jacques Panijel shows further complex links between past and present, the Algerian War and the Holocaust. Panijel, an academic and documentary-film maker, was a former Resistance fighter who had been tortured by the Gestapo, and was a member of the anti-torture collective, the Maurice Audin Committee. After having witnessed the police repression on October 17 in central Paris, and with the FLN's backing, he decided to make a documentary film called "October in Paris" to show the context of state terror in which Algerians had been living in Paris since 1957, and to better convey the reasons why Algerians had decided to demonstrate en masse against

---

59. However, the FLN viewed this decision to grant Jewish men French citizenship as an example of divide-and-rule tactics by the colonial state. See Claude Estier, "Les journées de Décembre," *Droit et liberté* 196 (January 1961): 5.

60. Gilbert Meynier, *Histoire intérieure du FLN* (Paris: Fayard, 2002), 252. See also Stora, *Les trois exils*, 141–43.

61. Marcel Péju, *Le procès du réseau Jeanson* (Paris: La Découverte, 2002), 174–75 and more generally (text first published in 1961). See also Nicolas Hubert, "Le 'camp,' paradigme indifférencié de la littérature anticolonialiste?, " *Matériaux pour l'histoire de notre temps* 92 (October–December 2008): 64–71.

such violence. Panijel described the violence of October 17, 1961 as "Nazism in the center of Paris."[62] This underground film contains reconstructions of the demonstrations and interviews with Algerians having been brutalized. The film was nearing completion just as the police killing of nine French antifascist demonstrators took place at the Charonne metro station on February 8, 1962. According to the scenario, the film's narrator says at the end of the film: "The door is closing on the Algerians. But don't go! October 17 is continuing! The door is going to open on us, who are not filthy Arabs, who were not Yids (*youpins*), twenty years ago!"[63]

In saying this, Panijel's aim was to show that, with Charonne, France was moving from one "state crime" to another, and that this, for him, exemplified the dangers of a slide into fascism, one of the left's key campaigning themes at the time. In this sense, while antifascism might be considered to be disenabling in memorial terms—the Communist-sponsored memory of Charonne did indeed obscure that of the October 1961 repression for at least two decades in France—antifascism could also be enabling of memory in the sense that the critique of state (police) violence provided a link from Vichy to October 1961 and then to Charonne and beyond that some people continued—and continue—to make. This continuity can be seen in the writings of the militant author Maurice Rajsfus, himself arrested by the Vichy police (his parents were murdered at Auschwitz).[64] It also appears as a leitmotif within demands for accountability governing what the State does in the name of its citizens that feature in the writing of (among others) Étienne Balibar,[65] who illustrates Paul Thibaud's useful idea of an "Algerian" or a "post-Algerian" generation.[66] For Thibaud, these terms refer to those who experienced the early part of the Algerian war as adolescents, and who then emerged as political actors near the very end of the war, often within the context of antifascist

---

62. Author's interview with Jacques Panijel, Paris, February 21, 2002.
63. Scenario reproduced in *Image et son*, 169 (March 1963): 22.
64. For Rajsfus' wartime experiences, see his *Paris, 1942. Chroniques d'un survivant* (Paris: Noesis, 2002). See also Rajsfus' book with Jean-Luc Einaudi, *Les silences de la police* (Paris: L'esprit frappeur, 2001).
65. Étienne Balibar, *Droit de cité. Culture et politique en démocratie* (La Tour d'Aigues: Éditions de l'Aube, 1998).
66. Paul Thibaud, "L'événement qui nous tourmentait," in *La guerre d'Algérie et les intellectuels français*, ed. Jean-Pierre Rioux and Jean-François Sirinelli (Brussels: Complexe, 1991), 377–85.

student politics. These people often have a particular sensibility toward the events of both October 1961 and Charonne. There are thus significant generational nuances to make regarding the age and historical consciousness of political actors when attempting to understand how and why links were made in 1961 between the past and the present.

CONCLUSION

All of the examples quoted above show that there was a small but determined group of people in France whose relationship to the Algerian War of Liberation, and decolonization more generally, was heavily influenced by their diverse experiences of World War II and, specifically, of anti-Jewish policies. These connections may be explicit or more indirect, but they are all, I would argue, significant and interesting.

The political "space" for an avowedly multidirectional memory may be larger, wider, and richer at some historical moments than at others, and the Holocaust may not always or explicitly be one of the vectors. It is clear, nonetheless, that during the Algerian War in France there developed a particularly strong repertoire of themes that drew analogies between the Occupation, the Holocaust, and the Resistance on the one hand, and, on the other, the Algerians' struggle for independence and the repression that this struggle met. Yet we have also seen that this rhetorical field did not emerge from a political and memorial void, just as generational factors were important in its elaboration and expression: they would also play a key role in its transmission.[67] Indeed, many of the examples discussed in this essay raise interesting questions about the articulation between individual and collective memory, and the interlinked nature of various types of memories within the same individual (or groups) that may inform decisions to intervene politically to resist oppression. This essay has sought to underline how, for some people, there are connections between historical events that appear "self-evident" due to either personal experience or transmitted memory. However, for some other people, these links need to be further explained since—superficially at least—they are either refused (due to "competing memories") or genuinely not understood as being connected. Making

67. See House and MacMaster, *Paris 1961*, Part Two.

those connections is part of both individual and collective political engagement. Yet what happens when we move from the personal, experiential register to the expression of such memories and links in the public sphere and its historically-determined idioms clearly remains an area for further study.

ROSS CHAMBERS

The Long Howl: Serial Torture

> In 1943, in the rue Lauriston, Frenchmen were screaming in agony and pain: all France could hear them. In those days . . . one thing seemed impossible in any circumstances: that one day men should be made to scream by those acting in our name.
> —Jean-Paul Sartre, "Preface" to Henri Alleg, *The Question.*

> We know that French specialists in "muscular interrogation" or "extreme questioning" (the habitual euphemisms for torture) were able to pursue new careers well beyond the borders of Algeria as soon as the conflict ended there in 1962.
> —Henri Alleg, "Afterword" to Henri Alleg, *The Question.*

> . . . this long human howl . . .
> —Jacobo Timerman, *Prisoner without a Name, Cell without a Number.*[1]

THE LOGIC OF DISAPPEARANCE

An event that is both violent and unprecedented in the experience of the victim is what we call traumatic: something is happening that has no referent to which it might be compared. Consequently it cannot be known because it cannot be recognized; it is the raw sensation of unfiltered violence, Timerman's "long human howl." A victim who nevertheless survives the trauma and may wish to bear witness to it for others is then faced with a rhetorical conundrum: how to make the traumatic at least recognizable to those who have not experienced it, how to provide a semiotic referent for an experience without such a referent, given that to do so would necessarily entail betraying the real character of such (referentless) experience? Without a referent there can be no communication, but recourse to a referent makes the traumatic untraumatic.

---

1. The Sartre and Alleg epigraphs are from Henri Alleg, *The Question*, trans. John Calder (Lincoln: University of Nebraska Press, 2006), xxvii and 101 respectively; the third from Jacobo Timerman, *Prisoner without a Name, Cell without a Number*, trans. Ilan Stavans (Madison: University of Wisconsin Press, 1981), 33. *Preso sin nombre, celda sin número* is described on the flyleaf as "copyrighted as an unpublished work."

This is the dilemma that survivors of the Nazi camps expressed by saying that only the dead (who cannot speak) were qualified to bear witness to their indescribable horror. But equally it accounts for the way people testifying to the AIDS pandemic, as it was experienced in the West during the 1980s and early 1990s, sometimes referred to it as a Holocaust, making use of the historical Holocaust as a referent for the terrifyingly unprecedented experience of the pandemic they were themselves undergoing, but incurring the ire of those who, failing to perceive the figurality of the move, insisted, understandably, on the absolute specificity of the Shoah. The Holocaust *is* an inadequate and inappropriate descriptor of AIDS, and vice-versa; but without the availability of the (by definition inadequate) figural mode, all traumatic events as they are actually lived would become literally unspeakable.

Allegory (or "speaking other") as a device for "speaking of" the unspeakable in this way, has characteristics that make it a particularly appealing figural mode for testimonial purposes. For although allegory has an object (it is an "allegory of" X or Y), it presents as objectless: the object is not necessarily identified, the recognition of its object being left to the reader, who may well discover it to be infinitely elusive. Allegory does not claim to "represent" its object as some kind of simulation thereof, but only to be structurally homologous with the object it thus fails to represent: it does not represent AIDS "metaphorically" *as* a Holocaust, but claims only that AIDS and the Holocaust are comparably structured events, members of a paradigm. Each of the two has the features of traumatic experience, including the absolute specificity of such experience, features that made AIDS and the Holocaust *each* terrifyingly traumatic, because unprecedented, but traumatic therefore in its own historical, that is specific, way. Thus allegory whose object is unidentified (and may be unidentifiable)—"modern" allegory, if you will—shares with the traumatic the ungrounded sense of an unknowable that baffles recognition, even though, unlike pain itself, as described by Timerman—"without points of reference, revelatory symbols or clues to serve as indicators" (32)—allegory is *nothing but* clues, indicators, symbols and referents. But it makes recognizable, in this way, what cannot be known by those who have not experienced it (or indeed, in a more philosophical sense, by those who have). Walter Benjamin's influential understanding of allegory as a set of ruins or a scatter of rubble that remain as aftermath indicators of an event now beyond knowledge, and thus as a stimulus for melancholic *Andenken*—a "thinking towards" whose object is beyond grasp—is thus an extremely suggestive one.[2] To the extent that it does make the object of allegorical reference recognizable, allegory thus understood does so only as a function of the kind of recognition that is an acknowledgement of one's not-knowing.

It is not literally true that history "repeats itself," as the saying goes. But it *is* certainly the case that, as Baudelaire recognized ("Andromaque, je pense à vous"), and as he may well have taught Benjamin, one instance of historical trauma may well allegorize, and simultaneously be allegorized by, another otherwise different disaster. Mediated by the figure of Andromache, the destruction of "old Paris" by the modernizing forces of the 1850s and the sack of Troy as recounted in the *Iliad* each reference the other, in a "dialectical" back-and-forth without sublation, a criss-crossing *jeu de reflets* producing the uncanny sense of de-differentiation that is such a Baudelarian trademark and, of course, a symptom of historical melancholy.[3] Similarly, a remarkable essay by Debarati Sanyal shows how the allegory of the Holocaust that is Alain Resnais's *Nuit et Brouillard* recurs, mediated by a landscape of watch-towers and barbed wire, in the colonial/postcolonial context of Sembène Ousmane's *Camp de Thiaroye*; and she goes on in her essay in this volume to describe the "crab-walk" history that arises in this way from the allegorizing imagination of recurrent trauma.[4] The "gray zone" she speaks of, following Primo Levi, is not only the ambiguity entailed in enforced participation in traumatic experience, such as our own fascination with the Holocaust and its representation, but appears also as a new version of "Baudelarian" de-differentiation and the historical mulling-over or *ressassement* that is historical melancholy.

But because my present concern is with the practice of political torture, my interest is in another aspect of the "night and fog" associated with allegory. This is the logic of disappearance, beginning with the disappearance of particularity, that enforces the to-and-fro of allegorical *Andenken* and "penser à" and so is constitutive of memorial multidirectionality or *noeuds de mémoire*. Resnais's title famously refers to the "Nacht und Nebel" edict that reinvented the ancient *ca-*

---

2. See Walter Benjamin, *Urspung des deutschen Trauerspiels* (Frankfurt: Suhkamp, 1963), trans. John Osborne as *The Origin of German Tragic Drama* (London: Verso, 1977). "Allegories are, in the realm of thoughts, what ruins are in the realm of things" (178).
3. My reference is to "Le cygne," poem 99 of *Les Fleurs du Mal*.
4. Debarati Sanyal, "Auschwitz as Allegory in *Night and Fog*," forthcoming.

chot for modern purposes, as the political practice of disappearance and torture that has flourished in the "dirty wars" of the latter two-thirds of the twentieth century and the early twenty-first. Disappearance takes the form of terror campaigns directed primarily against the ideological enemies of authoritarian régimes, often themselves characterized for that purpose as terrorists; but secondarily also against the population at large, which the practice seeks to reduce to a state of cowed submission.

If allegory is, as Benjamin so suggestively argued, a response to the disappearance of historical evidence entailing meditation on the remaining traces of what is no more, disappearance as a political practice aims to leave no traces. The Nazi camps were intended to be disappeared themselves, once they had done their work of eliminating large populations of Jews and others from the earth; the very disappearance of that population was itself to be a mystery. But likewise life in the camps, in the interim—if "life" is the word—was intended to be itself traumatizing in that the effect of the many degradations and deprivations meted out to the inmates was to be the inevitable depersonalization of individual subjects, the disappearance of their sense of personhood. The so-called *Muselmänner*, reduced to what Agamben was to call "bare life," were the living evidence of that policy's success, while the survivors who lived to bear witness to this vast "experiment," as Levi sardonically described it, concerning the meaning of the human, were those who managed somehow to resist, as Levi quite consciously did, and to cling to their sense of personhood amid the *Hier ist kein Warum* world of the camps. (Not coincidentally, "resistance" was the alternative word for the ideological enemies the Nazis called terrorists.)

Consequently, the act of bearing witness itself depends crucially on the witness's having successfully defended—or at least retained—the integrity of his/her personhood throughout the long ordeal, something that, in turn, seems to have depended on some combination of youth, faith, education, access to the support of a group, political commitment, and of course, sheer blind chance. For Holocaust witnessing narratives are generically readable as allegorical accounts, not solely of physical survival but also of the survival of the future witness's sense of being a person. And the same is true of the accounts of those who were subjected to political torture.

Indeed the brutality of torture's attack on the victim's personhood strongly suggests that depersonalization is the torturer's primary goal. The point is intuitively clear to anyone who has seen the infamous

Abu Ghraib photographs, or the distressing picture of a visibly damaged Khalid Sheikh Mohammed after the working-over he received at the hands of the CIA. The claim that the goal of torture is to obtain information that will "save lives" takes no account of the information's likely unreliability, or of the fact that torture is so frequently pointless in that respect (and indeed often arbitrary). Of the two best-known accounts of modern political torture, those of Henri Alleg and Jacobo Timerman, General Aussaresses himself has admitted that Alleg was a run-of-the-mill figure with no information of real importance to give, while Timerman insists on the circular, ideologically self-confirming nature of the information his torturers sought (an admission, for example, that he was Jewish and a Zionist—which was no secret—or that there was a Zionist scheme to settle large numbers of Jews in Patagonia, a plan "if not absurd, at least unfeasible" (73).[5] It seems highly likely on the other hand that the ideological satisfaction derived from reducing a perceived "enemy" to something like "bare life" derives from the "proof" such depersonalization offers of the other's supposedly deficient humanity, as when Nazis pointed to the degraded state of Jewish concentration camp inmates as evidence of their alleged racial inferiority. Similarly, René-Nicolas Ehni's harrowing account of his service as a conscript in the French army during the war of Algerian independence offers plentiful evidence both of the dehumanizing objectification, in the torturers' eyes, of tortured Algerians undergoing the "gégène," and of the confirmation these indignities provided of their status as "bicots."[6]

If we ask, then, why accounts like those of Alleg and Timerman are structured, not simply as stories of physical survival but more specifically as accounts of their resistance to depersonalization and thus of the survival of their human dignity and intellectual integrity, we can find the answer, therefore, in each man's ideological awareness and literate thoughtfulness (Alleg as the Communist editor of *L'Algérie Républicaine*, Timerman as the Zionist editor of the liberally-minded *La Opinión*). Each has the power to analyze what is happening to him. Alleg is explicit about his struggle to maintain a sense of self and self-control even as he undergoes the effects of, inter alia, electric shock,

---

5. Général Paul Aussaresses, *Services spéciaux. Algérie 1955–1957* (Paris: Perrin, 2001), 190.
6. René-Nicolas Ehni, *Algérie roman* (Paris: Denoël, 2002); see especially ch. 3, "Le bled." Thank you to Mireille Rosello for referring me to this astonishing account. (The "gégène" was army slang for the field dynamo used to deliver electric shock; "bicot" is a racialized term of contempt for North Africans.)

water-boarding and sodium pentathol. "Stupefied as I was by the blows and the tortures I had undergone, one single idea was still clear in my mind: 'To tell them nothing, not to help them in any way.'" (63); "I suddenly felt proud and happy not to have given way" (80).[7] At his final interview (when torture is still threatened), "I wish to be addressed as 'vous,'" (86) he coolly asks General Massu's aide-de-camp; and the lieutenant obediently switches from "tu" to "vous"—a signal confirmation of Alleg's victory. And throughout his account, Alleg makes clear the stakes of his struggle by reporting the crude speech of his torturers in the framework of his own correct and carefully controlled prose, with its past definites and pointed subjunctives.

Timerman, for his part, refers relatively reticently to the physical tortures he was subjected to, largely isolating them in a single chapter; but he demonstrates his intellectual survival by providing carefully analytic accounts of the ideological stakes of his many interrogations, as well as of the whole process of physical disappearance to which he was subjected. He appears to have adopted what he calls a stratagem of passivity and withdrawal into himself—"I was a professional stoic" (36)—as a self-disappearing counter to the disappearance of his person being inflicted from without. Consequently he is explicit and thoughtful in his assessment, not only of the "relation of mutual adversaries" that arises in torture from "the desire to destroy, to eliminate the individual" (66), but also of the *noeuds de mémoire* that result from the ubiquity of torture since Nazism as an unending scene of ideological confrontation—"On that day in September 1977, how many of us were seated upon the accused man's bench? . . . How many were judged for having been born?" (111)—and finally of the absolute irrationality of a process of interrogation that demands of "those who hold a fluid, pluralistic view of reality" that they conform to rigidly-held ideological convictions:

> It sounds absurd that my torturers wanted to know the details of an interview they believed Menachem Begin had held in 1976 in Buenos Aires with the Montoneros guerillas. It's less absurd when you're being tortured to extract an answer to that question. (72)

That is, ideological torture in Timerman's view seeks to destroy, to obliterate, to disappear the workings of the intellect by requiring submissive responses to "questions impossible to answer" (74):

---

7. All page references in the text are to Henri Alleg, *La question* (Paris: Ed. de Minuit, 2002).

At any rate, they found it necessary for me to declare myself a Marxist. This demanded many hours of questioning and harsh treatment, without my being able to make them understand the obvious contradiction between being a Zionist and being a Marxist, according to their understanding of Marxism. (75)

Only an abdication of the rational intellect, signaled by abject "confession," will satisfy the ideologically motivated torturer.

Neither Alleg nor Timerman uses the word *ordeal*, but each clearly structures his narrative in the thematic framework of that indeterminably ancient ritual of judgment, thereby linking the modern practice of torture to the long European history of martyrdom, initiation rituals (of which "hazing" is another descendent), and especially trial by ordeal, whether judicial or inquisitorial. ("Ordeal"—cf. the medieval French "ordalie"—is cognate with German *Urteil*, a verdict or judgment; and "trial" is a testing, implying examination and sorting, as in French *trier*: the "questioning" of Alleg—from "quaerere," to seek, as in a "quest"—takes place in a "centre de tri"!). In the way that the title *La question* alludes to the Inquisition, Timerman's *Prisoner without a Name, Cell without a Number* (*Preso sin nombre, celda sin número*) evokes the stakes of the practice of disappearance as an ordeal, i.e. the disappearing of human identity. The *ancien régime* practices of the *cachot* and the *oubliette*, with their nineteenth-century political versions, evoked for example in Piranesi's extraordinary *Carceri*, or in Stendhal and Dostoevsky, remain relevant. If Sartre's 1943 identifies a "year that keeps happening," and if a multidirectional memory-web, an allegorical "jeu de reflets," constructs a nonlinear history that links Guantánamo and the CIA's black holes to Gestapo prisons, to Algerian "centres de tri," to the ordeal of a Steve Bilko in apartheid South Africa, or that of thousands of disappeared persons in Argentina and many other countries of South America (and indeed the world, if we think of the Soviet Union or Franco's Spain or the practice of "ethnic cleansing" that became common in a disintegrating Yugoslavia), it is because the archaic structure of the ordeal, which links the brutality of torture to the *Nacht und Nebel* of disappearance and its assault on identity, provides the uninterrupted thread out of which this complex history is woven.

And since the enunciation of the *Nacht und Nebel* policy was clearly intended to resonate with the ideology of *Blut und Boden*—alliterative parallelism, rhythmic rhyming—the thought arises that modern political torture is the inheritance of a deeply rooted ideological authoritarianism, a generic fascism that, like the year 1943 for Sartre, simply will not go away, and indeed predates National Socialism itself. One of the attendant manifestations of this inheritance, as we shall see, is messy morality: the (also alliterative) morality of dirty-hands-but-clean-conscience that was persuasively epitomized most recently by Jonathan Littell's anti-hero, Maximilian Aue.[8] *Blut und Boden* is the ground; *Nacht und Nebel* the method; messy morality the enabling casuistry.

MESSY MORALITY AND THE EUPHEMIZING OF VIOLENCE

> The act of love (*l'acte d'amour*) bears great resemblance to torture or to a surgical operation.
> —Charles Baudelaire, *Fusées*.[9]

> They didn't even leave marks.
> —Jacobo Timerman, *Prisoner without a Name* (33).

> Political realism is not a set of doctrines but "a certain style of denial of the relevance of morality to politics, especially international politics."
> —Tamas Pataki quoting C.A.J. Coady.[10]

Baudelaire's striking insight about "l'acte d'amour" suggests that one might approach the ordeal of torture as a violent confrontation—indeed a conjunction—of bodies. To approach the question in this way will permit us to discern in the crabwalk history of modern political torture not only the erotics of violence the poet is interested in, but also a steady, and more or less unidirectional, evolution. For if torture is an archaic practice, it is in another sense strikingly anachronistic as well. Like the act of love in one way, it resembles a surgical operation in another, because it amalgamates extremely ancient features with strikingly up-to-date technological practices, a kind of modernity. It jostles the most distant past and the most immediate present into a strangely intimate encounter whose medium is pain.

Thus a close and violent physical or bodily confrontation having unmistakably erotic implications—most typically homoerotic, given

---

8. See Jonathan Littell, *Les Bienveillantes* (Paris: Gallimard, 2007), trans. Charlotte Mandell as *The Kindly Ones* (New York: Harper, 2009).
9. Charles Baudelaire, *Oeuvres complètes*, vol. I, ed. Cl. Pichois (Paris: Pléiade, 1975), 659 ("Fusées XI"), editor's translation.
10. Tamas Pataki, "Dirty Hands," review of C.A.J. Coady, *Messy Morality: The Challenge of Politics* (OUP, 2009), *Australian Book Review* (June 2009): 26–27.

that rape so often is the form of torture used in violence against women —simultaneously entails recourse to an apparatus of often ingeniously designed (or inventively adapted) tools and instruments, a whole evolving technology of violation whose history is as closely bound up with humanity's long howl as the enduring sexuality. Arguably, Baudelaire's "fusée"—not coincidentally, the term is itself in Baudelaire's usage an anachronism, substituting an aggressively technological and warlike metaphor for ancient concepts like aphorism, maxim or "pensée"—expresses a violent rejection of Romantic conceptions of love by linking it, through torture, to battlefield amputations and other operations performed—without benefit of anesthesia, of course—during the then recent Crimean War. Along with the American Civil War, the war in Crimea was the first to have been fought with recognizably modern weaponry, most notably the Gatling machine-gun, and was thus itself inescapably anachronistic in character (as Tennyson similarly noticed). So torture becomes the aphorism's central figure for the painful sense of wrenching anachronism that characterized, for a generation born just before the Industrial Revolution arrived in France, the brutal becoming-modern of a society still rooted in its *ancien régime* past. Experienced as the strange (and apparently unmediated) yoking together of nature and *techné*, of the ancient and the brutally new, modernity-as-anachronism for Baudelaire entails a strange erotics of pain.[11] And what I would like to suggest is that, in its own specific way, the world history we ourselves have lived through since, let's say Sartre's recurrent 1943, has been a similarly traumatic awakening to, or coming to terms with, a new and likewise devastating historical and political reality, a new form of modernity's anachronistic cruelty whose allegorical analogue—an equivalent of the violent act of love for Baudelaire—would be the "new" (and simultaneously "old") practice of political torture inaugurated in the rue Lauriston.

But the new semiotic referent for the practice of torture would not now be warfare and battlefield surgery but the softened, euphemized

---

11. The association of modernity with the Crimean War would have been readily made through the figure of Constantin Guys, "le peintre de la vie moderne": Guys's dispatches from the Crimea had invented the new journalistic genre of illustrated, on-the-spot reporting. On love-making, torture, and surgery as violent hands-on contact and their shared ordeal character, see Baudelaire's astonishingly cruel amplification of the "Fusées, XI" aphorism in "Fusées, III," with its key formulation: "Epouvantable jeu, où il faut que l'un des joueurs perde le gouvernement de soi-même" (Pléiade, I, 651). Incidentally, surgery ("opération chirurgicale") is etymologically "hands-on work" (Greek *kheiros*, a hand).

version of ordeal that is competitive athleticism. Like torture increasingly technologized as time went on, athletics as a mode of bodily competition and contact flourished in the militarized groups and *confréries* of ancient social organizations and survives today, not only as hazing but also as that other practice of (mainly) male bonding that is competitive sport. In this mitigated form of ordeal, "winning" becomes an absolute goal as a test of "discipline," that is of the ability, acquired through practice and "training," to withstand punishment (a semantic cognate of "discipline") by overcoming one's physical and other limitations. (One might note in passing that George Perec's *W ou le souvenir d'enfance* suggests an interesting triangulation of the practice of competitive sport, the concept of ordeal, and the phenomenon of disappearance.)

Whence the associations of ideas expressed by the young soldiers who visit Alleg in his cell in order to congratulate him on his success in resisting torture. "Were you tortured in the Resistance?" asks one, who clearly understands Alleg's powers of resistance—again the word is strangely resonant—as a matter of prior training, and who adds, when Alleg answers no, an admiring "You've done well. . . . You're very tough" (82). The other, a conscript and sports fan, gives him a broad grin and mentions that he has been present throughout Alleg's long ordeal, as if claiming the status of a loyal sports supporter: "My father talked to me about the Communists in the Resistance. They died, but they never talked." Alleg comments:

> I looked at this youth with the sympathetic face, who could talk of the sessions of torture I had undergone as if they were a football match that he remembered, and could congratulate me without spite as he would a champion athlete. A few days later I saw him, shrivelled up and disfigured by hatred, hitting a Moslem who didn't go fast enough down the staircase. (82)

So the point is that it's not just a matter of sport. Nor is it simply that in the minds of the torturers themselves, the "trials" undergone in the Algerian "centre de tri" replicate the sporting feats of the rue de Lauriston and other Gestapo prisons. If sports culture functions, as Alleg suggests, as a handy euphemization of the brutality of torture—one, perhaps, that salves the conscience of the torturer and makes it easier for him to do what he does—we must think also of the whole militarized culture of Nazi Germany, with its Prussian inheritance, its cult of the body and its capacity for strength, health, and athletic beauty, its own eroticization of painful effort and encounter, and of course the technological modernity of its whole apparatus of war, repression, extermination, and disappearance. The sports culture of Nazi Germany represented the acceptable face (think the Berlin Olympics and/or the filmmaking of Leni Riefenstahl) of a nightmarish ideological program, its euphemized twin.

But the Gestapo did not use sodium pentathol. If, as I'm proposing, the crabwalk history of modern political torture has also been a history of the euphemization of that form of bodily violation in the interests of its deniability—a history that includes and entails the eroticization of pain already present in Baudelaire's aphorism as it is in the practice of competitive sport—then an extremely significant component of that history has been the search for technologies of pain that do not leave a permanent trace on the victim's body. The methods of torture employed by the French in Algeria—notably the "gégène" and the "baignoire" (now called waterboarding), both of which were inflicted on Alleg, who gives stark descriptions of their excruciating effects—were already in that category of so-called "clean" (or sometimes "touchless") torture, which is why they have become such modern staples. But the experimental use of pentathol to which he was subjected also illustrates the de-emphasis on the torture-scene as an episode of bodily encounter, and the corresponding intensification of the search for "hygienic" technical devices (such as those that produce sensory deprivation or else unremittingly assault those same senses), that has accompanied this trend. So it is significant that Alleg's defense against the effects of pentathol was to inflict a degree of physical pain and damage on himself, by surreptitiously digging his nails into his own flesh. "Chassez le naturel, il revient au galop" (Send the natural packing, it comes back at a gallop): torture remains of course the dirty, hands-on, "unhygienic" form of physical violation that it has always been, despite all efforts to cleanse it, to make it touchless, or to assimilate it to supposedly harmless forms of sport. But it is clear that this technological hygienizing of torture is like the rhetoric of euphemism of which it is an implementation in that its function is to alleviate the guilt of those who practice it by disappearing, if not actually eliminating, the "dirty-hands" component of their messy, dirty-hands-but-clean-conscience morality.[12]

12. See especially Kristin Ross, *Fast Cars, Clean Bodies: Decolonization and the Reordering of French Culture* (Cambridge, MA: MIT Press, 1996), 108–122. Ross's landmark essay stresses the "ideologeme of cleanliness" in relation to the dirty war, and

For, from the point of view of "government" in particular, that is of pragmatic politics (another suspect alliteration), euphemized torture that leaves no physical evidence has many advantages. It seems, for example, to have made it possible in the United States to "train" military and other personnel to resist the ordeal of torture should they be captured, while thus contributing to the legitimation of "clean" torture techniques (which are made to appear sport-like and harmless), and incidentally teaching the same techniques to the trainees. "Harsh interrogation techniques" can also be contrasted with torture "proper" so that the latter can be plausibly denied. But deniability itself, however "plausible," has also always been a two-edged practice, since it makes it possible to claim the high moral ground while simultaneously allowing it to be understood (since denegation always entails a degree of acknowledgment of what is being denied) that torture is nevertheless being practiced. And this ambiguity, in turn, can have two, not necessarily mutually exclusive, uses: one, an atmosphere of uncertainty and a sense of threat arises and—especially in conjunction with "night and fog" practices of disappearance, but also independently—help to keep the general population cautiously submissive, and thus cowed. And/or two, an implied or explicit claim can be made that the government is relentless in its will to defend the population at large against "terrorists." Finally, in the case of an embarrassing disclosure, there remains the "few bad apples" defense (the thrust of the original proverb—that it takes only a few bad apples to turn the whole barrel rotten—being now forgotten). If it is an axiom of government that the powers-that-be must always be right, then, in addition to the boost it gives to the messy morality of political realism, the euphemizing of torture's physical, *corps à corps*, violence and of its brutal assault on selfhood has proved a most valuable asset.

But the ideological stakes remain, and in a sense emerge more starkly as a consequence of the backgrounding of bodily confrontation. Ultimately, as I argued in an earlier essay concerning Alleg, those stakes concern the character of the nation whose birthing is always in "question" when dirty wars rage and political torture flourishes. That

---

follows Sartre in viewing the goal of torture as the stripping of human dignity (my "personhood") from one's enemy. As for euphemism, it is something like the signature figure of messy morality for the reason that it stages a (partial) "disappearance" of the disavowable reality by means of a formulation that elicits its shadowy "return," reproducing in this ambivalent way the uncanny dynamics of denegation as of Freudian repression.

Baudelaire associates torture with "l'acte d'amour" on one hand and "une opération chirurgicale" on the other makes sense, then, if we think of political torture as a strange form of (mainly) male conception and birth, and at the same time as an obstetrics transferred from biological childbirth to the public arena of the formation of nations: a forceps birth or a Caesarean delivery, or course, a surgical operation ("opération chirurgicale") because, viewed in the most traditional terms, it has moved from the domain of women and fertility to that of men: politics, technology, and warfare.[13]

However, if we do so think of political torture, then what emerges with some clarity is the question posed by the long howl that is the *noeud de mémoire* of which I have given a necessarily partial account here, the profoundly symptomatic and characteristically modern inheritance of Nazism in France, Algeria, South Africa, Argentina (and other Latin American nations) as well as the (off-shore) United States.[14] That question is this: not just what kind of nation, but also what kind of world do we wish to inhabit? How might that world, in the various senses of the word, be "conceived"? And how "delivered"?

---

13. For a more careful reading of torture as male birthing, see my earlier essay on Alleg, "Ordeals of Pain," in *Entre Hommes: French and Francophone Masculinities in Culture and Theory*, ed. Todd W. Reeser and Lewis C. Seifert (Newark: University of Delaware Press, 2008), 206–223.

14. Is it necessary to point out that the outsourcing of political torture is yet another instance/implementation of its euphemizing? (It is also an unexpected exemplification of political torture as a matter of "simultaneous multidirectionality.")

DEBARATI SANYAL

Crabwalk History: Torture, Allegory, and Memory in Sartre

> "We listened as his soul cracked. The sound of his voice really twisted our minds and made our hearts stop" (prisoner recalling Manadel al-Jamadi's torture and death at Abu Ghraib).

How can writing do justice to the sheer violence of torture while investigating its interlocking meanings at a particular historical juncture? It is striking to note how often in literature the bodily encounter of torture gives rise to the allegorical imagination and its displacements: Kafka's executionary harrow, the scarred body of the barbarian at the heart and margins of Coetzee's Empire, or as I shall suggest in this essay, the allegorical registers in Sartre's neglected play, *The Condemned of Altona*. Of course, "speaking otherwise" about torture may be the only way to speak of it at all under regimes of censorship, where only the ruses of allegory can convey the state's dirty secret. Yet, at a structural level, there is a disquieting kinship or complicity between torture and allegory. For if torture, (from *torquere*, "to twist, turn, wind, wring, distort") is a process that twists and turns the body and psyche of its victims into distorted signification, allegory is a rhetorical figure that similarly disfigures or twists bodies and objects into emblems whose meanings shift according to different historical horizons. Indeed, allegory necessarily betrays the singularity of an experience by invoking it through substitution and analogy, a gesture that is particularly fraught when addressing historical events considered unique in the magnitude of their destruction, such as the Shoah. Yet despite the potential complicity (at the level of form) between a violent historical event and its evocation through the mode of allegory, the traumatic nature of experiences such as detainment, torture, and extermination often prompt the displacements of allegorical inscription in order to become legible and transmissible. More pertinent to this inquiry is that, while the allegorical mode could not be further from the identificatory, affective force of a documentary's testimony to an act of violence (as in the case of the first-hand witnessing of al-Jamadi's torture in Abu Ghraib), allegory's figural displacemernts force us to decipher its twists and turns in relation to our own cultural moment and its interlocking violences. Allegory opens what I will call here a kind of crabwalk history, in which distinct yet proximate genealogies of state violence are evoked to constitute a *noeud de mémoire* that helps us better read the aims and effects of torture both as an embodied confrontation and as the outcome of a structure of relations.[1]

In recent decades the absolute singularity of the Holocaust has become something of an established *doxa*. Yet as several pieces in this volume attest, in the immediate aftermath of World War II, the legacy of the Nazi genocide was woven into other histories in the making, and formed memorial knots that bound together distinct legacies and practices of violence. Thinkers such as Hannah Arendt, Aimé Césaire, Frantz Fanon, and Jean-Paul Sartre, among others, probed the affinities between Nazism and imperialism, as well those between the concentrationary and colonial experience, identifying analogies, continuities, and even intersections between these distinct legacies of racialized violence. Postwar French cultural production abounds with figures that put the traumatic legacy of the Holocaust in dialogue with other bodies and histories. Figures such as the victim-turned-executioner or the enemy whose face is one's own sought to shore up anticolonial dissent by underscoring France's paradoxical turn from victim of the Nazi occupation to perpetrator of internment and torture in service of its colonial occupations. Such allegories opened up proximities between the French Republic and the Third Reich, between imperialism and genocide, in a double reference that was both testimonial with regard to the Nazi terror and admonitory with respect to imperialism. Allegory, or speaking otherwise, evoked one history through another and bound them into a *noeud de mémoire* that

---

1. Torture is a devastating bodily encounter, yet its exercise is also embedded within a web of power and signification, a system of relations that both defines and exceeds its perpetrator and victim. As Marnia Lazreg observes, "Torture is a structured environment with a texture of its own, a configuration of meanings, a logic and rationale without which physical, let alone psychic, pain is incomprehensible and ineffective. In the social situation of torture, memory, identity and culture weave a network of ideas and perceptions, experiences and ideals that define a genuine battle between two embodied realities." *Torture and the Twilight of Empire: From Algiers to Baghdad* (Princeton, 2007), 6.

marked a memorial convergence rife with productive entanglements and troubling interferences.

Sartre's enigmatic *The Condemned of Altona*, ostensibly about postwar Germany and collective guilt but also an allegory of French torture in Algeria, offers a fascinating and complex example of such a *noeud de mémoire*. The play is set in the German mansion of old von Gerlach, a wealthy industrialist who collaborated with the Nazis during the war and sold his land to Himmler for the construction of concentration camps. Now dying of throat cancer, he bequeaths his shipbuilding empire to his younger son Werner, and commands him (along with his daughter-in-law Johanna and sister Leni) to remain in the house in order to look after his eldest son Frantz. A Nazi war hero who supposedly died in Argentina, Frantz von Gerlach in fact has sequestered himself upstairs in the attic, and only receives his sister Leni for food, care, and occasional bouts of incest. In flashback sequences, we discover that during the war, Frantz had stumbled upon a concentration camp built on the family's property. In order to atone for his father's collaboration, he attempted to save a mad rabbi who escaped from the camp. But the rabbi was caught and slaughtered by the SS before his very eyes and shortly afterwards, Frantz joined the army on the Eastern Front. At the end of the war he returned to his father's mansion and sequestered himself upstairs, presumably traumatized by Germany's defeat. Frantz now believes that mankind is doomed to extinction, and that crabs will reign over the thirtieth century. For much of the play, under the surveillance of these crabs, he records testimonies that will vindicate humanity to this post-human, crustacean posterity, but he also turns into a crab onstage, scuttling sideways when his mysterious wartime past comes up. The play ends on the disclosure that Frantz tortured villagers on the Eastern Front and was known as "the Butcher of Smolensk."

When *The Condemned of Altona* opened in Paris in September 1959, the play's audiences readily grasped its indictment of torture perpetuated by the French army. The Communist mathematician Maurice Audin had been "disappeared" from Algiers in 1957 and a committee led by Pierre Vidal-Naquet was investigating his fate; Henri Alleg's *La question*, on his torture at the hands of the French paratroopers, was also in clandestine circulation, and although censored, Sartre's powerful preface to Alleg's testimony appeared fragmentarily in the press of the day. Sartre at any rate was convinced that despite the public's disavowal of torture during what was euphemistically called *les événements,* and despite the play's German setting, his allegory of the nation's dirty secret had been deciphered by all: "behind this Germany everyone read Algeria."[2] Censorship had forbidden what Sartre described as a frontal approach to the problem of violence in French society.[3] Only an oblique, allegorical allusion—a *crabwalk*—could bring the question of torture home to French terrain.

If for Jean Améry torture was the essence of the Third Reich "materialized in all the density of its being," for Sartre torture materializes a far broader genocidal principle at work in distinct sites of violence, whether these are the Nazi camps, the Gestapo quarters of occupied France, the racialized spaces of French colonialism, or the torture chambers of the late-colonial state.[4] Torture embodies a battle for the species; it is an attempt to secure and consolidate the boundaries between the "human" and the "inhuman" from within a territorialization of bodies and spaces. This occupation of another's body/space and the forms of inhumanity it produces are at the heart of Sartre's play and its haunting allegory of posterity's crabs. The slippery distinction between the human and the inhuman is a leitmotif in *The Condemned of Altona*; indeed, the precarious threshold between the two is embodied by the protagonist, Frantz, who in the aftermath of torture, both defends humankind before an inhuman, crustacean future and periodically mutates into a crab himself.

The following reading traces a series of figures for inhumanity in *The Condemned of Altona* and other writings by Sartre along with a number of contemporary reflections on the concentrationary experience that bring the legacy of the Nazi genocide to bear on colonialism, torture, and empire. I will tease out how the protagonist's ethical trajectory from helpless witness of the Judeocide (figured by the Rabbi's slaughter) to torturer in the ruins of Hitler's empire may be deciphered in light of a postwar meditation on what constitutes the "human" in the aftermath of the Nazi concentrationary experience and as an allegory of France's historical mutation from victim

---

2. Jean-Paul Sartre, *Sartre on Theater*, trans. F. Jellinek (NY: Pantheon, 1976), 257 (translation modified).

3. "je tenais à avoir une assez large audience et . . . cela aurait été impossible si j'avais abordé de front le problème de la violence, tel qu'il se présente aujourd'hui dans la société française." Jean-Paul Sartre, *Un théâtre de situations* (Paris: Gallimard, 1973), 348 (my translation).

4. Jean Améry, *At the Mind's Limits: Contemplations by a Survivor on Auschwitz and its Realities*, trans. Sidney Rosenfeld and Stella P. Rosenfeld (Bloomington: Indiana University Press, 1980), 30.

to perpetrator of occupation, internment, and torture. Along the way, I hope to illuminate the political force and ethical ambiguities of such an allegorical approach to historical violence, while suggesting that allegory is precisely what makes Sartre's historical crabwalk through distinct sites of racialized violence speak to us with relevance today.

In 1941, Frantz von Gerlach stumbles upon the concentration camp built on his family's grounds and horrified by what he sees, goes to his father:

> *Frantz: (youthful voice; soft, affectionate, but worried)* Father, I would like to speak to you.
> *Father (looking at him):* Have you been down there?
> *Frantz:* Yes. *(Abruptly and with horror)* Father, these are no longer men.
> *Father:* The guards?
> *Frantz:* The prisoners. I am disgusted with myself, but it is they who fill me with horror: their dirt, their vermin, their sores. *(a pause)* They look as though they live in perpetual fear.
> *Father:* They are what they have been turned into.
> *Frantz:* You couldn't turn me into that.
> *Father:* No?
> *Frantz:* I would withstand it.
> *Father:* What makes you think they don't?
> *Frantz:* Their eyes.
> *Father:* If you were in their place, yours would be the same.
> (*CA* 32–33, trans. modified).

The distinct emphasis Frantz places on the possessive in his enumeration (their dirt, their vermin, their sores) suggests that he sees the signs of the prisoners' expropriated humanity as an expression of their inner inhumanity, as a failure to hold on to humanity under inhuman conditions. This confusion of what has been done to them with what they are constitutes a refusal of his vulnerability *and* complicity within a field of dehumanizing violence. Frantz represses the knowledge that these men are the abject face of his subjecthood, that their apparent inhumanity reflects a common condition of radical exposure to annihilation, one that Giorgio Agamben has termed bare life. Frantz's refusal of kinship is a failure to put himself in the place of the other (as his Father points out, if he were in their place, his eyes would be the same). His repulsed gaze upon the detainees is blind to the human element that remains in the wake of the "demolition of a man."⁵

Sartre later describes this repugnance for the detainees' abjection as a failure of human *contact* that triggers the protagonist's moral fall. If Frantz eventually succumbs to the temptation of torture, it is because in this critical scene, he failed to have an immediate, affective recognition of the prisoners as his human kin:

> I think he begins slipping (*il glisse*) from the start. . . . He has started to slip the moment he is filled with horror by the prisoners in the camp, the moment he condemns not only the system of concentration camps in the name of the dignity of man . . . but the prisoners too, emotionally, as it were by instinct, when he says "They are no longer men." From that moment he has slipped (*il a glissé*) . . . What he will always lack is . . . a human contact which will be strong enough, when he is tempted to become a torturer himself, to render him incapable of carrying it out because he is dealing with a human being.⁶

For Sartre, it is the missed encounter with the residual humanity that remains in the aftermath of Nazi dehumanization that precipitates Frantz into a murderous system of relations. The failure of contact with the detainees' human vulnerability will eventually unleash the violent touch of torture.

When Frantz confuses cause and effect upon witnessing the detainees' dehumanization, he voices the logic of the camps themselves, which produced in its victims the very inhumanity that legitimated their extermination. Robert Antelme exposed the mechanism of this conversion into abjection in his testimony *L'espèce humaine* (1947), a key source for Sartre's play. Antelme portrays in searing detail the ways in which the concentrationary universe challenged the detainees' belonging to the human species and forced them into a constant proximity to beasts and things, as if the "human" were a precarious zone that one could only partially inhabit or from which one could be exiled ("Father . . . these are *no longer* men," Frantz declares). In his ironic portrayal of the Nazi gaze, Antelme identifies the same confusion of cause and effect that leads Sartre's protagonist to banish the detainees from the human realm into abjection: "We are becom-

---

5. Primo Levi, *Survival in Auschwitz*, trans. Giulio Einaudi (NY: Collier Books 1993), 26.
6. *Sartre on Theater*, 292–93.

ing very ugly to behold. For this the fault lies with us. It's because we are a human pestilence.... If we weren't pestilential we wouldn't be violet and gray; we'd be clean and neat; we'd stand up straight."[7] Yet the Nazi attempt to sunder the species and force a mutation that expels its victims from humanity is foiled by an ineradicable relationality. As Antelme recalls, if a civilian recoils in horror at the sight of Buchenwald's skeletal survivors, it is not because their faces are irrevocably alien but because their kinship cannot be masked: "it is the human in me that makes her back away," for even the most ruthless degradation of a victim cannot mask the underlying unity of the species.[8]

As we shall see, Antelme's meditation on the inescapable relationality of victim, executioner, accomplice, and witness within a field of dehumanization is at the very heart of *The Condemned of Altona* and will allow Sartre's allegory to invoke multiple frames of historical reference simultaneously. Sartre's protagonist is initially an idealist who, horrified by the camp's production of inhumanity, tries to redeem both his father's collaboration with the Nazis and his own repulsion for their victims by trying to save a Polish rabbi who escaped from the camps. Frantz finds the mad and frightened rabbi wandering about the property and hides him in his room, in a gesture that prefigures his own mad sequestration after the war. However, his efforts to save the rabbi fail and he is forced to watch him killed like an animal by the SS—the rabbi's throat is slit before his very eyes. At the end of the play, Frantz discloses that the memory of his impotence made him embrace Hitler's cult of pure power, when for ten days he tortured Russian partisans and villagers to death on the Eastern Front. As the Butcher of Smolensk, Frantz was no longer forced to watch another human being slaughtered like a beast. Instead, he could produce the inhuman with his very own hands:

> The rabbi was bleeding, and I discovered at the heart of my impotence some strange sort of approval. *(He is back again in the past.)* I have supreme power. Hitler has made me an Other, implacable and sacred: himself. I am Hitler and I shall surpass myself.... Never shall I fall

---

7. Robert Antelme, *The Human Race*, trans. J. Haight and A. Mahler (Marlboro, VT: Marlboro Press, 1992), 76.
8. Ibid. 244. For a summary of recent debates on the status of Antelme's category of "the human," as pure internal difference (Blanchot, Levinas), or as irreducible, residual humanity, see Colin Davis, "Antelme, Renoir, Levinas and the Shock of the Other," *French Cultural Studies* 14/1 (2003): 41–44.

prey to abject powerlessness. I swear it. It's dark. The horror is still chained . . . if anyone unleashes it, it shall be me. I will claim evil, I will display my power by the singularity of an unforgettable act: change *living* men into vermin (*changer l'homme en vermine de son vivant*). I alone will deal with the prisoners, I will hurl them into abjection: they will talk. Power is an abyss and I see its depths. It isn't enough to choose who shall live and who shall die; with a penknife and a cigarette lighter, I will determine the reign of the human (*je déciderai du règne humain*). (CA 163–164, trans. modified).

Once repelled by the concentration camp victims' proximity to the inhuman, Frantz now enforces a radical divide between human and inhuman, himself and his victims. Under the Swastika, he inscribes his absolute power upon the body of another. Not content with extermination, with choosing who will die, as would be the case in a selection, Frantz instead will change living humans into vermin and materialize the Third Reich's enemy as an abject, inhuman thing. Given the homonymy of Frantz and France, the protagonist's trajectory from powerless witness and imaginary "proxy victim" of Nazi violence to accomplice and perpetrator of torture in the name of the Reich would have harbored allegorical resonance for a nation whose recent, albeit repressed, memory of defeat, occupation, and imperial loss played a role in the generalization of torture during the Algerian war.

From his postwar writings on, Sartre portrays torture as a deadly combat for ontological sovereignty. The torturer not only wields absolute power over the life and death of another, but seeks to expel the victim from the species altogether. The vermin is a recurrent figure in Sartre's thought for the vulnerability of a human body facing its imminent devastation at the hands of another. As the protagonist of *The Wall* (1939) awaits his execution, for instance, he perceives his body as an enormous vermin to which he is tethered. In the immediate aftermath of the Occupation, Sartre once again vividly evoked this sense of a radical banishing from the species through the disquieting image of the vermin. He imagined the Resistance fighters' experiences of torture by the Gestapo as a mutation from one species to another. As they suffered under the watchful gaze of their tormentors, the *Résistants* come to believe that they would awaken on the other side of pain not as human beings, but as vermin: "these faces bent over them, this pain inside them, all this led them to believe that they were only insects, that man is the impossible dream of cockroaches and woodlice, and that they would awaken as vermin, like everybody else."[9] In this hallucinatory vision, the victims of torture are imagined to experience their suffering as a forcible expulsion from the human condition and an awakening to their dehumanized abjection as vermin, or bare life.

Sartre revisits this vision of torture a few years later, during the Algerian war, when he observes that "it is for the title of *man* that the torturer pits himself against the tortured, and the whole thing happens as though they could not both belong to the human species," here deliberately echoing Antelme on Nazism's attempt to sunder the species.[10] For audiences in 1959, the portrayal of the inhuman as vermin in *The Condemned of Altona* would not only evoke familiar anti-Semitic Nazi propaganda of Jews as vermin, but also French designations of North Africans as parasites, as *ratons* or rodents, thus opening a dialogue between these two legacies of racialized violence and their construction of the enemy as external to the human species. This sense of expulsion from the human species haunts the contemporary testimonies of Algerian victims of torture as well. Djamila Boupacha will later declare that: "When I endured the pain from my torturers' blows, I was sure that we no longer belonged to the human species."[11] To the extent that the discourse of torture as dehumanization had been well established in discussions of the Third Reich, such declarations in Algerian testimonies of French torture produce an eerie echo of the archive of the Nazi genocide. Sartre's writings operated within an ambient tropology of dehumanization that wove the concentrationary experience, occupation, extermination, and torture into a *noeud de mémoire*.

Sartre's vision of the human as a dream of cockroaches under the Nazi Occupation thus returns a decade later in the context of decolonization, informing both his political and literary writings. In *The Condemned of Altona* and its allegory of the crabs, however, the dehumanizing trauma of torture is portrayed through its effects on the

---

9. Sartre, *Qu'est-ce que la littérature?* (Paris: Gallimard, 1948), 219 (my translation).
10. Sartre, *Colonialism and Neocolonialism*, trans. A. Haddour, S. Brewer, T. McWilliams (London and New York: Routledge), 85.
11. *Djamila Boupacha* (Gallimard, 1962), 72. The legacy of Nazism saturates the testimonies of torture at the hands of the French from the 1950s on: Henri Alleg, of course, who notes how French paratroopers themselves sought to model their practices and techniques on the Gestapo, but also H.G. Esmeralda (a Jewish Berber tortured for giving medical aid to the FLN) in *Un été en enfer: Barbarie à la française* (Exils, 2004), a testimony that also appeared in fragments in 1957.

perpetrator and not the victim of such an act. The possibility that Frantz could "awaken as vermin, like everybody else" and encounter his vulnerability as bare life is precisely what he disavows. Initially repelled by the detainees and their vermin, as torturer he seeks to turn other human beings into vermin, yet paradoxically he comes to embody the vermin he reviled when he declares humankind to be an impossible dream, not of cockroaches or woodlice, but of crabs.

Frantz von Gerlach thus comes to embody the inhumanity from which he recoiled as witness and attempted to produce as perpetrator. In a scene that stages this paradoxical turn, he imagines the future as a tribunal of good, beautiful men and it is he who is the crab scuttling under their gaze: "The crabs are men. (Pause.) What? (He sits down.) . . . Real men, good and handsome, on all the balconies of the centuries. Me, I was scuttling in the courtyard; I thought I heard them saying: 'What's that, brother?' And that, that was me. (*He stands up, springs to attention, gives a military salute, and speaks in a loud voice.*) I the Crab" (*CA* 132, trans. modified). Frantz's designation of himself as an abject inhuman thing, as *that* (*ça*), recalls his youthful response to the abjection of the camp inmates, when he declared to his father that "they couldn't turn me into *that*," that is to say, into vermin. Yet his military salute under Hitler's portrait in this scene suggests that his abject crabhood is the result of his participation in the circuit of Nazi dehumanization. Frantz's will to torture produces within him the very metamorphosis he seeks to inscribe on others. His crustacean mutations occur whenever the memory of having tortured comes up and vividly illustrate the point that, from consecrating the sovereignty of one species over another, the boomerang effect of torture unravels the distinction between human and inhuman altogether in a reciprocal petrification where both victim and perpetrator become insect, vermin, cockroach, or crab.

These figures of mineral hardness and impermeability recurrently link the Final Solution to colonialism, occupation, and empire in Sartre's thought. In his *Antisemite and Jew*, Sartre portrays the anti-Semite's desire to become a "ruthless rock" (*un roc impitoyable*), a gleaming knife, even a towering stone cathedral, "anything but a man."[12] Colonialism is similarly diagnosed in his preface to Frantz Fanon's *The Wretched of the Earth* as a petrified and petrifying ideol-

---

12. Sartre, *Réflexions sur la question juive* (Paris: Gallimard, 1954), 64, my translation, and "L'enfance d'un chef."

ogy, for in order to occupy the colonial space—one that Fanon himself described as a quasi-*mineral* setting—the colonizers must transform the native into a "speaking beast" and in turn, "they must harden, give themselves the opaque consistency and impermeability of stone; in short, they must in turn dehumanize themselves."[13] Sartre's figures of petrification draw analogies between distinct sites and regimes of violence. Their crabwalk through history suggests that the battle of the species enacted with such bodily immediacy in torture is a genocidal matrix at the core of the concentration camp, the occupied territory, and the colonial empire alike. By figuring particular historical forms of dehumanization through images of petrification (such as the cockroach, vermin, or crab), Sartre points to the productivity of allegory as a vector of multidirectional memory.

Torture is the territorial occupation of another's body and as such, it is the most concrete embodiment of imperialism: the prisoner is reduced to abject sentience or vermin in contrast to the torturer's self-extension, the boundaries between the human and the inhuman are thus secured, and as Elaine Scarry puts it in her analysis of its structure, real pain is converted into the fiction of absolute power.[14] For Jean Améry, who was tortured in Fort Breendonk, torture's inscription of power upon the human body is structurally akin to imperial conquest; both are forms of occupation whether bodily or territorial. Améry's own account is imbued with the rhetoric of imperialism: the Gestapo's blows upon him were felt as a terrifying border violation, an orgy of unchecked self-expansion in which his torturers' "faces were concentrated in murderous self-realization" as they exercised their "agonizing sovereignty" upon his body and mind.[15] For Améry, who was then deported to Auschwitz, Buchenwald, and Bergen-Belsen, torture was both the most tangible incarnation of the Third Reich ("materialized in all the density of its being") and the summation of its imperialist logic. This imbrication of torture and imperialism has been echoed more recently in J.M. Coetzee's haunting allegory of apartheid, *Waiting for the Barbarians*, where the body of the tortured victim is both the material foundation and the symbol of Empire, for

---

13. Frantz Fanon, *Les damnés de la terre* (La Découverte, 2002), 53; Sartre, *Colonialism and Neocolonialism*, 61.
14. Elaine Scarry, *The Body in Pain: The Making and Unmaking of the World* (Oxford: Oxford University Press, 1985), 27–59.
15. Améry, *At the Mind's Limits*, 36.

it is by marking the body of its enemy as an illegible barbarian that imperial boundaries are traced and consolidated.[16]

The imperial structure of torture is unveiled at multiple levels in Sartre's *The Condemned of Altona*. Indeed, Frantz's own acts as a perpetrator are rhetorically linked to his family's shipbuilding empire: just as the Father's fleet of ships "traced" the von Gerlach name on the seas, similarly, with the cruder instruments of a penknife and lighter, Frantz will inscribe his name on the bodies of his prisoners:

> *Johanna:* To act means to kill?
> *Frantz* (to Johanna): That's acting. Writing one's name.
> *Klages:* On what?
> *Frantz* (to Klages): On what's there. I write mine on those fields there.
> (145)

It is no accident that Frantz resorts to torture, or writing his name on what is there, in the ruins of the Third Reich's eastward imperial expansion. The analogy with France faltering in Algeria as its soldiers labor upon the bodies of insurgents would not have been lost on contemporary audiences.

In Sartre's play, the Nazi camps' production of inhumanity enables the idealist Frantz's descent into torture. Similarly, the late-colonial French state produced the racialized hatred that Sartre describes as an anonymous magnetic force field passing through and corroding its agents, thereby enabling perfectly decent French soldiers to torture in Algeria: "In this business, the individual does not count; a kind of stray, anonymous hatred, a radical hatred of man, takes hold of both torturers and victims, degrading them together and each by the other. Torture is this hatred, set up as a system, and creating its own instruments."[17] Numerous testimonies of perpetrators in Algeria illustrate the colonial system's role in conditioning this racialized dehumanization even before the conscripts landed, offering ample evidence that torture is not the result of "a few bad apples" but of an established and sanctioned system of relations. As one conscript recalls, "From the start we were taught to consider and to treat them (the Algerians)

---

16. Like Sartre's play, Coetzee's *Waiting for the Barbarians* is a parable of complicity, for the magistrate who makes love to the barbarian woman in fact seeks to recover the traces that her torturers left upon her body, casting one net of meaning over another to make this body readable and to possess the significance of its damaged history.

17. Sartre, *Colonialism and Neo-Colonialism*, 81.

like dogs. Really like dogs. Even when we were in France at school, all they talked about were *bougnoules*."[18] One might recall a more recent illustration of this institutionalized rhetoric of dehumanization in the US military, when Major General Geoffrey Miller, who implemented Guantanamo's interrogation techniques in Abu Ghraib, declared to his officers that if they didn't "treat these prisoners like dogs," they had lost control of the interrogation.[19] For many young French soldiers in Algeria (as with their recent counterparts in Iraq and elsewhere), the descent into torture mirrors Frantz's own "slippage" into a murderous relation with the other, when he fails to see the abject detainees as human beings. A French conscript in the Aurès remembers the slippery slope of torture in remarkably similar terms: "We let ourselves slip (*on se laissait glisser*). And then we became indifferent, the slaps, the insults, the blows we inflicted on the prisoners, it didn't affect us anymore. We were caught in a dirty game, everything seemed natural."[20] This *glissement* into murderous dehumanization—its incarnation as a system of naturalized relations under colonialism and its bodily enactment in torture—is what Sartre seeks to convey and denaturalize through his eerie dialectic of vermin and crab. In this sense, Sartre's crustacean allegory knowingly staged the kind of alienating shock produced by the diffusion of Abu Ghraib's photographs, which made the unacknowledged beast of state-sanctioned torture rear its ugly head. As Mark Danner has observed, "Abu Ghraib made torture televisual. For the first and only time in the nearly five years of the war on terror, torture raised its repellent form from the grey swamp of newspaper reporting and pundit commentary to stand front and center in the American consciousness: shocking, bewildering, disgusting—undeniable."[21] Sartre's play performed a similar function in its time, albeit with the twists and turns of allegory required by censorship; it continues to evoke distinctive historical iterations of torture within a multiplying network of memories and legacies of violence.

If the enigmatic crabs of Sartre's play portray "the burning judgment of some unimaginable and alien posterity," such allegorical fig-

---

18. *Le monde*, 11/11/2000.
19. See the testimony of Former Brigadier General Janis Karpinski, http://www.fidh.org/IMG/pdf/doc_20_-_Karpinski_Testimony.pdf.
20. *Le monde*, 11/11/2000.
21. Mark Danner,"Bodies Under Stress," http://www.markdanner.com/articles/show/106.

ures also spoke eloquently of contemporary torture to audiences during the Algerian war, as they continue to do so today.[22] As Kristin Ross has argued, Algeria during the war became France's monstrous double, a place in which banal household items such as a telephone or a bathtub became alien instruments of unimaginable pain. The *magnétophone* or tape recorder used to record Frantz's testimony would have reminded audiences of the homonymous device designed for electrotorture, the *magnéto*, a field telephone adapted with alligator clips. In an image that may well have inspired Sartre's crabs, Henri Alleg recalls the shiny steel claws attached to electrodes that will be applied to his earlobes and genitals, noting with grim irony that these were called "crocodile clips" by telephone engineers.[23] More generally, Sartre's diagnosis of torture as the face-to-face outcome of a mechanized set of relations, as well as its mutually petrifying effects, resonates with contemporary testimonies by its victims. In his sober account of the excruciating pain he endured at the hands of the *paras* in El Biar, Alleg describes torture as a petrifying technology that transforms the human into a machine: Alleg is virtually plugged into his torture device when an electrified wire is inserted into his mouth and his jaws are soldered to the electrode by the current, such that he cannot unlock his teeth. In another horrific ordeal of electric torture, Alleg describes how "At each shock, I started but did not cry out. I had become almost as insensitive as a machine" (*presque aussi insensible qu'une mécanique*).[24] In his agony, Alleg feels himself to be an inhuman machine, an extension of torture's instruments. The victim's sense of petrification and insertion into an implacable machine is powerfully captured in Chilean painter Roberto Matta's *La question ou Le supplice de Djamila* (1961). Matta's title was a double reference to Henri Alleg and to Djamila Boupacha, a young Algerian freedom fighter tortured and raped by the French army. Both Boupacha's ordeal and Matta's disquietingly erotic representation underscores the linkage of torture and the sex act in the cultural imagination that Ross Chambers examines in this volume. *La question ou Le supplice de Djamila* depicts a disjointed, splayed body that is virtually "processed" by the machinery of torture. The victim's limbs and those of

22. Fredric Jameson, *Sartre: The Origins of a Style* (New York: Columbia University Press, 1984), 305.
23. Henri Alleg, *The Question* (New York: George Braziller, 1958), trans. John Calder, 54.
24. Ibid., 79.

the tormentors appear fused by metal instruments, making visible Alleg's sensation of fusion with the apparatus of torture. Matta represents Djamila Boupacha's ordeal as a mechanized process that imbricates the victim with her executioners in a chilling image of torture's reciprocal petrification. The mechanical imagery of Sartre, Alleg, and Matta suggest torture to be the material incarnation of an existing web of relations. Far from consecrating the victory of one species over another, torture is a magnetic force field that processes victims, perpetrators, and accomplices alike into anonymous vectors of terror. As Frantz's own mutations illustrate, the boomerang effect of violence inevitably infects perpetrators, locking them into a mutual dehumanization with their victims.

The boomerang effect so vividly corporealized as a dialectic between vermin and crab in *The Condemned of Altona* gives a concrete —if hallucinatory—bodily image to Aimé Césaire's critique of colonialism's mutually dehumanizing effects. But it also gives us an image for Césaire's historical diagnosis of Nazism as the *choc en retour* or historical rebound of European colonialism come home to the metropole.[25] Indeed, in Sartre's play, the figures of the camp detainees, the dead rabbi, and the tortured partisans in Smolensk are implicitly linked in their racialized abjection. Frantz's victims, turned into vermin within their lifetime, also remind viewers that Hitler's own eastward production of *Lebensraum* was a racialized imperial project in which Slavs were cast as a sub-human slave population occupying a space to be conquered in the model of European colonial rule ("The Russian space is our India," Hitler declared).[26] It is probable that these silent, indeed silenced, figures in Smolensk and their links to Jewish victims would have simultaneously evoked the Algerian subject during decolonization. Sartre's figures of petrification thus brought Nazi barbarism and its own colonial archive home to French terrain. While the dialectic of vermin and crab conveys something of the phenomenological texture of torture's effects, the migration of victims in the

---

25. Aimé Césaire, "the colonizer, who in order to ease his conscience gets into the habit of seeing the other man as an animal (*la bête*), accustoms himself to treating him like an animal, and tends objectively to transform *himself* into an animal. It is this result, this boomerang effect (*ce choc en retour*) of colonization that I wanted to point out," *Discourse on Colonialism*, trans. J. Pinkham (New York: Monthly Review Press, 1955), 5. For a powerful analysis of Césaire's *choc en retour* in relation to colonialism and genocide, see Michael Rothberg, *Multidirectional Memory: Remembering the Holocaust in the Age of Decolonization* (Stanford: Stanford University Press, 2009), 66–107.

26. *Hitler's Table Talk*, 1941–1944, (Oxford: Oxford University Press, 1988), 32.

play, from the Nazi camps to Hitler's imperial expansion and its *Ostpolitik* come to allegorize the genocidal kernel of French colonial rule and its bodily materialization as torture both in the colony and the metropole.

This figural dislocation of imperial violence and its migration across different historical contexts and geopolitical sites does come at a price, however. In *The Condemned of Altona*, the victims of distinct histories of racialized violence are never represented on stage. They are precarious ghosts invoked in dream-like flashbacks, who exist only in their somatic incorporation by the von Gerlach family. The rabbi whose throat is slit resurfaces metaphorically as the Father's throat cancer and suggests that the specter of the Holocaust continues to contaminate postwar Germany's industrial empire. Similarly Frantz, the mad crab in the attic, comes to allegorize the gangrene of torture infecting postwar France. Both father and son are subject to forms of psychic and bodily occupation by the ghosts of their past, yet their victims are never embodied or given voice. Instead, they are incorporated by the agents of their death. Frantz's thirst for martyrdom, his case of survivor's guilt, his willed incarceration in a dank cell reminiscent of concentrationary barracks, emaciated and in rags, even his obsession with crabs, are attempts to embody the victimized inhumanity he disavowed. Haunted by a suffering that he once inflicted and yet was unable to feel, his anguish is a form of ontological hunger that usurps his victims' voices. In sharp contrast to Sartre's *The Victors* (*Morts sans sépulture*), a play that in 1947 shocked audiences by portraying the torture of resistance fighters by the French *milice*, *The Condemned of Altona* never represents the victims' bodies or voices. They are only invoked through the traumatic imprint they leave behind on their murderers.[27] This dramaturgical choice turns the victims of torture and extermination into so many ghosts that inhabit, haunt, and indeed "occupy" the play's embedded historical landscapes.

This ghosting of bodies and histories can, and of course should, be linked to Sartre's tendency to subsume the specificity of racial and cultural identities under totalizing analyses of violence. Indeed the ghostly, silent rabbi recalls Sartre's postwar vision of the Jew as a "phantom personality at once strange and familiar, that haunts him

---

27. Sartre touches upon a nascent interest in the phenomenon of perpetrator trauma that dominated in *la mode rétro* of the 1970s and that seems to be resurfacing in France, with the prize-winning novel by Jonathan Littel on the traumatic testimony of Nazi officer Maximilen Aue, *Les Bienveillantes*.

and is nothing but himself—himself as others see him," that is to say, as a spectral construct that circulates in French culture.[28] This analysis of Jewishness as the reactive product of anti-Semitism is replicated in Sartre's definition of the colonial subject as locked in an embrace with the colonizer: "the colonialist and the native are a couple, produced by an antagonistic situation and by one another."[29] Throughout Sartre's writings, the colonized subject and the Jew are evacuated of their historical, religious, or racial specificity, in a gesture decried by Frantz Fanon and others.

Yet as Walter Benjamin has observed, this hollowing out of bodies and histories is also a feature of allegory itself, a rhetorical figure that unmoors image and meaning and whose structure of substitution turns its objects of representation into so many ghosts or "phantom proxies" that can be pressed in service of other times, bodies, and places. The allegorical registers of Sartre's play erase the particularity of the Final Solution, to be sure. Yet it is this betrayal of testimonial specificity that opens up a politics of memory in the play. Allegory's separation of objects and bodies from the meanings invested in them is precisely what allows Sartre to mobilize the memory of ghosts such as the mad rabbi and the mute Russian partisans in service of contesting other histories of imperialism. By projecting France into the mirror of Nazism, Sartre gave an allegorical face to the "war without a name," a face whose monstrousness exploded the fiction of France's incorporation of Algeria into its national body, and exposed the moral petrification that was its price.

In his preface to Alleg's *La question*, Sartre denounced the appalling irony of France's Gestapo tactics in Algeria, noting that it had only taken fifteen years to turn victims into perpetrators: "Depending on the circumstances, anyone, at any time will become a victim or a perpetrator. . . . Victim and perpetrator are one and the same image: and it is our image."[30] This vision of history as an unstoppable wheel of violence that turns victims into perpetrators, witnesses into accomplices, vermin into crab is at the heart of *The Condemned of*

---

28. Sartre, *Anti-Semite and Jew* (New York: Knopf, 1995), 78. For a discussion of the "spectralization" of Jewishness in Sartre's postwar thought, see Jonathan Judaken, *Jean-Paul Sartre and the Jewish Question* (Lincoln, Nebraska: University of Nebraska Press, 2006), 145.

29. Sartre, *Critique of Dialectical Reason*, vol. 1, trans. A. Sheridan-Smith (London and New York: Verso, 2004), 721.

30. Sartre, *Colonialism and Neocolonialism*, 76.

Altona and illuminates the play's bewildering conclusion. Frantz's final ravings, which are recorded and posthumously played on an empty stage, explain his century's inhumanity in the following terms: "The beast was hiding, we would suddenly catch its gaze in the intimate eyes of our fellow men; so we struck. I caught the beast, I struck, a man fell and in his dying eyes I saw the beast, still alive, myself" (178, trans. modified). Whereas Frantz had previously recoiled from the camp inmates because of the inhumanity he saw in their eyes, in the end it is his own inhumanity that is reflected in his victims' eyes. This mutation into the very beast that is to be destroyed also characterizes France as a nation. Once horrified by the atrocities committed by the Nazis, the French public has imperceptibly slipped into their footsteps: "everything occurred unnoticed, by imperceptible abdications; and then when we looked up we saw in the mirror an alien, hateful face: ourselves."[31]

"I saw the beast, still alive, myself," "we see an alien and hateful face ... ourselves": both Frantz the protagonist and France the nation are compelled to assume a face that appears murderously alien and yet turns out to be intimate, if not constitutive. The enemy whose face is our own is, as I have mentioned, a recurrent figure in the postwar rhetoric that analogized Nazism with French colonialism. One recalls Resnais and Cayrols' *Night and Fog*, which also sought to illuminate Algeria through Auschwitz in its final warning that the face of tomorrow's executioners may be no different from our own. This mutation from victim to executioner, from human to alien, is brilliantly staged in the closing moments of Sartre's play. As Frantz's disembodied voice emerges out of the inhuman technological medium of the tape recorder from a stage that is voided of human presence, the spectators become the tribunal that will pass judgment on his life and century. Yet these spectators are not positioned as fellow human beings but as the crabs of the future. In fact, in one of its few (American) productions during the Vietnam War, Frantz addresses all of his crab monologues directly to the audiences, thus underscoring the play's anti-imperial valences.[32] Frantz's final address, voiced by a tape

---

31. Ibid. (trans. modified)

32. Directors R.G. Davis and Peter Berg made the following remark on this production: "Let's do it backwards. That's how it was learned anyway. The past is only understandable from the present. We'll start from now: the U.S. must be destroyed. This is what Sartre's *Condemned of Altona* taught me." "Sartre through Brecht," in *The Drama Review* (1967–1968) 12 (Autumn 1967): 132.

recorder to a crustacean audience, by one dehumanized entity to another, staged the petrifying consequences of sanctioning torture in establishing the sovereignty of one species over another.

"I lacked imagination . . . Out there," Frantz says of his days as torturer in Smolensk (CA 162), in a pivotal moment in the play, where Sartre's usually systemic approach to violence opens into a dialogue with Albert Camus's call for an imaginative approach to history through what he termed "the eyes of the body," that is to say, through a sensory and affective reception of its violence and injustice, one for which the figural displacements of literary form, and of allegory itself, are paradoxically most suited. Camus's embodied apprehension of history haunts Sartre's own *oeuvre* and the phenomenology of racialized violence that it offers through its metaphors of petrification. The sheer strangeness of the crustacean imagery in *The Condemned of Altona*, its final address to an audience of future crabs, were ways of restoring to torture some of its alien horror and of wrenching the postwar French public out of its "tetanus of the imagination."[33]

In a recent novel titled *Crabwalk (Im Krebsgang)*, a meditation on the infernal repetitions of history in postwar Germany, Günter Grass describes historical investigation in terms that capture Sartre's use of allegory, as "sneak(ing) up on time in a crabwalk, seeming to go backward but actually scuttling sideways, and thereby working . . . forward."[34] In *The Condemned of Altona*, it is through the back door of the Nazi past that Sartre sneaks up on France's late-colonial present, and works forward to illuminate the ever-actual centrality of torture to Empire. In a climate that tends to privilege monolithic representations of trauma and victimization, and when the Holocaust itself has been constructed as a singular and unrepresentable event, Sartre's allegory reminds us of a time when its legacy was actively pressed in service of other struggles. Yet what is distinctive about Grass's figure for historical inquiry is the sideways motion of the crabwalk, and the alternative it offers to *reading* allegory in univocal, chronological, or hierarchical terms, as even Sartre did when he positioned Algeria "behind" Germany in his play. The spatial figure of the crabwalk invites us to read time allegorically, such that Nazism and imperialism, genocide and colonialism, the Holocaust and decolonization are addressed

---

33. Simone de Beauvoir on the French public's incapacity to grapple with the phenomenon of torture during the Algerian war. Cited in Rita Maran, *Torture and the Role of Ideology in the French-Algerian War* (New York: Praeger Publications, 1989), 143.

34. Günter Grass, *Crabwalk*, trans. K. Winston (New York: Harcourt, 2003), 3.

side by side by side in relations of proximity and mutual illumination rather than of petrified equivalence and identity. The crabwalk suggests a circuit of communication that travels forward and backward in time as well as sideways in space; it offers a mode of reading that brings different histories into proximity and adjacency without reducing one to the other or positing them as analogous, symmetrical, and reversible. Finally, crabwalk history opens the possibility of tracing intersections and interferences between multiple histories that are bound together in the fabric of the cultural imagination and yet distinguished by knots of historical specificity, of attending to "noeuds de mémoire" as well as to "lieux de mémoire." In such a formulation, the Nazi genocide, late colonialism, and postcolonial iterations of imperialism would inevitably inform one another, but they would not necessarily be abstracted into the same unwavering historical paradigm. Similarly, these histories might continue to be invoked to illuminate our own present without suggesting that contemporary political configurations mirror those of the past. Indeed, the very fact that "occupation," "torture," and "genocide" are terms suffused with distinctive histories and yet, at the same time, are markers of an unfolding present suggest that Sartre's crabs are still speaking to us in allegories that have yet to be deciphered.

II. Entangled Lives

ESTELLE TARICA

Jewish Mysticism and the Ethics of Decolonization in André Schwarz-Bart

The three novels published by French author André Schwarz-Bart are primordially concerned with human suffering on a grand scale. His first novel was an immensely popular prize-winning Holocaust novel, *Le dernier des justes* (1959), published to great acclaim and some controversy. His second novel, *Un plat de porc aux bananes vertes* (1967), was co-authored with his wife, Guadeloupe novelist Simone Schwarz-Bart; set in 1952, it is about an elderly Martinican woman living out her final days in a Paris hospice. His third novel, *La Mulâtresse Solitude* (1972), is a historical novel set in eighteenth century Guadeloupe and based on the life of a legendary rebel slave named Solitude.[1] These works focus on traumatic Jewish and African diaspora experiences—the Holocaust, West Indian slavery, postcolonial immigration to France—and appear to have been directly influenced by developments in the author's life: the fate of his family in the Holocaust,[2] his alliances with West Indians in postwar Paris, his marriage to Simone and move to Guadeloupe with her, and his engagement with decolonization and national liberation movements in North Africa and the Caribbean.

Beyond the biographical connections, however, these works are linked by Schwarz-Bart's conviction that Jewish and black collective identities have been similarly shaped by a history of slavery and stigma; what they have in common is the burden of a traumatic past.

---

1. André Schwarz-Bart, *Le dernier des justes*. (Paris: Éditions du Seuil, 1959); André Schwarz-Bart and Simone Schwarz-Bart, *Un plat de porc aux bananes vertes* (Paris: Éditions du Seuil, 1967); André Schwarz-Bart, *La Mulâtresse Solitude* (Paris: Éditions du Seuil, 1972).
2. Schwarz-Bart survived the Holocaust in hiding. He managed to save three of his siblings from deportation; the rest of his family perished.

Schwarz-Bart's view of this shared relationship to the past produces a particular ethical and affective vision, a significant aspect of his work that has yet to be fully explored. That vision draws on a combination of political and theological sources and often takes a mystical form in his novels, in which we find the problem of the existence of suffering in the world to be an important source of conflict. As Michael Rothberg and Bella Brodzki have each pointed out, Schwarz-Bart's view of the past is mythical and spectral, a turn away from historicism.[3] These elements of Schwarz-Bart's work have sometimes been treated by critics with a degree of skepticism because they suggest a redemptive or even escapist relationship to the violence of limit events from the past, especially the Holocaust. Yet these aspects of Schwarz-Bart's work need to be re-evaluated in light of his own quite sophisticated, learned, and politically-committed approach to the traumas of Jewish and black history. In fact Schwarz-Bart's turn to mysticism is not an escapist turn away from history, but rather the result of his confrontation with the ruptural effects that the Holocaust and African slavery occasioned for Jewish and West Indian historical consciousness. The political force of Schwarz-Bart's ethos, meanwhile, lies precisely in its reparative and metaphysical character, for it is this aspect of his thought that guided his relationship to decolonization in the 1960s and drew him into a complex dialogue with anticolonial thought, which involved an implicit rejection of ethno-nationalism but respect for other forms of ethno-particularism.

The mystical current that circulates through the works is perhaps the most salient feature linking together his three novels and their Jewish, African, and Caribbean themes. It produces a particular ethos of sympathetic awareness, what I will call Schwarz-Bart's *reparative intent*, which underlies the human relations the novels depict and lends them an other-worldly dimension. In each of his works we find a recurring situation: the characters display a capacity for an inter-subjective encounter that allows them a metaphysical transport away from indignity. Schwarz-Bart's vision of this encounter was influenced by Emmanuel Levinas and Martin Buber, and his work as a whole can thus be said to participate in the "retrieval of humanism" associated

---

3. Michael Rothberg, *Multidirectional Memory: Remembering the Holocaust in the Age of Decolonization* (Stanford: Stanford University Press, 2009), 138–53; Bella Brodzki, "Nomadism and the Textualization of Memory in André Schwarz-Bart's *La Mulâtresse Solitude*," Yale French Studies 83/2 (1993): 224.

with the postwar efforts of these Jewish philosophers.[4] To understand the significance of Schwarz-Bart's linkage of the Holocaust to African and Caribbean history, we must therefore look to the phenomenologies of racism and anti-Semitism that he explores, and to the reparative, consoling nature of his response.

In essays and interviews, Schwarz-Bart established that the affinity between Jews and the people colonized and enslaved by France was central to the conception of his novels. He once said of his overall project that he aimed to write a "reversible book," one that would operate like a reversible garment, as Francine Kaufman describes it, which "can be read on both sides at the same time: a black side and a Jewish side."[5] Yet when the three novels are assessed individually their shared origin and "reversible" vision can be difficult to perceive, a limitation that Schwarz-Bart himself was apparently conscious of (Kaufman, 34). Indeed, one of the difficulties of interpreting the significance of Schwarz-Bart's project of bringing Jewish and Antillean histories together is that the link between them is so fleeting and allusive, in each novel quite marginal to the story at hand. The awareness of a common legacy hardly appears in the individual novels, if at all. Here it is important to remember that Schwarz-Bart envisaged these three works as part of a series of nine volumes that he never completed. Presumably the full significance of the relationship between the two collective histories would have been revealed across the projected cycle of novels. As the work stands now, however, the link between the Shoah and the black diaspora can only be tentatively sought in the fragments of this vast unfinished history, as some critics have already done.

For instance, Michael Rothberg has shown that what links black and Jewish histories together in Schwarz-Bart's work is the deliberate use of anachronism, establishing a relationship to the past as spectral that can be found in Schwarz-Bart's Holocaust novel *Le dernier des justes* as well in his Caribbean novel *La Mulâtresse Solitude*; in both works, "a strong drive toward historical continuity coexists with

---

4. Matthew Calarco, "The Retrieval of Humanism in Buber and Levinas," in *Levinas and Buber: Dialogue and Difference*, ed. Peter Atterton, Matthew Calarco and Maurice Friedman (Pittsburgh: Duquesne University Press, 2004), 250–61.

5. Francine Kaufman, "André Schwarz-Bart, entre mémoire juive et mémoire noire: une oeuvre réversible," in *Dossier: Hommage à André Schwarz-Bart*, ed. Diana Rammassamy and Kathleen Gyssel, *La tribune des Antilles* 53 (October 2008): 34. Translations are my own unless otherwise noted.

ghostly discontinuity" (*Multidirectional Memory*, 142). This awareness of history as ghostly appeared first in the Holocaust novel but in fact, Rothberg argues, it was inspired by Schwarz-Bart's conversations with his West Indian friends about black slavery, making the Holocaust text the product of cultural and intellectual cross-pollination and producing a kind of mutual haunting of Jewish and West Indian histories across all of the author's works. Meanwhile, Ronnie Scharfman, drawing primarily from *Un plat de porc*, has argued for an allegorical relationship between the black diaspora experience in France and the Holocaust. She argues that because Schwarz-Bart could not confront the concentrationary universe head on—he recounts that various reasons prevented him from doing so, including sheer terror[6]—he turned instead to the old-age home and to the legacy of the black experience of slavery and exile embodied in the novel's main character; these can be seen as stand-ins for the Holocaust and other inexpressible aspects of the Jewish experience, making the novel "a metaphor for Jewish suffering during the Shoah."[7]

What is clear is that Schwarz-Bart was interested in what a relationship to black history could illuminate about Jewish history, and vice-versa, perhaps more so than in using one as a vehicle to represent the other. Indeed, to read *Un plat de porc* as an extended allegory of the Holocaust runs the risk of diminishing the overall importance Schwarz-Bart lent to the themes of black slavery and racism, because it suggests that an absent and unsayable referent—the Holocaust—determines the greater significance of the novel. It is instead the "contiguity" between the two, as he put it,[8] their mutual encounter, that is most important. Such encounters, many of which took place in 1950s Paris, appear as key moments in the author's various autobiographical accounts of how he came to work on the Caribbean and become involved in Caribbean lives.

The symbolism of the biblical Exodus structures Schwarz-Bart's account of one such formative encounter, an epiphany inspired by the word "slavery." In his lengthy 1967 essay in *Le Figaro littéraire*, he

---

6. André Schwarz-Bart, "André Schwarz-Bart s'explique sur huit ans de silence: Pour quoi j'ai écrit La Mulâtresse Solitude," *Le Figaro littéraire*, 26 January 1967, 8.
7. Ronnie Scharfman, "Exiled from the Shoah: André and Simone Schwarz-Bart's *Un plat de porc aux bananes vertes*," in *Auschwitz and After: Race, Culture and "the Jewish Question" in France*, ed. Lawrence Kritzman (New York: Routledge, 1995), 262.
8. Diana Rammassamy and Kathleen Gyssels, "André Schwarz-Bart: Oeuvres," in *Dossier: Hommage à André Schwarz-Bart*, 32.

explains that in postwar France he heard that word in reference to black history, but that it then awakened in him an intimate memory of a Passover Seder, when his father had explained to him, as is the custom, that like all Jews he is a child of slaves under Pharaoh—a condition that Schwarz-Bart would then extend to the Jews under Hitler ("André Schwarz-Bart s'explique," 1). In this relationship to slavery, and from the perspective of that Jewish child who listened to his father, he found himself "taken by definitive and fraternal love" for West Indians, by a "great, keen sympathy" (Ibid.). It is a theme he echoes in an interview with the American Jewish journal *Midstream* later in 1967. He says that before his contact with West Indians, "I had always thought that what happened to the Jews was without comparison with anything that had happened to other human beings. . . . I remained sealed within the solitude of Jewish destiny. But when I found myself face-to-face with people who carried upon their shoulders an experience about which it can be said—without meaning to establish an exact correlation—that it is similar to our own [as Jews], that this suffering still serves to shape them today, I came to know a feeling of fraternity that I had never before felt toward non-Jews."[9]

In Schwarz-Bart's appeal to the existence of a common experience of past trauma, his thinking slides between the mystical and the historical. The Exodus event recalled in the Passover Seder is not only a past event; it also refers to an experience that continues to be actualized across history—even into the very recent past. Thus, Hitler becomes another Pharaoh, and the Holocaust, a re-enslavement. This approach loosens the Jewish past from its moorings in temporal history, making it available as a parable for the continued instruction of Jewish children and a means of interpreting the significance of present-day events and experiences. Brought into the timeless realm of biblical parable, the Jewish past thus framed also becomes available as a template for more universal instruction. Here the Exodus story has been invested with meaning that responds to the contemporary moment of decolonization, much as happened in Latin American liberation theology in the 1960s. Peruvian priest Gustavo Gutiérrez, one of the movement's most important theologians, wrote in his seminal *Liberation Theology* (1971), "The Exodus experience is paradigmatic. It remains vital and contemporary due to similar historical experiences which the people of God undergo."[10]

9. André Schwarz-Bart, "Interview with Michael Salomon," *Midstream* (1967): 4.
10. Gustavo Gutiérrez, *A Theology of Liberation*, Revised Edition, trans. and ed. Sister Caridad Inda and John Eagleson (Maryknoll, NY: Orbis Books, 1988), 90.

He saw the biblical Exodus as an event with an explicitly political meaning pertinent to contemporary national liberation movements: "The liberation of Israel is a political action. It is the breaking away from a situation of despoliation and misery, and the beginning of the construction of a just and comradely society" (88). The Exodus represents for Gutiérrez the "'desacralization' of social praxis," putting the transformation of society into human hands (90).

Schwarz-Bart's renewed appreciation of the meaning of slavery brought him into kinship with West Indians, but he still had to work out the terms of this affinity. Schwarz-Bart's re-encounter with the Exodus story loosed it into a stream of universal history, but his encounter with the anticolonial thought of intellectuals from Africa and the Caribbean brought home the power of particularism, or what he referred to as the "unfathomable hard core" at the heart of each collective cultural entity ("André Schwartz-Bart s'explique," 9). He feared that bringing the black and Jewish experience to bear on each other might violate this particularity, especially because it ran the risk of obscuring, in his words, the "singular," "sentimental" and "folkloric" character of the racism experienced by blacks, by which he seems to have meant its historical, emotional, and cultural specificity (8). Schwarz-Bart was interested in capturing what he called the "great universal stream of violence and degradation," but not at the expense of an appreciation of the singularity of its instances (8). He thus placed tremendous authority in figures who could provide his work with political and cultural authenticity. Conscious that a white man could no longer serve, morally or politically, as the mouthpiece for the aspirations of people of color, he sought approval from leading black intellectuals, especially Aimé Césaire—the publication of his West Indian novels was conditional on Césaire's approval (9). Even more significant, he asked his wife Simone to become a co-author because she provided the knowledge of the Creole language that he lacked. This, he admitted, was the greatest obstacle that he faced when composing his Caribbean novels: "I believed in the limitless power of human sympathy, which was my only weapon in this adventure. . . . Nothing in my text, it seemed to me, represented a betrayal of my West Indian brothers. Nothing, except precisely the absence of that inexpressible element which I was discovering, and which is the flower of any work that springs from a *terroir*, from a spiritual soil" (9).

But by far the most important aspect of Schwarz-Bart's ongoing dialogue and collaboration with West Indians was his loyalty to the sympathetic awareness engendered by his re-encounter with the biblical Exodus and to the reparative urge that it inspired. He wrote, "I believe, according to the terms that Levinas uses with respect to Martin Buber, that the essence of dialogue is not in the universal ideas that interlocutors hold in common nor in the ideas that one has of the other, but in the encounter itself, in the invocation, in the power of the I to say You."[11] Everywhere in his work we see the hard kernel of identity give way to enigma and infinity, to a vast, borderless space opened up when "I" invokes "You."

In the mid-1950s, still while writing *Le dernier des justes*, Schwarz-Bart had a conversation with a West Indian friend on the Paris metro. She was depressed because acquaintances had wounded her, unintentionally, with their racist comments. Schwarz-Bart recounts that he attempted to comfort her by showing her how much progress had been made world-wide in the struggle for black liberation. He pointed to the imminent independence of Africa and predicted the end of racism. Yet his friend refused to be cheered by his optimism. Faced with her refusal, he had a kind of depressing epiphany. He writes, "I had the impression that I was butting up against a mysterious, oppressive reality whose existence I had never before suspected." She says to him, some things will change, but "in a hundred years, in a thousand years . . . a *négresse* will always remain a *négresse*" ("André Schwarz-Bart s'explique," 1; ellipsis in original). He recognizes her "naïve fatalism," as he calls it, as the one he himself had experienced as a Jewish child, and vows to try to convince her that she is wrong—by writing a book.

The novel series, then, originates in his desire to intervene in his friend's negative relationship to herself, a relationship of suffering and despair—his aim is to repair this particular effect of racism, what he calls, in *Un plat de porc*, "metaphysical indignity" (53). This effect, this "mysterious, oppressive reality" in which identity and punishment are indissociable, in which identity is stigma and indignity, and of whose existence he becomes aware in talking with his friend and which he recognizes as having once been his own, permeates *Le dernier des justes* as well as the two subsequent novels. How can writing a book prove to his friend that she need not despair? It seems that

11. Ibid. Schwarz-Bart may have been referring to Levinas's article "La pensée de Martin Buber et le judaïsme contemporain," in *Martin Buber: L'homme et le philosophe*, Introduction by Robert Weltsch (Brussels: Éditions de l'Institut de Sociologie de l'Université Libre de Bruxelles, 1968), 42–58.

this book will not only contain a lesson. The fact of its existence will also be a lesson, a kind of proof or rebuttal. The resulting works—for eventually the author came to think in terms of a cycle of several books—are not simply descriptions of this oppressive reality, but also refutations of it, attempts to deny its claim on reality. This is not to say that the works deny the strength of the experience of stigma; rather, Schwarz-Bart was intent on showing that a certain kind of inter-subjective encounter can generate another, more powerful reality than stigma, and so heal the breach.

Of all the formative experiences that Schwarz-Bart recounts in his story of the genesis of his novel series, it is this reparative intention that has left its most enduring trace in the novels themselves, both formally and thematically. What links the three existing novels together is the presence of an exemplary character—Ernie Lévy in *Le dernier des justes*, the narrator Marie of *Un plat de porc*, Solitude herself—who responds to surrounding brutality or indignity with the attitude of sympathetic awareness that Schwarz-Bart had described in his essay in *Le Figaro littéraire*. This attitude infuses the entire narration—even those moments of violence so unbearable that they would seem immune to consolation. One of the principal aims of this sympathetic awareness appears to be to offer evidence of the existence of an alternative reality more powerful than the oppressive reality in which the characters live. The appearance of this awareness at critical junctures has a mystical effect, for it seems to transport those whom it reaches out of the world and into a better place; such characters, or more precisely, the awareness embodied in these characters, is a kind of bridge between two worlds. These moments thus have the trappings of the mystical "escape from history," the escape from the temporal and finite world to a world of timeless infinity.[12]

Hence the recurrence of a certain gesture on the part of Schwarz-Bart's characters and narrators toward the existence of a more profound reality underlying that negative reality of "metaphysical indignity" in which their daily lives unfold—whether as European Jews, West Indians in contemporary France, or Africans and West Indians living in slavery. Repeatedly, we are brought to their consciousness of standing before a vast and enigmatic reality, quite often embodied in the form of another person. In the novel *La Mulâtresse Solitude*, the

---

12. Gershom Scholem, *Major Trends in Jewish Mysticism*, Third Edition Revised (New York: Schocken Books, 1971 [1946]), 20.

awareness of enigma comes to the title character through her mother, whose mystery the child attempts to decipher: "she would concentrate very hard in the earnest hope of penetrating Man Bobette's secrets . . . she resumed her delicate, exacting task, winding and unwinding the thread of her reverie."[13] Solitude in turn grows up to be a mystery to those around her, a strange presence in their midst of whom they ask, "Is she of this world?" (129). At the end of the novel, in the chaos of the last battle between the rebel slaves and the French army, her thoughts turn outward to consider the sky "as vast as the sea, where all things . . . are confounded in insignificance" (145).

The appearance of this mystical "escape from history" derives not only from a theological inspiration. It was also guided by a formal problem Schwarz-Bart confronted as he was composing the novels of the Solitude series. He realized that West Indian identity cannot be grasped in the traditional way, by tracing back a line in time and using genealogy as the narrative backbone of the novel. This is because (and here he seemingly anticipates Glissant), "the true depths of the Antilles is the rupture (le déchirement)" ("André Schwarz-Bart s'explique," 1; ellipsis in original). For a novelist who wants to write a historical novel, this realization poses a serious dilemma. His answer, he writes, was to create a character who is internally vast, as vast as the world, a "Carrier of Times" (porteuse du Temps), to encompass that history of rupture not from some point outside it but from within the subject herself. Schwarz-Bart's turn to the mystical is thus caused by the limits of conventional history imposed by the fact of African slavery.

The enigmatic beings who people the novel thus become symbols in the mystical sense of the word. As Scholem explains, "[I]n itself, through its own existence, [the mystical symbol] makes another reality transparent which cannot appear in any other form. . . . A hidden and inexpressible reality finds its expression in the symbol" (Scholem, 27). Solitude's capacity to perceive a hidden and formless reality "expressed" through or by the people-symbols whom she meets across her life sets her at odds with the all-too-concrete and visible reality of the slave plantation. It lends that brutal reality, filled with torture and ruled by the punitive visual economy of the phenotype, a baroque air of unreality, of *mere* appearance. Solitude's "delicate, exacting task" of

---

13. André Schwarz-Bart, *A Woman Named Solitude*, trans. Ralph Manheim, Introdoction by Arnold Rampersad (San Francisco: Donald S. Ellis Publisher, 1985), 53–54.

deciphering the people-symbols around her, a task everywhere associated in the novel with love and tenderness, works a kind of magic on the "real" environment, effectively diminishing it. Eventually, Solitude herself becomes a symbol, especially in her after-life as a figure of legend.

Working backwards chronologically to Schwarz-Bart's second novel, *Un plat de porc aux bananes vertes*, co-authored with Simone, we find similar gestures performed by Marie, the narrator. We learn that Marie is the great-granddaughter of the rebel slave Solitude. Like Solitude, Marie has a special capacity to recover from the indignity and despair caused by her miserable circumstances. She is often insulted by other patients in the old-age home with the lacerating lip-smacker "miam miam" (yum, yum), absurd references to cannibalism whose effects, the narrator reports, "send me back to my nothingness [*néant*] as a *négresse*" (*Un plat de porc*, 52–53). The phrase recalls Schwarz-Bart's conversation with her friend on the Paris Métro, her pessimistic "believe me, my dear André, in a hundred years, in a thousand years . . . a *négresse* will always remain a *négresse*"—"néant" and "négresse" are fatally and fatalistically conjoined. In one instance the insult to Marie is followed by an act of physical assault, the swiping of Marie's glasses from her face, leaving her blind. From this sightless nothingness, Marie responds desolately to her assailant with the cry, "Mademoiselle! . . . Infinitely! . . . *Infinitely,* . . . I tell you!" (*Un plat de porc,* 53; emphasis and ellipsis in original). The words are short-hand for the polite "Merci infiniment," whose meaning in this context could be both sardonic and obsequious (thank you for insulting me). The reference to "infinity" can hardly be literal, and yet absent the requisite "merci," and so closely following on the idea of the "néant," the word takes on a life of its own, a spontaneous, outraged rebuttal that draws the speaker back into her dignity. Nothingness transmutes into infiniteness. Later, when the narrator is seized by dark thoughts about the past and wonders "how many lives . . . [have been] reduced to ashes?" (206), she turns inward to that infinity, addressing herself as "my sweet little World," and enjoins herself, "oh remember . . . recognize . . . admit . . . never to be able fully to unfold the map of the Universe: because behind these islands, these seas, continents. . . ." (206; ellipses in original). The words end in a suggestive ellipsis, but the thought goes on, as a kind of mantra, to encompass "all those little people perched up there, with all their little eyes but immense, perhaps, in their own suffering," and ending, finally, on a note of her own insignificance, with the question, "what is this but the sigh of a *négresse* into the infinite?" (206).

These gestures lend the novels a recognizably mystical air, but although the presence of mysticism in Schwarz-Bart's work is unmistakable, it is of a nontraditional sort, adapted for secular ends. The people-symbols of *La Mulâtresse Solitude* make a timeless or infinite reality manifest, but that reality consists essentially of their inward selves in relationship to others. Schwarz-Bart was not apparently troubled by the co-existence of a religious and secular worldview in his novels.[14] This may have been due in part to his exposure to the ideas of Martin Buber, whose infusion of Jewish mysticism into a universalist existential and psychological language had already established this possibility. The slippage between mystical and historical registers in Schwarz-Bart's work correlates loosely to Buber's I-You/I-It distinction. Like most novels, those of Schwarz-Bart depict what Buber called "the It world," the object world that one knows and experiences, in which a person, "He" or "She," appears as a "dot in the world grid of space," as "a loose bundle of named qualities."[15] But the novels also seek to transmit something of the I-You relationship, its infinite space of encounter, its timelessness: "It cannot be surveyed: If you try to make it surveyable, you lose it.... The You world does not hang together in space and time" (Buber, 186). Schwarz-Bart's novels are filled with depictions of what Buber called "You moments," an opening onto a dialogue or relation with no borders: "Whoever says You does not have something; he has nothing. But he stands in relation" (182). This kind of I-You relation is not knowing or experiencing an other, but rather "a world in itself" (175).

With Buber serving as a loose intertextual key, it is perhaps less surprising to note the similarity between the Tzaddikim, the Just or Righteous men found in *Le dernier des justes*, and figures such as Marie and Solitude. The Tzaddik is, among other things, a "bridge be-

---

14. For a nuanced account of the co-existence of secular and religious appoaches to the past in Schwarz-Bart's work, especially in *Le dernier des justes*, see Neil Davison, "Inside the Shoah: Narrative, Documentation, and Schwarz-Bart's *The Last of the Just*," *Clio* 24/3 (Spring 1995). (Accessed June 30, 2008). http://gateway.proquest.com/openurl?ctx_ver=Z39.88-2003&xri:pqil:res_ver=0.2&res_id=xri:lion-us&rft_id=xri:lion:ft:mla:R03021037:0

15. Martin Buber, *The Martin Buber Reader:Essential Writings*, ed. Asher D. Biemann, (New York: Palgrave Macmillan, 2002), 183.

tween the divine and the material world."[16] Here too Schwarz-Bart may have been influenced by Buber's early writings on Hasidism, which included material on the Lamed-vov. According to Buber, for the Tzaddik "what matters is not what can be learned; what matters is giving oneself to the unknown" (Buber, 69). The task of the Tzaddik is to fulfill the relation or bond with the infinite (84).

In *The Last of the Just*, that power is accorded, ambiguously, to the protagonist Ernie Lévy as he confronts what Geoffrey Hartman calls "the limit of sensibility," the inability of the senses to assimilate certain events as real, a limit that recurs throughout Holocaust survivor testimonies because of the overwhelming horror of their circumstances.[17] Schwarz-Bart brings this limit, this sense of unreality, to the fore in the penultimate episodes of the novel which recount the cattle-car transport to the death camp and the annihilation in the gas chamber. In the cattle-car Ernie has taken a group of children under his charge. Many of them have already died in the transport, and to soothe the ones still living, he tells them a story of messianic redemption. He says, the dead are just sleeping, and will awaken later on when we arrive in the Kingdom of Israel, a place of joy and comfort. Ernie's voice has a hypnotic effect on his listeners; the children's eyes take on a dreamy expression, though they, like everyone else in that place, are covered in filth and dying of pestilence and thirst. For this reason, Ernie's act enrages another adult in the cattle-car, who hisses at him: "How can you tell them it's only a dream?" Ernie responds politely: "Madame, there is no room for truth here."[18]

The formula recalls a famous line from Primo Levi's *Survival in Auschwitz*, "Hier ist kein warum" (Here there is no why), uttered by an SS guard at the camp when Levi first arrived.[19] The phrase marks the inmate's entry to an arbitrary world utterly divorced from reason. For Levi, it is this aspect of the camp, perhaps more than any other, that crushes him and renders the experience senseless; reason and reality have parted ways. Schwarz-Bart's phrase, meanwhile, under-

---

16. J.H. Laenen, *Jewish Mysticism: An Introduction*, trans. David E. Orton (Louisville, Ky.: Westminster John Knox Press, 2001), 236.
17. Geoffrey Hartman, "The Book of the Destruction," in *Probing the Limits of Representation: Nazism and the Final Solution*, ed. Saul Friedlander (Cambridge, MA: Harvard University Press, 1992), 326.
18. André Schwarz-Bart, *The Last of the Just*, trans. Stephen Becker (New York: Atheneum Publishers, 1961), 366.
19. Primo Levi, *Survival in Auschwitz*, trans. Stuart Woolf (New York: Collier, MacMillan, 1961), 25.

scores the extent to which the Nazis have destroyed the human faculty for a sensory apprehension of the truth. The reality they have created is too awful to be recognized as true, the mind cannot accept it; what the eyes see simply cannot be believed.[20] Truth and reality have parted ways. To live in this reality, we require a lie; hence the messianic tale. Ernie's awareness of this does not comfort him, because he does not believe the lie himself. There is no room for the truth here, he says; left unsaid is the fact that there is nowhere else to be *but* here. The statement is thus an expression of despair. But the phrase opens up to its opposite if we put ourselves in the position of the children's caretaker and allow that consolation in such circumstances might also be a real imperative. If the truth is not here, then where is it? The phrase suggests the displacement of truth onto some other plane of reality. From such a perspective, the cattle-car takes on an aspect of mere appearance. How could Ernie deny this to the children? Laden with metaphysical import, this meaning of "there is no room here for the truth" diverges radically from Levi.[21]

Though unfinished, Schwarz-Bart's work demonstrates the power of the Holocaust to evoke other historical traumas but also, equally important, the power of other traumas to shape the memory of the Holocaust, as Rothberg has argued, suggesting a tangled pathway of interconnected memories. If memories need social authorization to flourish, then Schwarz-Bart offers an interesting form of authorizing Holocaust memories: through a critical perspective on French colonialism. Such a gesture was not uncommon in its time, though from the vantage point of the present day it has a controversial ring, in part because of the prevailing tendency in the United States and elsewhere to view the Holocaust as unique and incomparable, in part because of the questionable purposes for which comparisons between the Holocaust and French colonialism were invoked in the 1980s during the trial of Klaus Barbie.[22]

---

20. See Hartman for the recurrence of such expressions of disbelief in Holocaust survivor testimonies. "The Book of the Destruction," 326.

21. See also Davison, "Inside the Shoah," for an analysis of this passage.

22. See Pierre Vidal-Naquet, *The Assassins of Memory: Essays on the Denial of the Holocaust*, trans. and foreword by Jeffrey Mehlman (New York: Columbia University Press, 1992), which offers a thorough account of the dilemmas that resulted when two otherwise valid historical insights concerning the Holocaust—one, that it could be inserted into world history and thus "compared, confronted, and even, if possible, explained" (126), and two, that the logical contradictions and expediency that characterized the French legal proceedings against Barbie were problematic (131–35)—were put to use in the attempt to acquit Barbie of his crimes.

Yet it is Schwarz-Bart's metaphysical approach to past trauma, his reparative intent, consoling tone, and mystical turn away from history, *not* his comparative framing of the Holocaust, that have been the target of criticism, whether because the mystical "escape from history" that his works depict suggests that Jewish and black victimhood is eternal and inevitable or because the works' reparative intent suggests redemption for suffering that many believe to exceed all possibility of redemption. Sidra Dekoven Ezrahi, referring to both *La Mulâtresse Solitude* and *Le dernier des justes*, says of Schwarz-Bart that he "transmutes the bloodbath into a gentle lyrical parable" in which the suffering of Solitude and Ernie Lévy "is ultimately redeemed by the harmony and ascendancy of [their] being."[23] Ezrahi faults the author for "a message of comfort" and compassion that is—she claims—more Christian than Jewish, and in fact it is not clear if her criticism is based on her objection to consolation as an appropriate response in the face of genocide or her objection to Schwarz-Bart's (highly debatable) departure from the Jewish tradition. Lawrence Langer also objects to the martyrological thread running through *Le dernier des justes*, arguing that because Schwarz-Bart places the suffering of Auschwitz within the long history of Jewish oppression and endurance, he gives such suffering a millennial meaning. Yet, Langer says, the horror of the camps is unsurpassed, unprecedented and unparalleled, thus it cannot be enveloped by Jewish history. "Ernie Lévy's pathetic desire to link his fate with a universal pattern," writes Langer, is nullified by the nature of the Holocaust experience, which "imprisons the survivor in an uncycled moment of time."[24] Langer claims that Schwarz-Bart's turn to the Jewish martyrological tradition offers a false redemption; it reaffirms our capacity to "translate . . . suffering into the exemplary" and pretends "a spiritual meaning to redeem the horror"—yet nothing can redeem the horror of Auschwitz, Langer argues (265).

Implicitly, both Langer and Ezrahi reject Schwarz-Bart's belief in the existence of "inexact correlations"—to recall an expression by Schwarz-Bart in his *Midstream* interview—between the millennial past and the recent past, and between the Jewish response to oppression and the response of other peoples. In contrast, Michael Rothberg

---

23. Sidra DeKoven Ezrahi, *By Words Alone: The Holocaust in Literature* (Chicago: University of Chicago Press, 1980), 137.

24. Lawrence L. Langer, *The Holocaust and the Literary Imagination* (New Haven: Yale University Press, 1975), 263–264.

seeks to rescue the comparative element of Schwarz-Bart's approach to the Holocaust, arguing that the author's linkage of Jewish and black histories "disrupts the sacralized uniqueness of the Holocaust."[25] Yet, he continues, the desacralizing potential of these "intersecting stories" is nullified by Schwarz-Bart's use of myth, which "seems to transfer historical losses into a de-historicized realm." Echoing a claim made by Ezrahi,[26] Rothberg argues that in Schwarz-Bart's work black and Jewish victimhood come to seem eternal, a "transcendent, extra-historical inevitability."[27] By this reading, Schwarz-Bart's desacralization of biblical history and Hasidic theology in order to bring them to bear on contemporary situations of alienation and dispossession has the precise opposite of its intended effect: it sacralizes contemporary politics, because it appeals to the existence of a realm that transcends the material world.

However, it bears noting that Schwarz-Bart's characters are victims of historical circumstances that the author describes in precise, grim detail. If their victimization seems timeless, it is due to its long-lasting effects, which outlive the original circumstances that gave rise to it and which are compounded by continued pervasive racism. In other words, he is responding to a traumatized and stigmatized condition, though Schwarz-Bart uses other language to describe this state: solitude, indignity, hopelessness, sorrow. Schwarz-Bart does not portray it as eternal and inevitable, but he does confront the despair of those who fear it might be, including himself. He seeks to intervene in a situation of sorrow and despair in a way that both acknowledges its hold *and* tries to break it. The point is not to diminish the extent of the original suffering, but rather to diminish its hold on the psyche. Thus his novels transcend their realist and historicist devices in order to re-frame the past as a parable for the present day. His depictions of an ethos of sympathetic awareness circulating in situations of deep and systemic violence constitute an element of that parable. So too does his mystical loosening of the bonds of material reality, which generates *noeuds de mémoires* linking together disparate histories, much like Gutiérrez's re-interpretation of the Exodus and God's plan in terms of national liberation, and, to a lesser extent, Buber's "I/You" encounter.

25. *Multidirectional Memory*, 152.
26. *By Words Alone*, 133.
27. *Multidirectional Memory*, 152.

Is Schwarz-Bart in fact *redeeming* the Holocaust and slavery by finding in these stories of suffering "an affirmation of faith and solidarity," as various critics imply?[28] It seems rather to be a salvage operation, an incomplete rescue rather than a full-blown redemption, for it is all too conscious of its own limits. Langer is aware of this when he concludes his analysis by saying, dismissively, that "Ernie's consolations are surely only that—not revelations of a higher reality, a deeper truth, a spiritual meaning to redeem the horror."[29] But here Langer misattributes to Schwarz-Bart his own value system, whereby consolation falls miserably short of true revelation, whereas Schwarz-Bart's work seems to subsume these two together: the revelation of another reality is itself a consolation, but only modestly so, a temper of despair. Furthermore, what is transcendent about such moments in the novels is not precisely the opening onto a deeper truth, but the fact that such opening happens inter-subjectively in a context of dehumanizing hatred. It thus offers an alternative social web, beyond the web of violence and injustice, and serves as a reminder that another world is possible.

Even if we agree with Hartman that the Holocaust "challenges the credibility of redemptive thinking,"[30] it does not necessarily follow that the challenge is absolute. The question can still be posed: can the credibility of redemptive thinking be restored? This question circulates throughout Schwarz-Bart's work, although reformulated toward more modest and limited ends—not, is it possible to recover the belief that human suffering is justified by a greater good? But, is consolation, the alleviation of sorrow and despair, still possible? Schwarz-Bart's representations of past horrors, though graphic and at times quite brutal, remain fundamentally lyrical and consoling—not in order to evade history, but in order to respond to the challenges to historical thinking that such events engendered and to the ethical imperatives they call forth. His stance toward catastrophe is guided by the need for psychic repair, and he finds an answer precisely in the *noeuds de mémoires* he perceives between the death camp and the slave plantation. Sympathy joins these disparate memories of suffering together and, once conjoined, transmutes them mystically into evidence of fellowship.

---

28. The quoted phrase is Neil Davison's, from his analysis of the tension between secular and transcendent elements in *Le dernier des justes*. "Inside the Shoah."
29. *The Holocaust and the Literary Imagination*, 265.
30. "The Book of the Destruction," 326.

RONNIE SCHARFMAN

Reciprocal Hauntings: Imagining Slavery and the Shoah in Caryl Phillips and André and Simone Schwarz-Bart

"Memory, that untidy room with unpredictable visiting hours."
—Caryl Phillips, *The Nature of Blood*

"J'habite une blessure sacrée
J'habite des ancêtres imaginaires"
—Aimé Césaire, "Calendrier lagunaire"

In April 2009, an unusual scene occurred at the White House. Picture this: in an elegant room, a long table, laden with all the symbolic foods for the Passover celebration of the Seder, surrounded by 18 people of all ages. And at the head of this table, in the White House, reading from the *Haggadah*, the story of the Exodus of the Hebrew slaves from Egypt, the first black President of the United States, Barack Obama.

Another historic allusion to this Jewish symbolic reenactment of liberation can be found in a short essay for the French newspaper, *Le Figaro littéraire*, in 1967, in which André Schwarz-Bart, the French-Jewish novelist and survivor of the Shoah, whose work will be explored in this essay declared:

> I remember that in 1941, on the first night of Passover, the honor of posing the ritual question to the head of the family came to me . . . and I remember the response that my father gave me in Hebrew: "My child, it was during a night like this one that our ancestors came out of Egypt, where they had been held as slaves." And I believe that it is that Jewish child whose fathers were slaves under Pharaoh, before becoming so again under Hitler, who was taken by a definitive, fraternal love for West Indians.[1]

---

1. André Schwarz-Bart, "Pourquoi j'ai écrit *La Mulâtresse Solitude*," *Le Figaro littéraire*, January 26, 1967, 1,8, 9. My translation.

If I choose these two episodes to introduce my essay on "Reciprocal Hauntings," it is because they strike me as paradigmatic of the community of questions at the heart of this volume, and because they function as relevant examples of what Michael Rothberg conceptualizes as "multidirectional memory" in his new book of that title, "which is meant to draw attention to the dynamic transfers that take place between diverse places and times during the act of remembrance."[2] Rothberg's definition and his own juxtapositional reading practice inform my interrogations here, as I seek to foreground interconnected histories and open paths of communication and transference, in the psychoanalytic meaning of that term, between two novels from the twentieth century that deal with blacks and Jews, with slavery and genocide. The concept of multidirectional memory that articulates an ethics of comparison gives us the tool that allows us to read them together. As a reading practice as well as a conceptual model, multidirectional memory uncovers surprising juxtapositions, teases out the dialogic, porous aspects of complex narratives and articulates the ways these histories relate. Without conflating the memories dramatized in these narratives, such a practice exemplifies the values of tolerance and reciprocal enlightenment.

The Martinican novelist, poet, and theoretician of postcoloniality in the Caribbean Édouard Glissant has expressed the concern that Caribbean culture be constituted as a "prophetic vision of the past." And the Nobel laureate Toni Morrison has defined fiction as the "fully realized presence of the haunting of history."[3] The novels I shall read together here face each other across diasporas, dialoguing with history and memory, supplementing lacks and erasure through the powers of fiction. These works of the literary imagination cross borders of culture, race, and gender, nomadizing across oceans and centuries, questioning and dilating our understanding of two of the most tragic episodes in modern Western history, the black experience of the Middle Passage and slavery at the hands of the colonizing Europeans, and the Jewish experience of persecution and genocide, reaching its culmination at the hands of the Nazis in the Shoah. From Paris to Venice

---

2. Michael Rothberg, *Multidirectional Memory: Remembering the Holocaust in the Age of Decolonization* (Stanford: Stanford University Press, 2008), 11.
3. Édouard Glissant, *Caribbean Discourse: Selected Essays*, trans. J. Michael Dash (Charlottesville, VA: University of Virginia Press, 1999), 64; Toni Morrison, "Unspeakable Thoughts Unspoken: The Afro-American Presence in American Literature," in *Michigan Quarterly Review* 28/1 (1989): 1–34.

to Martinique to Africa to Palestine and Israel to Eastern Europe, Germany and the extermination camps, Caryl Phillips's *The Nature of Blood* (1997) and André and Simone Schwarz-Bart's *Un plat de porc aux bananes vertes* (1967) audaciously traverse emotional territory in ways that force us to reexamine any essentializing or exclusive claim to a monopoly on human suffering.[4] I shall also briefly interpolate a discussion of André Schwarz-Bart's unfinished, posthumous novel, *L'étoile du matin*, published in Paris in the fall of 2009, just as I had completed this essay.[5] Schwarz-Bart's last work, which, by his own avowal, he struggled with for over 35 years without being able to bring it to fruition, was pieced together from fragments organized into this book by his wife Simone. It not only prolongs the themes and issues that my essay discusses, it also broaches the subject of hauntings in a very personal way, as if Schwarz-Bart's life were indistinguishable from his literary project. I shall return to this text more specifically further on.

Caryl Phillips, a black British writer born in the Caribbean, textualizes multiple narratives in his novel, including a version of the Anne Frank story, where a young survivor of the camps hallucinates her past, present, and future, and where years later, her aged Zionist uncle finds himself alone in the Israel he helped to build. At the novel's end he dances with a much younger, black Ethiopian Jew who forces him to confront racist attitudes in the young state, and Phillips implies that the tragedies suffered by various marginalized groups must be confronted reciprocally, even if particular suffering can never be shared. To this family saga Phillips juxtaposes a re-imagined account of the Othello story, and a related historical narrative about a blood libel event in medieval Italy that resulted in the persecution of Jews in a small town. His characters are exiles and orphans—even the powerful, successful Othello—all vulnerable to pervasive, insidious forms of racism, anti-Semitism, and genocide. He mixes historical, literary, and invented figures as he incarnates a chorus of voices, echoing in multiple directions anachronistically, refusing any facile resolution to the problems posed in his text.

Similarly, in his collection of travel essays and meditations, *The European Tribe*, written in 1987, Phillips describes his visit to Anne

---

4. Caryl Phillips, *The Nature of Blood*, (New York: Knopf, 1997); Simone and André Schwarz-Bart, *Un plat de porc aux bananes vertes* (Paris: Seuil, 1967). This novel remains untranslated in English. All page numbers within the text refer to these editions.
5. André Schwarz-Bart, *L'étoile du matin* (Paris: Seuil, 2009).

Frank's house in Amsterdam by remembering his early sense of identification with her as a black child growing up in Britain in the early 1960s. Watching a TV series on the "World at War," he relates his shock, outrage, and terror at first learning about the Shoah: "I thought to myself, if white people could do that to each other, what the hell would they do to me?"[6] But it is especially Anne's own book, its survival both as witness to racial persecution and its adolescent hope in humanity's fundamental goodness, that inspired the young Phillips in Leeds when there was no African diasporic history taught in school, and before he discovered the writings of Richard Wright, James Baldwin, and Ralph Ellison. "As a result I vicariously channeled a part of my hurt and frustration through the Jewish experience" (54).

Phillips's literary project from the beginning incorporates and juxtaposes multiple diasporic voices. As both a product and producer of postcolonial literature, and a contemporary citizen of the world familiar with the psychological literature of trauma theory and survivor guilt, Phillips's audacious experiments with voice build on and extend Schwarz-Bart's fragmented narrative in *Un plat de porc*. Yet like Schwarz-Bart, he is looking for those sites of encounter in order to relate, that is, both to connect and to tell, the ghosts of racial violence that haunt both blacks and Jews, through acts of hallucinatory remembering.

Similarly, André Schwarz-Bart, the French Jewish writer of Polish origin whose family was exterminated by the Nazis, and his Guadeloupean wife Simone, explore the ghosts of slavery and the traumas of its sequelae by creating the character of an old Caribbean woman, descendant of slaves and sole survivor in her family of the catastrophic eruption of the Mt. Pelée volcano in 1902. She ends her days hallucinating voices and scenes from her Antillean past in an old-age home in Paris. This writerly novel—difficult, fragmented, experimenting as it does with mixing memories, nightmares, hallucinations, journal entries, nonlinear narratives—testifies to the formal challenges, as does Phillips' text, of textualizing multidirectional memory. It has received very little critical attention, and remains untranslated into English. I have argued elsewhere that, despite its slave-descendant protagonist and its settings in Martinique and Paris, *Un plat de porc* resonates in profound ways with the *univers concentrationnaire* of André Schwarz-

---

6. Caryl Phillips, *The European Tribe* (Boston and London: Faber and Faber, 1992), 66–67.

Bart's award-winning epic of Jewish persecution through the ages, *The Last of the Just*.[7] But it is as if readers did not know what to make of its porous opening out onto a multiplicity of modern traumas, exile and alienation being the most obvious ones for our purposes here. Like Phillips in *The European Tribe*, Schwarz-Bart explains the origins of his sense of identification with the West Indian community living in Paris in the *Figaro* article quoted above. It is based on what he perceives as their common experience of the "phantomlike shadow of slavery." Yet he struggled with his own scruples about "representing the other," more ego ideal for him than menace, questioning his right to speak from within their voice, seeking nonetheless a totalizing fictional experience that could bridge the Shoah and slavery. Not surprisingly, Schwarz-Bart dedicated this novel both to the Martinican negritude poet Aimé Césaire and to the literary chronicler of the Shoah, Elie Wiesel, underscoring the multidirectionality of its themes and purpose.

Given the backgrounds and cultures of these authors, I would like to suggest in this essay that a chiasmatic relationship obtains when their works are compared, a relationship that interrogates the mutually imaginative, metaphorical, and ethical links that are established when they look at the ghosts from the other's past—a black writer exploring the scars of the Shoah, a Jewish writer exploring the scars of slavery. Each project represents a gesture toward empathic identification, via the means of that imaginative leap that literature provides. The ghosts function as repositories of the memory knots and nodes that this issue of *Yale French Studies* is concerned with.

What, after all, is a ghost? Is it a legacy, an effect of loss? The return of the repressed? What repressed? Do ghosts appear as a matter of voluntary or involuntary memory? Psychoanalytic theory has a great deal to say about the subject of ghosts, generally conceiving them as internalized "bad objects." In "The Therapeutic Action of Psychoanalysis," Hans Loewald quotes Freud as speaking of the "indestruc-

---

7. André Schwarz-Bart, *Le dernier des justes* (Paris: Seuil, 1959). See my "Exiled From the Shoah," in *Auschwitz and After*, ed. Lawrence Kritzman (New York: Routledge, 1995), 250–63. In particular, Schwarz-Bart's quote from the *Figaro* article where he states: "through the intercession of the old age home, it seemed in my eyes that the delicate joint was established between slavery and the concentration camp theme that has been preoccupying me for a very long time. Since 1945, the greatest part of my intellectual life has developed under the sign of the camps" (256). Schwarz-Bart's work anticipates the concept of multidirectional memory here.

tibility of mental acts as being like the ghosts in the *Odyssey* which awoke to new life as soon as they tasted blood." Loewald continues: "Those who know ghosts tell us that they long to be released from their ghost life and laid to rest as ancestors. As ancestors, they live forth in the present generation, while as ghosts they are compelled to haunt the present generation with their shadow life."[8] Can fiction, the "fully realized presence of the haunting of history," which gives lifeblood to these ghosts, also lay them to rest, exorcise them?

In the two primary novels I am analyzing here, each of the main protagonists is both a *survivor and* a ghost herself, and each hallucinates a ghost ancestor. (This proves to be the case for the protagonist of Schwarz-Bart's last narrative as well, where Haim is one of the living dead survivors of Auschwitz.) I want to ask if these ghostly presences are discursive strategies for examining a "past that won't pass," in these stories that look at each other across a chasm of experience, and dialogue with each other in chiasmus. The characters live and relive personal trauma as the authors interrogate the other's historical tragedy. In so doing, they pose an implicit question: can we be haunted by the other's ghosts?

In his chapter on their work, Rothberg cites Schwarz-Bart's and Phillips's juxtapositions of black and Jewish histories as "self-conscious acts of the imagination that work through deliberate anachronism," and he formulates a critical reading practice that identifies what he calls "anachronistic aesthetics," premised on hospitality to the histories of the other (136, 137). According to Rothberg, "recognizing memory as multidirectional entails understanding how all acts of remembrance involve relays and ricochets between places and times that prevent the kind of arbitrary closure that attempts to canonize events as unique and sacred presume."[9] The two novels in question here are attempting, each in their own way, to find a literary form adequate to their intuitions of multidirectional memory as ways to explore minority history.

Turning now to Schwarz-Bart's novel, I will present a crucial scene where the haunting by ghosts is doubled in a *mise-en-abyme* that opens onto a gaping chasm of horror, terror, and immeasurable suffer-

---

8. Hans Loewald, *Papers on Psychoanalysis* (New Haven: Yale University Press, 1980), 248–49.
9. Michael Rothberg, "Writing Ruins: The Anachrontistic Aesthetics of André Schwarz-Bart," in *After Representation? The Holocaust, Literature, and Culture* (New Brunswick: Rutgers UP, 2009), ed. R. Clifton Spargo and Robert Ehrenreich, 101.

ing. Mariotte, the isolated protagonist of the story, a 72-year-old Martinican decaying in an old-age home in Paris, shuttles back and forth in her narration between the recent past, the distant past, and the present, between Martinique and Paris. What allows memory to come is the physical touch of a plant leaf from the Antilles that she has kept among her meager personal effects as a kind of transitional object. She hides with it in the toilet, ironically the only locus of privacy in the nursing home, and rubs it on her cheek like Aladdin's magic lamp. It is the ghost of her grandmother Man Louise who first emerges. At this moment in the narrative the native land returns to Mariotte, the way we say the repressed returns, but here, as in Proust's cup of tea, as a whole childhood universe—intact, with all its sights, sounds, smells, and, especially, with grandma's ghost:

> Frissons of foam, eddies of deep water: and here it is suddenly that a high wave of Time deposits on the desolate beach of my mind the silhouette of grandma seated in her creole rocking chair under the veranda, two meters away from the toilet bowl where I myself am seated, with an ancient leaf in my hand. (42; my translation)

How and why is it the ghost of this particular ancestor who erupts first in Mariotte's memory-return? In creole cosmogony, with its traces of African cultural heritage, the boundaries between the dead and the living are of course more fluid. Moreover, in this novel where tenderness is so cruelly lacking, it is the psychoanalytic bad object, grandmother's phantom, that seems to have been forever hovering at the edge of Mariotte's consciousness. We realize in this scene that the granddaughter had long ago internalized the stern, guilt-inducing judgments of this powerful character whose branded breast is an eternal reminder of her slave past and Mariotte's desertion. Freud reminds us that the unconscious is timeless, and Mariotte immediately regresses to grandmother's frightened little girl in their first encounter, while Man Louise's cruel ghost observes with glee, "You are almost as old as I now, Madame" (43).

Grandma's ghost, whose reprimands in this first scene focus on Mariotte's traitorous, alienated use of French rather than Creole, functions, I would argue, not only as super ego, but as alter ego. I would like to suggest that there is yet another ghost who haunts the pages of this story, and it is that of André's wife Simone, whose co-authorship of this novel is difficult to identify and tease out except, precisely, at those moments where the ghost of the native(s) language returns to haunt its dominant French, follows it like a shadow, refuses to be assimilated, forces its hospitality, by inserting all sorts of proverbs and lyrical turns of phrase.[10]

For Simone Schwarz-Bart, the ink of this first effort at fiction will become the lifeblood that allows her to pass from ghost writer to novelist in her own right, author of the 1972 chef d'oeuvre *Pluie et vent sur Télumée Miracle*. André describes the "birth of the writer" in his *Figaro* article and in an interview the two gave to the Antillean academics Héliane and Roger Toumson. These texts reveal the process of writing *Un plat de porc*, a novel for four hands, as they tell it, where André was blocked in his writing and Simone, unexpectedly for them both, supplied a scene. His struggle here is the same one that haunted him during his entire career as a writer; how to represent the other, Holocaust victim or descendant of slavery, without betraying their experience by merely aestheticizing it. "I felt that I risked falling into exoticism, that is to say, into a form of writing that envisions a human reality from afar, in what it has that is picturesque, curious. . . . Simone knows Creole as a total language, a veritable expression."[11] She will provide the specificity, the otherwise "unfathomable core." He credits her by identifying in a brief piece of her writing what he calls "a translucent, silken equivalent for each one of the turns of phrase and expressions of the Creole language [and] also . . . her imagination had interpreted, transformed, added all those details by which one recognizes a true writer."[12]

At the level of language itself, Mariotte's sensibility could not have been rendered without Creole working its way into French at strategic moments where she must reconstitute herself in discourse. The apparition of grandma's ghost is one such moment. The textualization of Creole here functions itself like a postcolonial ghost that cannot be laid to rest. It is interesting for the purposes of our problematic that the tensions over language usage as related to memory and identity are played out within the text between two different generations, and from two different geographical loci on the postcolonial map. Thus grandma's very first words at being conjured up by Mariotte in Paris are in Creole, and they belie and anthropomorphize the loneliness of

---

10. In all their interviews, Simone has always claimed that "he" wrote the novel, whereas André has always told the story of their "accidental collaboration." See notes 11 and 12 below.
11. André Schwarz-Bart, "Pourquoi j'ai écrit *La Mulâtresse Solitude.*"
12. André Schwarz-Bart, "Pourquoi j'ai écrit *La Mulâtresse Solitude.*"

"being left behind": *"Par la pitié di Dié, par la clarté di Saint-Esprit, est-ce que ni an moune par ici?"* (For God's sake, for the Holy Spirit's light, is there no like-minded soul around here?) (43). We might coin the term "like-languaged" to translate Man Louise's anxiety as it is articulated in this question. If "becoming French" represents an unstable, evolving identity position for the postcolonial subject coming from a nonhexagonal part of the francophone world, like Mariotte, it is also thematized, textualized dialogically in the very writing of this text. In the example above, it is Creole itself that erupts in the French, emphasizing the disruption between Mariotte's Martinican past and her Parisian present. She can only recuperate and reverse that distance, both temporal and spatial, by resorting to Creole herself. But what she longs for is a nostalgic, impossible return, an expression of sentiment for which the mother tongue should be the vehicle, but which the withholding grandmother cannot confer. Mariotte needs to be recognized in the warmth and affection of hearing her name pronounced in her maternal *créolité*. But the rupture of her departure represents a point of no return.

Mariotte is taken to task by Man Louise for having tried to escape her "negress's place," and her ghost serves as eyewitness to the truth of the past, a bridge to history, both personal and collective, and a constant reminder chiding Mariotte as to the inauthenticity of her identity choices, which sought a genealogical interruption when Mariotte left Martinique to travel the world.

The apparition of Man Louise's ghost, despite her guilt-inducing reminders of betrayal and abandonment, allows Mariotte to effect a genealogical reconnection and with it, to recuperate her lost Antillean past in all its plenitude, both painful and joyous. Once the phantom reappears, Mariotte begins to remember all the little quotidian details of her Martinican childhood—the people, places, perfumes, flavors, including an episode revolving around the delicious eponymous dish of the book's title, and her child's desire for these released memories in all of their materiality, constitute the bulk of the novel.

Who then is Grandma Louise? Instantly recognizable by the mark of the master's iron brand on her breast, she is a former slave whose subsequent existence is built around distrust, fear, paranoia of all things having to do with the whites. Mariotte describes her as "she who wore chains in her soul throughout her life—more deeply inscribed than the mark of the branding iron on her right breast" (47). Her severity toward Mariotte, which takes the form of insults and humiliation, is the other side of her impotence to affect her own circumstances. As Man Louise's ghost facilitates the return of memory for Mariotte, she in turn remembers Man Louise hallucinating a ghost of her own. This haunting *mise-en-abyme* opens on to the primal scene of trauma whose scars, both physical and mental, transmitted to little Mariotte as witness, constitute the painful sequelae of slavery that haunt all people of the African diaspora. In this pitiful and terrifying scene (Aristotle's definition of tragedy), Man Louise regresses deliriously, just before dying, to her former slave self. Ironically mistaking her own daughter for her former white mistress, she relives the terrors of being whipped and, more tragically, of being severed from her babies. In her grotesque reenactment of that moment, she prostrates herself at her daughter/mistress's feet, begging for mercy for her son. Mariotte recounts this in her notebook:

> The morning of her death she was screaming . . . and then suddenly I saw her again as the old "fresh water slave . . . " and she grabbed one of Moman's legs kissing it with fury, angrily, and going down to the naked toes that she licked with big, avid strokes, like a cat: "Oh for the grace of God, don't take away my second son, don't go selling him to Mister Saint-James, leave him to me, sell him to someone more Christian. With all due respect, mistress, with all due respect, he nails ears too much, you know, too much, ears. . . ." While Moman, immobilized with terror, her face grey, contemplated with wide open eyes the spectacle of Man Louise hanging on her leg and covering her dusty feet with slave kisses. (65)

This scene of haunting stages not only the ghosts of traumas past, but also their ghostly, ghastly transmission from one generation to the other. Mariotte sees her own Mother transformed into a ghost/mistress by Grandmother's hallucinatory substitution. But Moman herself *also* becomes a ghostly subject as she witnesses this incarnation of her *own* Mother as slave, as creature, as "nègre." "Moman, immobilized . . . her face grey." This primal scene of loss, fear, and powerlessness, lived, witnessed, reenacted, remembered, recorded, transmitted, of course opens onto the collective memory of suffering for Afro-Caribbeans, in that it re-calls and re-presents the history of the slave past. But it functions in another way as an example of multidirectional memory in that it echoes scenes from another tragedy that is always present in Schwarz-Bart's fictional project.

It is around the experience of motherhood that Mariotte's bewildered and frightened empathy for Grandma Louise's ghost is voiced.

There is no pain or terror greater than the arbitrary and irrevocable separation of parents from children. During the Nazi deportations of the Jews to the death camps, at the moment of selection this horror was lived by thousands of Jewish families. Since *Un plat de porc* was published *after*, but conceived during the writing of Schwarz-Bart's famous saga *Le dernier des justes,* we can deduce that he is textualizing these reciprocal, multidirectional hauntings.

Multiple renditions and accounts of such scenes clearly remained part of Schwarz-Bart's haunted imaginary throughout his entire literary career. For some forty years after writing *Un plat de porc* we can identify a symmetrical, if inverted scene in the autobiographical *L'étoile du matin*. In this recent text we see a reformulation of the moment of deportation, where the mother of the Schuster family of Polish Jews makes the ultimate sacrifice by urging her children to run off as the Nazis ready to take the family away. Schlomo, the eldest brother, and Haïm Lebke, the younger protagonist of the story's first part, "Kaddish," are exhorted to escape with their younger siblings and hide. In this moment their mother is described like a hunted animal whose survival instincts are acutely put into play by the soldiers' actions:

> The soldiers were sweating, helping the old and the sick to get up into the trucks.... One foot on the steps and one foot on the street, Haïm's mother stretched the folds of her neck towards the neighboring house and her ears quivered, her eyes folded like a cat's. Suddenly she turned around to the household that was waiting in the shadows, and addressing herself dryly to the eldest: "Run away with the little ones, quick, quick, I entrust them to you before God." She pushed Schlomo who himself pushed the little ones hurriedly towards the back of the shop opening onto the prairie and the river, the forest.... Haïm Lebke had stayed close to his mother and grabbing her arm strongly: "I don't want to, I don't want to," he screamed. A slap of an incredible violence sent him back to the little group of children that was moving away toward the grass, the light. As Haïm moved on, his mother held Schlomo's prayer bag out to him, turned around without a word, shut the little door.... Once arrived at the edge of the woods, they heard the departure of the trucks and the screams of the ecstatic Polish peasants who were rushing towards the inside of the empty houses. (106–107, my translation)

The pain of traumatic wrenching of mother from child is reversed in this later text. This time, it is the child Haïm who expresses his distress by grabbing his mother's arm, rather than Mariotte's grandmother grabbing her mistress's leg. Haïm's mother's determination to try to save her children is expressed impersonally, as if the pain she must inflict on her child in order to save him exceeds her subjective agency—"a slap of an incredible violence sent him back"—such that we do not actually witness her administering it. It's as if the gesture, in its desperate cruelty, can only be inscribed if it is depersonalized. In another reversed mirror image of these two scenes that constitute a multidirectional remembering, Haïm's mother is figured as a canny "cat," whereas Mariottes's grandmother is reduced to a cat's creatureliness in its desperate licking. In both cases, I would argue, Schwarz-Bart uses the animal imagery to depict the dehumanization wrought by terror and despair.

How can we read this scene juxtaposed with the ghostly one in *Un plat de porc* cited above? Can multidirectionality imply some kind of corrective to the writing or reading of devastating historico-personal events such as these? Although Haïm's mother appears to be empowered by her decisiveness at the crucial moment of deportation, her sacrificial gesture will prove futile. Schlomo sneaks back to the ditch where his parents have been dumped, and is murdered along with them. Haïm will watch all of his little siblings die of disease and starvation in the Warsaw Ghetto, the same Ghetto Schwarz-Bart evoked poignantly at the end of his 1972 novel of resistance in Guadeloupe, *La Mulâtresse Solitude*.[13] Schwarz-Bart thus seems to be going over the same territory, obsessively, remembering across cultures, tragedies, histories, geographies. Both intertextual and metatextual commentaries foreground what was always already the multidirectional aspect of his project. In the *Figaro* article, for example, there is a reference to the brave resistance of the black leader Delgrès and his forces fighting the French, ending in their collective suicide, that is *already* compared to the Warsaw Ghetto uprising. And although he doesn't mention it in the *Figaro* piece that dates from 1967, he uses a similar event, this time one taken from Jewish history, to set the opening scene of his previous novel, *Le dernier des justes*, that of the collective murder/suicide of a group of persecuted, besieged Jews in York, England, on March 11, 1185.

Let us turn now to the ghostly hauntings in Phillips's novel.

13. See Bella Brodzki, "Nomadism and the Textualization of Memory in André Schwarz-Bart's *La Mulâtresse Solitude*," in *Yale French Studies* 83 (1993).

In *The Nature of Blood*, Eva, the protagonist of the Holocaust narrative sections of the novel, is herself almost a ghost when we first hear her voice as her camp is being liberated by British soldiers. One of the last of the living dead, she apprehends herself in the mirror of the soldiers' reactions to the decaying bodies around them: "They are struggling . . . Skeletons facing men. Bodies twisted in bony gestures of supplication. I have no strength to be happy" (12).

Eva's narrative alternates between past and present, without transition, an internal monologue that, like the unconscious, is timeless (as I have mentioned with respect to Mariotte's monologue). But her fragmented stories and memories reconstruct little by little the family's history, their forced deportation, the selection, and her Mother's death, which will occupy the last part of my analysis. As a survivor, it would seem that Eva cannot go forward without going backward. Yet hallucinating her mother's ghost in a regressive need for fusion that also hints at survivor guilt con-fusion, only serves to underscore her sense of loss and abandonment:

> My Mama has left me alone. One morning she did not wake up. She lay asleep and I spoke to her all day long in the hope that she might answer back. I had managed to convince myself that by the time the spring arrived and the leaves were on the trees, Mama and I would be able to *begin the task of forgetting*. But one night, her strength ran out. I spoke to her all day long, but I never received a reply (13; my emphasis).

Eva's voice here, regressed to that of a little girl who cannot quite realize what she is describing, is *pathétique* by dint of the very affectless understatement that never pronounces the word "dead." Her illusion that spring would bring a kind of rebirth, articulated as "the work of forgetting," is reminiscent of Freud's concept of the work of mourning, that which allows us to move on after we have lost a love object. But Eva's monologue tells us that she cannot accomplish the task alone. She is now condemned to remember for them both, and, by extension, for the whole family, perhaps even the entire community. She will be burdened with the survivor's dilemma: the paradoxical moral obligation to keep the ghost alive.

It is interesting to compare this survivor's burden of Eva's to the introduction to *L'étoile du matin* in which Simone Schwarz-Bart explains, as she is grappling with publishing the fragments her husband could not, " . . . he sincerely wanted to offer this work. . . . [H]e couldn't do it in his lifetime because that would be, for him, to abandon those dead ones, while he wanted to keep them present in himself up until the end" (16). And within the body of the text, the writer says of Haïm, his autobiographical alter ego, "He had sought a thousand approaches for writing about this planet Auschwitz, but he never arrived at the end: each time, the shame of writing about the dead overtook him, and he had destroyed everything" (205). Writing is construed here not as conferring immortality on the dead, bearing witness to their story, but rather as a form of betrayal. It is as if the ghosts keep the living dead alive, as a reciprocal responsibility.

In Eva's case, although her body slowly regains strength after the camp's liberation, her fragile psyche begins to decompensate. She will not survive her survival. One might argue that her suicide in the English asylum where she is placed after a psychotic break is the result of her being abandoned by a British soldier with a rescue fantasy. But I want to suggest, rather, that the reuniting with Mother's ghost serves the psychic function at first of allowing Eva to actually leave the camp physically: it is the condition of possibility of her futurity. When the ghost abandons *her*, that is, when Eva can no longer deny that her Mother *is dead*, the absence of haunting will impede her ability to make a new life for herself. Her Mother's hallucinated return, as a ghost who cannot yet be recognized as one because Eva has repressed the truth of her death, revives the dialogue Eva wishes for in the scene above. In her fantasy projection, they plan their life after the camp together and the daughter gets to mother her own Mother, symbolically saving her:

> Today Mama arrived back at the camp. . . . Before I could say anything, the woman turned her face towards me and I saw it was Mama. I wasn't frightened. I was expecting her to return, for I never truly believed that she had gone. And now she is back. I hold her hard and encourage her to tell her story once more. Of how they took her from the hut and left her for dead. She touches my face as though still unable to believe her luck. But Mama, I ask, why did you not come and look for me? Mama looks sad now. "They told me that you were dead, and I believed them." "Dead?" I touch my Mama's face, her lips, her eyes, her nose. Mama is back with me. I can now begin to plan a future for both of us. (35–36)

In this poignant conversation, figured as though mother and daughter were mirroring each other, fused with each other, the living and the dead exchange properties. The hallucinated ghost of the Mother is figured as seeing her living daughter as a ghost. This confusion of boundaries, where it is no longer possible to distinguish who is living and who is dead, is the first symptom of Eva's madness. But the Mother's ghost allows Eva to face other truths that the unconscious already knows—that is, that the rest of her family—her sister and Father, have died in the camps. What role does the ghost serve here? In this scene where death and mourning are relayed, where the ghost dreaming a ghost announcing death is structured in the abyss, Eva, as subject of multiple loss, displaces her grief, impossible to digest, onto her Mother's ghost. By projecting her mourning for all the dead family onto the ghost, Eva psychically effects a series of substitutions that momentarily allow her to be the comforter—"I hug Mama"—rather than just the guilty survivor. Similarly, once Eva and her imaginary Mama have, in her mind, planned their separate departure from the camp in order to meet up in town two days later, Eva "sends her off" with food, like a mother would a child: "I hand the small bundle to her, with its piece of bread and other meager provisions. And then we embrace" (40).

In these pages that slip in and out of the past and Eva's hallucinations, there is another passage where Phillips effects a *mise-en-abyme* whereby Mama's ghost dreams a ghostly visit from Papa. It is by interrogating Mama's ghost that Eva allows herself to "learn" of her Papa's and sister's death:

> "Last night, Eva. I had a dream in which Papa told me that we were on our own now. Just you and me, my child."
> "And Margot?"
> Mama begins to shake her head and sob.
> "Just you and me."
> I hug Mama, but I am not sure if she is aware of me. (39)

Here, too, we move in and out of Eva's consciousness of reality. She needs this internal monologue with the ghost in order to come to terms, slowly, with the truth of her bereavement. Once again, she is the comforter. But the devastating observation, "I am not sure if she is aware of me," speaks to what Eva knows and doesn't know at the same time. Her Mother is not there, and yet the illusion of her presence, the promised reunion outside the camp, and the fantasy plan for a future in America are what allow Eva to move on and move out. By "seeing her Mother off" at the gates of the camp, by having her leave first, Eva is not abandoning her when she herself leaves.

Phillips's ghostly young survivor, haunted by the impossibility of forgetting, understands the mysterious truths of trauma's effects on the unconscious far better than the psychiatrist who reports on her suicide.

And as her aged, lonely Uncle Stephan realizes many years later, at the novel's end, looking back on the loss of his family to the genocide, "he now understood that to remember too much is, indeed, a form of madness" (211). For Schwarz-Bart's aged protagonist, on the contrary, when memory comes it is both recuperative and integrative. Remembering her grandmother's suffering releases Mariotte from self-hatred and valorizes her yearning for her Caribbean childhood.

In Schwarz-Bart's unfinished *L'étoile du matin*, the novelist's years of silence seem to dissipate as he demonstrates the same preoccupations with giving form to memory and catastrophe, specifically as it relates to the Jews in the Shoah, but also in a more universal and linked way. Is it coincidence that this novel ends with a scene first in Israel, and then the protagonist's return to Auschwitz where he had been in the camp during the war, this time as "tourist," accompanied by his young love Sarah, newly pregnant with their first child? Both scenes allow Schwarz-Bart to meditate on the meaning of the genocide from the distance of many years, as well as to question the multiplicity of human tragedies over time, views consistent with his concerns, both aesthetic and ethical, since his first novel. The conceit of the narrative is that it is "discovered" by an alien from outer space after the destruction of earth, in the year 3,000. What is his science fiction setting if not a future directed version of the mythical setting that opens *La Mulâtresse Solitude*? I mean to suggest here that with his last novel, and despite the fragmentary, and ultimately failed nature of Schwarz-Bart's larger project as sketched out by him in 1967, we have a coherent literary oeuvre, and one that yet again reflects Phillips's concerns in *The Nature of Blood*. Both novels end with surprising encounters that re(con)textualize the multidirectional echoes inherent in the novelists' audacious figuring of blacks with Jews. The two endings function as intertexts and, to return to my notion of the chiasmus that obtains when we compare certain aspects of these two writers' works, as book ends. A comparison of these two endings will constitute my conclusion.

As an old man, Haïm Schuster, survivor of Auschwitz, travels to Israel at the request of his young companion, Sarah. In this last part of the narrative, entitled "A Song of Life," Sarah seeks through this pilgrimage to reaffirm both Jewish survival after the genocide, and the multiplicity of possible Jewish identity positions for Haïm, who sees himself as one of the living dead. She observes:

> They had come from all the continents, witnesses from all the races and all the traditions, Jews from the East and the West, white Jews, black Jews, yellow, red, and even those mysterious Jews of Cochin, whose eyes seemed to contemplate another sky, and even those beings come straight out of legend, Falashas of Ethiopia, who still remembered the Queen of Sheba, and even the Jews of Harlem, who carried on their shoulders the two heaviest heritages of human history.... It was a planetary tribe: it all happened as if the totality of the human past had been poured out in this place that thereby reflected, by the simple nature of things, the entirety of contradictions of the modern world. (222–23)

What is striking here is the way Schwarz-Bart figures Israel as a place of intermingling, where people can actually be both black and Jewish, but not of utopian resolution. It functions, rather, as a microcosm of all of the contradictions of diasporic identity. Nor is it a question of Haïm "settling" there, as if it could ease the existential dilemma of the survivor. It is as if the only way beyond Auschwitz is back through Auschwitz.

Is it ironic or coincidental that Haïm and Sarah meet a young *métis* in the train going to the museum at Auschwitz? Doesn't Schwarz-Bart also want to deessentialize this icon of Jewish suffering? Their discussion in the train is telling. The young man identifies himself as a Guadeloupean *métis* whose mother is Jewish and father Antillean "a two hundred per cent: one hundred per cent Jewish and one hundred per cent black" (234). This is the crux of Schwarz-Bart's concerns, of course. How can one be fully both, fully faithful to both origins, unique and universal, biological and imagined? Isn't it only through exploring the other's history and memory? And isn't that precisely what the young black man is looking for in Auschwitz? They trade comico-serious banter about the unforgiveable crimes both groups have committed toward humanity: the Jews in "Giving God to the world," and the blacks in inventing jazz and the blues, "hitching the earth to the heavens" (235). And they agree that both excel, both meet, on the soil of self-denigration. The purpose, then, of introducing this character briefly is to desacralize the pilgrimage. Schwarz-Bart has Haïm contemplate, with some amazement, the transformation of the site into a tourist destination. But his protagonist meditates on something different at the end of this story. "He did not understand the atmosphere of sacredness that surrounded the Shoah" (245). In his nighttime ruminations after visiting the site, he has a kind of epiphany of the simplicity of the horror. "Jews died for nothing, absolutely nothing . . . tomorrow anybody else could be susceptible to dying for nothing . . . people would die without understanding, beaten down by the absurd" (246). Far from being a cynical conclusion to the conundrum of finding meaning in catastrophe, this revelation brings a kind of peace to tortured Haïm. The specificity of the tragedy is its time and place, and its particular victims. But as to its nature, "since the beginning of time, nothing, nothing new under the sun" (246). André Schwarz-Bart's instincts to link tragedies across epochs and diasporas through the explorations of the literary imagination were the same from the beginning of his literary career through the unfinished attempts to complete the story of his personal, familial disaster.

At the end of *Un plat de porc*, an enlightened Mariotte will also find comfort in espousing the human condition, an enlightenment that dissolves her sense of herself as unique victim:

> . . . you carry within yourself one of each kind . . . a beast named Jesus, another beast called Hitler, an anonymous Hindu coolie, the cannibalistic butcher on the corner, a Roman gladiator, one of our local women pregnant for the ninth time . . . a newborn, all white, yellow, black or red . . . (204–206)

True to his ethics and aesthetics of juxtaposition, Phillips ends *The Nature of Blood* in a far more troubling and ambiguous way. Yet it is no less multidirectional in its surprising pairing of Eva's Uncle Stephan and a young, black Ethiopian woman he dances with at a men's club outside of Tel Aviv. Phillips, too, introduces a new character at the end of the story, as if to complicate and prolong the sequelae of the Holocaust narrative. Uncle Stephan moved to Palestine before the war, leaving his family behind. His Zionistic zeal is put into question at the end of the novel, since he remains alone with his survivor's guilt. But the interaction between him and the unnamed black woman points to more complex fault lines in the nature of the new state of Israel itself. Founded in part in reaction to the Nazi genocide of the Jews, Israel's own difficulties in absorbing all of its immigrants, and in particular here, its black immigrants are figured as an unfortunate, ironic echo of racist attitudes.

The woman's internal monologue even recounts the famous airlift of Ethiopian Jews in terms of deportation, now a familiar scene for the reader, an uncanny, but not unconscious reference on Phillips's part to the uprooting and rupture, for this community, from their homes to the "promised homeland." This echo of deportation imagery adds yet another fold to the complexity of multidirectional memory in this novel, and between the two authors. It is worth noting that for both authors, Israel is a site of knotted memories.

> *(Together with my parents and my brother and sister . . . then you herded us on to buses . . . and yes, it was frightening . . . People looked around. Not everybody was here. It was impossible to take everybody. Relatives were being abandoned. And then on to the embassy compound, where we were stored like thinning cattle . . . I was lucky, for my parents and my brother and sister were relatively healthy. But many people were weak with malaria. And it is true, many people were dying.)* (199)

Phillips textualizes her version of this event in italics, and in parentheses. How are we to read this, if not as a silent relating that cannot tell its tale, that is not "communicated" to the other, as if she could claim no subjective agency over her own discourse, does not have the right to it or as if, distrustful, she refuses to share her story? Is she a victim, or is she locked in the isolation of her experience, or invisible, in some sense, like a ghost in this new country? The themes of forced uprootings, separation of families during the journey, herdings of people like animals, fear and chaos, disease and death are unmistakable markers of the multidirectional memory of deportations, traumas shared by both blacks and Jews across the centuries.

Later on, we actually "hear" her voice. After she has symbolically numbed her mouth with an ice-cube, she will ask, "You can be honest with me. You do not want us here, do you?" (208). This simple, direct question problematizes an irresolvable dilemma. Israel may have been created as a haven for all diaspora Jews, but racism still persists. It is Phillips's quiet indictment of essentialism. Is pernicious prejudice in the nature of blood? The novel ends on a scene of profound loneliness, with Uncle Stephan hallucinating his murdered nieces as he once played with them long ago. Phillips refuses any neat, facile closure, leaving us to ponder the multiple tragic narratives this novel has set in play.

By feeding the ghosts with the blood and ink of their respective chiasmatic, trauma-crossed stories, Phillips and Schwarz-Bart have given us texts that honor the multidirectional capacities of the literary imagination to empathize with the other. Catastrophe has no canon, ghosts have no color.

By way of honoring the ethics of comparison that is exemplified in this volume of *Yale French Studies*, I would like to conclude with a recent poem of mine that speaks to and of the criss-crossings of memories and stories from the traumas of diasporic exile and violent collective tragedy. Its title and first line, "These Are the Names," are taken from the opening of the book of "Exodus" in the *Hebrew Bible*, which in Hebrew is called "The Names."

THESE ARE THE NAMES

These are the names:
Shards of loss.
On the walls of the Pinchas synagogue, inscribe them:
Shlomo, Malka, Anshul, Motek.
On the slabs of Maya Lin's granite, incise them:
Johnny, Jimmy, Daisy, Leroy.
At the site of Ground Zero, recite them:
Sean and Singh, David and Pedro, Yuki and Luba.
At Whitney Plantation, memorize them:
Jean-Baptiste, Amélie, Dieu-Donné, Emile.
As you walk among walls of remembrance,
Hum them, like a chant of gratitude.
On the paths of the righteous,
Mumble them like the litany of a dirge.
On the field of angels
Whisper them and you might hear a prayer.
Handle them delicately
As you would butterfly wings.
None are begotten by their ghosts.
But none are forgotten by your witness.[14]

---

14. A version of this poem and an earlier version of this paper were read at the conference held at Purchase College in April, 2009: "All Over the Map: Transnational, Diasporic, Postcolonial Culture" to celebrate my retirement.

FRANÇOISE LIONNET

"Dire *exactement*": Remembering the Interwoven Lives of Jewish Deportees and Coolie Descendants in 1940s Mauritius

> I held on to the barbed wire with a rage I had rarely felt before. . . .
> With clenched teeth, *I pressed the palms of my hands on the barbed knots, pain shooting through my anger*. . . . Everything in me stopped.
> . . . I remember . . . the smell of rust and blood on my hands. . . . I sniffed up my palms as if they were a drug, each inhalation causing me to be filled with hope and serenity.
> —Nathacha Appanah, *Le dernier frère*[1]

> In the middle of nowhere, on that island with tens of ethnic groups, *a page of history completely heterogeneous to the environment is engraved*. That cemetery is guarded by the two Mauritians responsible for the upkeep of the adjoining Christian cemetery. On the wall of the shack that they use as an office, a naively drawn poster that appears to have been spontaneously put up by the municipal employees simply states that *intolerance and exclusion are murderous*.
> —Jacques Hassoun, "Préface"[2]

The Mauritian writer Nathacha Appanah published her acclaimed fourth novel *Le dernier frère* in 2007. It is the first fictional engagement in French with an episode of World War II that had only been documented in scant archival materials, one brief historiographic text, and a handful of testimonials: the internment of a group of Central European Jews in a "camp," a colonial prison in the British Crown Colony of Mauritius. This event, all but erased from historical records and local memory, remains a problematic and awkward chapter in the intersecting histories of British imperial interests, resistance to Nazism, and wartime survival in the Middle East and the Indian

---

1. Nathacha Appanah, *Le dernier frère* (Paris: L'Olivier, 2007), 100–101.
2. Jacques Hassoun, preface to Josef Deutsch, "Prisonniers sur l'île de la fièvre," *Le monde juif* 157 (May–August 1996): 77.

Ocean region. *Le dernier frère* is Appanah's personal foray into this silenced past, and an occasion to reflect on childhood, language, memory, ethical responsibility, and the intertwined losses of an Indo-Mauritian family and a young Czech-Jewish deportee named David Stein.

Mauritius is a multiracial, multilingual, multiconfessional, predominantly Indian diasporic and independent nation, populated by the descendants of indentured laborers and coolies who crossed over the "dark waters" or *kala pani* of the Indian Ocean during the nineteenth century. Mauritius is also a vibrant outpost of *francophonie*, the legacy of its former status as one of the slave cultures of the "vieilles colonies" of Ancien Régime France. The nation's most talented twenty-first century writers—whether established or currently emerging—are award-winning francophone Indo-Mauritians who publish with the main Parisian houses: Rishy Bukoree, Ananda Devi, Yusuf Kadel, Shenaz Patel, Barlen Pyamootoo, Amal Sewtohul, Khal Torabully, among others. Some focus on what Torabully has termed the dynamics of "coolitude;"[3] some are concerned with the aesthetics and politics of belonging (Bukoree, Kadel, Pyamootoo);[4] others scrutinize the gendered legacies of slavery and colonialism (Devi, Patel);[5] yet others embrace a global perspective on history and identity (Sewtohul);[6] and at least one has denounced with poetic eloquence the neocolonial militarism that led, in the 1970s, to the forcible displacement of some 1800 native Chagos islanders to Mauritius in order to make room for the US base of Diego Garcia (Patel).[7]

---

3. See Khal Torabully, *Chair corail, fragments coolies* (Guadeloupe: Ibis rouge, 2000), and *Coolitude: An Anthology of the Indian Labour Diaspora*, ed. Marina Carter and Khal Torabully (London: Anthem South Asian Studies, 2002).

4. Rishy Bukoree, *Poezi enn Rebel* (Port-Louis: Ledikasyon pu Travayer, 2007); Yusuf Kadel, *Un septembre noir* (Vacoas: Le printemps, 1998) and *Surenchairs* (Vacoas: Le printemps, 1999); Barlen Pyamootoo, *Bénares* (Paris: L'Olivier, 1999) and *Salogi's* (Paris: L'Olivier, 2008).

5. Ananda Devi, *Eve de ses décombres* (Paris: Gallimard, 2006); Shenaz Patel, *Sensitive* (Paris: L'Olivier, 2003) and *Le silence des Chagos* (Paris: L'Olivier, 2005).

6. Amal Sewtohul, *Histoires d'Ashok et autres personnages de moindre importance* (Paris: Gallimard, 2001) and *Les voyages et aventures de Sanjay, explorateur mauricien des anciens mondes* (Paris: Gallimard, 2009).

7. On October 17, 2009, the 2008 Literature Nobel winner J. M. G. Le Clézio, a citizen of Mauritius, published in *Le monde* an eloquent open letter to President Barack Obama, the 2009 Nobel Peace Prize winner, in which he urges the American president to end the forty-year-old ban that prevents deported *Chagossiens* from returning home to their islands. J. M. G. Le Clézio, "Lavez l'injustice faite aux Chagossiens," *Le monde*, October 17, 2009, http://www.lemonde.fr/opinions/article/2009/10/17/lavez-l-injustice-faite-aux-chagossiens-par-jean-marie-g-le-clezio_1255254_3232.html.

Geographically unique narratives of memory and displacement are an integral part of world literature today. Mauritian writers contribute to that trend, and Appanah is not the first to write fiction about the role of her island in providing refuge from militarism and political discrimination. Nor is she the first to write about the group of Jewish deportees who arrived in Mauritius in 1940. The Anglophone novelist Maureen Earl did so with *Boat of Stone* in 1993,[8] and the Francophone Alain Gordon-Gentil gives this history a small presence in *Le voyage de Delcourt* in 2001.[9] But *Le dernier frère* is the first text that actually strives to capture the voice and perspective of a native Mauritian as he lives through, and later in life recollects, the unusual events of his childhood. Appanah's narrator is the seventy-year-old Raj, a descendant of indentured laborers whose family had to move around the island in search of job stability. He recalls those summer months of 1944–45 when he was barely ten and his life was transformed by his friendship with David. In the epigraphs above, the emotional tone of Raj's narrative, his alternating feelings of anger and pain followed by the serenity and hope that sensory memory provides, contrast sharply with the matter of fact style of the French visitor, the Cairo-born Jewish psychologist Jacques Hassoun who discovers in the early 1990s both the traces of this past in the cemetery and the dispassionate humanistic poster put up by the caretakers: "intolerance and exclusion are murderous."

In this essay, I want to bring into dialogue the different points of view and modes of writing about injustice exemplified by these epigraphs. My goal is to draw attention to the events themselves and to Appanah's invaluable contribution to a cultural conversation that can take as many forms as there are sites of encounter for groups vying for recognition or seeking reparation for their apparently divergent histories of subjugation. Ethnic groups that cohabit peacefully can also harbor persistent feelings of suspicion, as has historically been the case in Mauritius between Hindus and Muslims, and between Indians and Creoles (whites, blacks, or mixed-race). In two of her four novels, Appanah's approach is to raise ethical questions about the relative status of historical discourse and literary representation with regard to events and traditions generally viewed as divergent and disconnected. She insists instead on presenting those as convergent and interwoven within

---

8. Maureen Earl, *Boat of Stone* (Sag Harbor, N. Y.: The Permanent Press, 1993).
9. Alain Gordon-Gentil, *Le voyage de Delcourt* (Paris: Julliard, 2001).

the broader framework of European political domination, with its long-term consequences on the formation of group identity in and across many geographical sites.

In her first novel, Les rochers de Poudre d'Or (2003), she stages a productive encounter between two different communities, coolies and slaves whose lives were marked by settler colonialism in the Indian Ocean.[10] In Le dernier frère, the fortuitous meeting of Creole-speaking Raj and Czech- and Yiddish-speaking David is an unusual and poignant opportunity for both to behave, despite their respective traumas and the dramas unfolding around them, like the children that they really are: "Play was our fraternal language," says Raj.[11] They learn to communicate in French, a language both have learned in school:

> Words, in the French language, were foreign to both of us. We now had to mold that language to our thinking, to what we wanted to say, and not be content, like at school, with simply deciphering and repeating words . . . maybe that is why we quickly became able to say important things such as I am alone. Me too. (81)

Play provides reprieve from loneliness, while the artificiality of French forces them to use simple words that paradoxically communicate more honest, direct feelings about "important things." This laborious use of language—the painstaking production of "foreign" words that is at once a joyful effort and a serious form of labor—encourages self-revelation and sharing. Their predicament mirrors the situation of the Francophone writer who succeeds in revealing muted histories, altering the landscape of memory, and articulating real—if heretofore unspoken—connections and feelings perhaps too painful to express in the quotidian medium of their own native or mother tongue. For Appanah, contrary to politically expedient statements either in favor of or against this "global" language, French becomes a *neutral* vector that enables more heartfelt and genuine communication between the young protagonists who have to work at using it playfully as well as seriously.

In Les rochers, Appanah uses French to create a narrative bridge between Creoles and Indians. In Le dernier frère, she gives a strong affective dimension to her portrayal of children of diverse origins, and her goal once again is to underscore the surprising parallels be-

---

10. Nathacha Appanah, Les rochers de Poudre d'Or (Paris: Gallimard, 2003).
11. Appanah, Le dernier frère, 84.

tween their completely unrelated communities. In the first epigraph, the image of the barbed wires that surround the Jewish prison are a metaphor for the barriers that intolerance and exclusion create as they demarcate and artificially separate discrete populations that might otherwise become bound together by feelings of mutual empathy and understanding, if only they could articulate and share what is truly "important" (81, 171), or what might simply be termed, after Agamben, the dispositions of "bare life."[12] The narrator implies that to use the codes of ordinary language in a rote, mechanical, or habitual fashion that blunts the force of words is also to submit to a dangerous status quo, one in which the performative goals of communication can get lost in clichés. By focusing on the lives of two young boys who have to use the only "artificial" tongue they share —French—and whose tragic destinies unfold against the lush background and ferocious storms of the tropics, Appanah is consciously echoing the mythical world of Bernardin de Saint-Pierre's *Paul et Virginie*[13] while also foregrounding the problems of cultural contact in a colonial context of generalized racism and distrust, one in which competition for recognition and survival are the rule. The novel thus provides a unique opportunity to engage in a creative dialogue with the long history of Mauritian literature as well as with the Jewish memoirists who were baffled by the island and its inhabitants, ignorant as they were of the historical specificities of this "exotic" country to which they were deported and where they survived, but which they failed to describe adequately because they could only perceive it through the tired clichés and set linguistic codes of their own European mind-sets.

DEFAMILIARIZING THE REAL: LANGUAGE AND TRUTH

What can we make of Appanah's choice to focus on an episode that is unknown to most Mauritians and marginal at best to the concerns of nation building in the postcolonial context of "unity in diversity" that subtends the political and cultural ideology of the country? What can

---

12. Giorgio Agamben, *Homo Sacer: Sovereign Power and Bare Life*, trans. Daniel Heller Roazen (Stanford: Stanford University Press, 1998).
13. Françoise Lionnet, "Critical Conventions, Literary Landscapes, and Postcolonial Ecocriticism," *French Global: A New Approach to Literary History*, ed. Christie MacDonald and Susan Suleiman (New York: Columbia University Press, 2010).

historical knowledge about this event, on the one hand, and the *creative* fictionalizing of daily life in this prison camp, on the other, add to our understanding of world history and world literature today?

In an interview, the writer explains:

> When I began writing my fourth novel, I told myself that I really had to deal with the Second World War. I pondered the encounter of a young Mauritian and a young Jew who knew nothing about each other's existence. In fact, most of the Jewish refugees had absolutely no idea of the existence of the island of Mauritius. And I figured that these two forms of misrecognition, and the simultaneously deep understanding that they all had about the difficulties of their individual lives needed to be put into perspective. . . .
>
> It is also a way for me to ask, with regard to the Second World War, what attitude would have been the right one. I think there are a lot of judgments on what one ought to have done, on what one did. *And I am fascinated by that: what does one do when one comes face to face with History? You don't know it when it is happening. You don't know how it is going to be recounted years later.*[14]

Personal responsibility and the flexibility of remembrance are Appanah's major concerns, and she stages a narrator, the adult Raj, who struggles with the need to recall as precisely as possible what was going on in Beau-Bassin in the 1940s. His poignant and increasingly intense anxiety about the need to "dire" [say] or "décrire" [describe] "exactement" [exactly][15] what he knows of this episode reveals a concern akin to that of a professional historian's search for truth rather than a fiction writer's imaginative re-creation of the past. Appanah makes her reader aware of the problems of representation, the inextricable bonds between truth and fiction, the tangled knots that give texture to, and complicate, the fabric of memory. *Le dernier frère* is not a historical novel, yet it attempts to provide an *effet de réel* [reality effect] by "quoting" what appears to be an entirely fictive newspaper account of 1973 as the sole source of illuminating historical information for Raj (208–210). The narrative foregrounds the work of remembering and narrativizing these "real" events, since the 1973 journalistic account that Raj comes across on a blissful Sunday afternoon at home is

---

14. Appanah, Interview, http://livres.fluctuat.net/nathacha-apanah/interviews/2432-un-autre-horizon-mauricien.html (emphasis added).

15. Appanah, *Le dernier frère*, 171; 175; 185; 189.

revealed to be the factor that turns his life upside down, and motivates him to plunge back into the past with the urge to remember as exactly as possible the childhood moments spent with the friend who filled the hole left by the death of his brothers.

"On Friday morning . . . a ten-person delegation from the United States gathered at the graves of the 127 Jews who died in exile in Mauritius," the quoted article states, adding that the Jews had arrived on the liner *"The Atlantic"* which "docked in Port-Louis on 26 December 1940 with some 1500 Jews on board" (208). Among those present, a former detainee, "Hannah," who has returned "after twenty-eight years" is reported as saying: "we were treated like plague-victims, our daily life was hard and we were not allowed out" (210). The irony, which will certainly be lost on the average reader, is that this (3-page) account, cannot possibly be copied from a "real" newspaper story, since it is only in the late 1980s that information about the 1940s began to appear in the public media; in addition, as I will explain below, the *S. S. Atlantic* did not make it to Mauritius, and many inmates regularly spent time outside the camp. These rather simple facts —easily verifiable from multiple archival and testimonial sources— underscore, *but only for the informed reader*, the constructed nature of the so-called journalistic account. Its insertion, at the end of the novel, further contributes to the blurring of the line between fact and fiction by transposing onto the structural level of the text a non-diegetic fragment of questionable status that is meant to provide an objective, public confirmation of the avowedly tentative private memories of the narrator.

On the face of it, this structural element of the narrative cancels out the main thematic thread of the story, namely, the uncertainties of Raj's memory and the public invisibility of the Jews. The text thus appears to disown on a structural level what it has embraced on a thematic and ideological one, since historical logic and causality appear to be underwritten by the "real" document that negates the provisional aspect of Raj's struggles with his *souvenirs*. But this narrative equivocation, which could be read as a way of *confirming* the reality of internment as against the tentativeness of memory, results instead in an (unwittingly?) ironic—and ethically troubling—unraveling of the very notion of "truth" that actually rules this genre of discourse (the news report), but that is in fact never questioned by the text. The straightforward news account, coming as it does at the end, provides closure but it thus arrests meaning and limits the thematic potentialities of the discourse of and on memory.[16]

By contrast, Raj struggles all along to make sense of his personal experience of survival and victimization by an abusive father. He relives his past physical and emotional pain, the loss of his brothers Anil and Vinod in a flood, then that of his "last brother" and friend David to disease: "Maybe memory is playing tricks on me";[17] "This is surely not the truth but that's what my memory tells me, that's what's left after sixty years" (142); and "My memories have been fermenting for so long that sometimes I cannot trust them" (163); he keeps repeating. Appanah dwells on these uncertainties as she thematizes Raj's efforts to recall his escape from violent surroundings, and to understand a Jewish presence that had been "completely heterogeneous to the environment" of Mauritius, as Jacques Hassoun puts it in my second epigraph. After the war, Raj endeavors to comprehend what "exactly" brought the orphan David (and the other inmates) to the prison where his father worked as a guard, but his quest is repeatedly thwarted by his family and teachers, who have remained ignorant of the full dimensions of that history.

His search provides Appanah with a narrative device that becomes a useful form of cultural mediation. By focusing on the unusual plight of the Central European Jews, she breaks open the common binaries along which Mauritian literature and culture traditionally tend to be defined: white/black, Hindu/Muslim, Indian/Creole, British/French, perpetrator/victim. The Jewish presence puts into perspective all local histories of conflict; those histories, in turn, create a new ground from which to understand both the specificity of Jewish victimization and what it shares with other forms of discrimination. Appanah builds unexpected analogies by means of a descriptive language that establishes connections and undermines received claims of uniqueness about the European concentration camp as the "new biopolitical *nomos* of the planet,"[18] since here the Mapou camp indexes patterns of exclusion that date back to early colonial forms of space management and population control (if not always extermination).

---

16. For an important discussion on questions of narrative closure, see D. A. Miller, *Narrative and Its Discontents: Problems of Closure in the Traditional Novel* (Princeton: Princeton University Press, 1981). I come back to this point in the last section of this essay.

17. Appanah, *Le dernier frère*, 130.

18. Agamben, 176.

When referring to the living conditions of the Indian laborers who came to work on the sugar estates, Raj recalls:

> On the Mapou sugar estate, on edge of the immense, green, undulating sugarcane field, there was a series of ramshackle boxes, huts, *so-called houses built from whatever our elders could lay their hands on, and that we used to call the "camp."* [*de soi-disant maisons faites de tout ce qui tombait entre les mains de nos ainés et que l'on appelait le "camp."*][19]

The use of the word "camp" and the defamiliarizing quotes around it provide an immediate and altogether different meaning from the one suggested by Holocaust narratives, while also echoing (with) them. The quotes highlight patterns of exploitation and colonial confinement that produced their own egregious and unjust living conditions for hundreds of thousands of indentured migrants ("nos ainés" [our elders]) and their descendants. That the same ordinary word can both denote and connote dissimilar histories is precisely the point here, since such polysemy forces the user, and the reader, to put more weight onto each word, just as the young Raj and David do in their candid use of French to communicate their naked existential feelings, their basic human needs as victims of such spatial and racial segregation.

But what does it mean, for Appanah, to represent such divergent histories by way of personal experiences that happen to converge through the hazards of a war waged ten thousand kilometers away and that would otherwise share no other common ground? And to do so by means of an unreliable narrator whose failing memory the text is at pains to foreground? Raj's point of view is at best limited—he was nine when he met David: "I was too young to understand what was happening in front of my eyes" (94)—and at worst, prejudiced since he cannot verify any of the "facts" linked to the atmosphere of familial and social violence that must have skewed his sense of reality. Of course, *all* Mauritians who came into contact with the Jews would have similarly been unable fully to comprehend what was at stake, just as the detainees themselves, as we know from their memoirs, did not yet know the full extent of the genocide. Appanah's purposive use of a limited point of view aims to achieve greater awareness of the intertwined destinies of the victims of both Nazism and colonialism. But can her novel trigger a *local* sense of collective national empathy

---

19. Appanah, *Le dernier frère*, 17 (emphasis added).

(if not responsibility) with regard to an era that most Mauritians today consider far removed from their daily concerns? That she succeeds in providing a *global* reading community with a much more nuanced literary and cultural understanding of Mauritian culture as well as Jewish history is now clear from the fact that her book is slated to be translated and published in a half-dozen or so different languages.

As mentioned before, the majority of the Jewish detainees were baffled by their life on the island. Those who wrote about their fifty-five-month long sojourn gave their memoirs provocative and exoticizing titles such as "Prisonniers sur l'île de la fièvre" [Prisoners on Fever Island],[20] a title that is actually contradicted by another detainee's narrative. "The climate of the island is not bad, but for Europeans it is very difficult because of the humidity rather than of high temperatures," writes Aaron Zwergbaum in his "Exile in Mauritius."[21] Zwergbaum tries to be admirably balanced but he cannot help orientalizing the island and its people. His descriptions echo Karl Lenk's in *The Mauritius Affair: The Boat People of 1940–41*: "The natural beauty of the place was breathtaking. . . . Coloured people lined the streets of the village and threw flowers as we passed."[22] Deutsch, Zwergbaum, and Lenk provide invaluable but equally limited insights into the complicated cultural and political dynamics of 1940s Mauritius.

It is hardly surprising that different narrative genres and diverse cultural voices would produce different effects and create different limitations: for the Jewish witnesses, the island is but an exotic and uncomfortable prison from which they hope to be delivered soon; for Appanah, the Jewish presence serves as ground for evoking broad problems of ethics and identity that exceed the specificities of the 1940s. Is it fair, then, to ask whether her narrative instrumentalizes the experience of the Czech boy in order to solve problems specific to the postcolonial nation and its ethnic issues? This is a question to which I will return in my last section, and which will be mirrored in the way Raj himself worries that he has unwittingly used David's presence to his own benefit. On one important critical level, however, Appanah's interweaving of two young lives in the textual space of this novel pro-

---

20. Deutsch, "Prisonniers sur l'île de la fièvre," *Le monde juif* 157: 86–111.
21. Aaron Zwergbaum, "Exile in Mauritius," *Yad Vashem Studies* 4 (1960): 191–257.
22. Karl Lenk, *The Mauritius Affair: The Boat People of 1940–41* (Brighton: Lenk, 1993), 80.

vides the reader with an example of a successful "minor transnational"[23] or "multidirectional"[24] approach to the surprising *mémoires croisées* of two seemingly unconnected ethnic groups: cultured Central European Jews and uneducated coolies. By foregrounding their parallel experiences of loss and the relational nature of identities and histories beyond geographic coincidences, even when connections might seem tenuous at best, the novel demonstrates that, in Rothberg's words, "remembrance both cuts across and binds together diverse spatial, temporal, and cultural sites" (11). For Appanah, then, remembrance can—and thus must—construct an ethical ground where the formation of both individual and collective identity in a global context can produce empathy and dialogue, and not "murderous intolerance and exclusion."

IN THE WAKE OF HISTORY: TRAUMATIC ARRIVALS

Contrary to the narrator's injunction to "say *exactly*," Appanah takes some major liberties (or unknowingly makes mistakes) about the facts of the 1940s in Beau-Bassin. It seems therefore useful to proceed by looking more closely at how those years have been described by individuals who lived them. Only then might we arrive at a full understanding of the contributions that Appanah's fiction makes to the cultural imaginary of her contemporary readers—be they Mauritians or Europeans. What are, then, the actual circumstances that brought the Jewish refugees to Mauritius, what liberties does the writer take with that history, and why? My own narrative here will borrow from and summarize details provided by several heterogeneous sources: personal memoirs, oral testimonies, and one historiography.

On 26 December 1940, two Dutch chartered vessels, requisitioned by the British colonial authorities in Haifa, Palestine, arrived in Mauritius after a seventeen-day journey. The *Nieuw Zeeland* and the *Johan de Witt* carried 1581 passengers on board. All were Jewish refugees who had been among the last to leave Nazi-occupied Central Europe. Some had started out in early September 1940 in Danzig, Berlin, and Vienna, while others joined them in Prague and Bratislava. On the

---

23. *Minor Transnationalism*, ed. Lionnet and Shu-mei Shih (Durham: N.C.: Duke University Press, 2005).

24. Michael Rothberg, *Multidirectional Memory: Remembering the Holocaust in the Age of Decolonization* (Stanford: Stanford University Press, 2009).

Danube, they were grouped in a convoy of four small ships that took them to Tulcea, Romania, on the Black Sea. There they boarded the S. S. *Atlantic* to Istanbul, crossed the Aegean to Crete and Cyprus, and finally arrived in Haifa in late November. All were bound for *Eretz Israel* to be re-united with family members who had reached those shores just weeks or months before. But none of them would be allowed to stay.

After the infamous *White Paper* of 1939, the British Colonial Office had decided to put a stop to illegal Jewish immigration to Palestine. Those who arrived on the *Atlantic* were temporarily housed in the Atlit detainee camp some twenty miles south of Haifa while the Colonial office considered other possible colonial destinations for their onward journey, namely Australia, Jamaica, and Trinidad, before settling on Mauritius. Since the *Atlantic* was by then in a deplorable state and taking water, the passengers embarked on the chartered *Nieuw Zeeland* and *Johan de Witt*, which set sail for Mauritius on 9 December 1940 via Port Said, the Suez Canal, Aden, and a weeklong Indian Ocean crossing.[25] That year, the first day of Chanukah coincided with Christmas. No special celebrations were permitted, but passengers were exceptionally allowed to use the swimming pool to cool off in the sweltering austral summer heat. In the afternoon of the 26th, the mountains of Port Louis and the island's lush green vegetation appeared on the horizon.[26]

This arrival in Mauritius elicited friendly curiosity as well as suspicion. Residents of the island had heard for weeks that a contingent

25. As Pitot documents, the *S. S. Atlantic* was originally built in 1870. Geneviève Pitot, *The Mauritian Shekel: The Story of the Jewish Detainees in Mauritius, 1940–1945*, trans. Donna Edouard and ed. Helen Topor (Lanham: Rowan and Littlefield, 2000), 46.

26. One has to wonder if Mauritius was chosen not only because of its relative "nearness" compared to Trinidad, Jamaica, or Australia (as was officially declared) but also because some British officials might have approved of an early Nazi plan to expel all the Jews of Europe to the neighboring (and much larger) island of Madagascar, then under Vichy control. This "territorial solution," which predated the articulation of the Nazi "final solution" had in fact been proposed as early as 1885 by the Orientalist scholar and anti-Semitic thinker Paul Anton de Lagarde, and later reiterated by the Polish government in the 1930s, with the support of the French Colonial Minister Marius Moutet. In 1937, a joint Polish-French commission actually went on a fact-finding mission to Madagascar and produced a report that ruled out the plan as too "expensive." Paul Anton de Lagarde, "Über die nächsten Pflichten deutscher Politik," *Schriften für Deutschland* (Stuttgart: Kroener, 1933), 288. Magnus Brechkten, *"Madagaskar für die Juden": antisemitische Idee und politische Praxis, 1885–1945* (Munich: Oldenbourg, 1997).

of refugees from Europe were on their way to the island. Most Mauritians were sympathetic to their plight. But rumors also circulated that some of them might be spies and Nazi agents; those coming from Germany and Austria were technically considered to be "enemy aliens." Furthermore, there were no Jews living in Mauritius, except for one single businessman, Isaac Birger, who had arrived there from Lithuania in 1937 with the Czech shoe company Bata. He had settled on the island after marrying a Franco-Mauritian woman. The ethnically and religiously diverse population of Mauritius would have had no particular stake in the Jewish question, even if they were no doubt influenced by a long tradition of British and French anti-Semitic discourses as transmitted through the literary, historical, and religious texts that formed part of the common educational and cultural experiences of educated Mauritians. From the perspective of the British colonial government, the refugees were *illegal* Jewish immigrants who, having attempted to land in Haifa, were in breach of the laws of Palestine. That was the ostensible reason for keeping them in punitive detention, for the duration of the war, in the Central Prison of Beau-Bassin, one of three colonial penal institutions on the island. A few of the detainees volunteered to go and fight in the war, and some men, primarily Poles and Czechs who had obtained official clearance from the British government, were actually able to leave the camp and join the Allied Forces.

The Beau-Bassin prison is a rather beautiful two-story stone building that dates back to the eighteenth-century French colonial period.[27] The refugees were housed in this "camp" under conditions of relative discomfort and crowdedness, but very far from the systematic genocidal madness underway in Europe. Despite their difficult circumstances, they were able to devise a semblance of normal living. Some fifty couples were married religiously by the camp rabbi, and were also allowed to "legalize" their union in civil ceremonies conducted at the closest municipal magistrate's office outside the camp, in Rose-Hill. Some fifty-three babies were born in the camp; two died. Some of the children and one young adult woman fell victim to the polio epidemic that raged in Mauritius during those years. Several refugees contracted malaria or other tropical ailments, from typhoid to dysentery; others suffered from a variety of respiratory or digestive difficulties and mal-

---

27. For a contemporary photo of the Central Prison, see the Republic of Mauritius government website, http://www.gov.mu/portal/site/prisons

nutrition. Those who died—127 including two suicides—in Beau-Bassin were interred about a mile away in the Saint-Martin multiconfessional cemetery's Jewish section, which continues to be maintained today by the *Amicale Maurice-Israel* (Mauritius-Israel Friendship Society), a local association of approximately 125 Mauritian members from the various ethnic and religious communities of the island. Yet others were also able, for a time, to participate in professional and cultural activities outside the camp, thus contributing to the lives of ordinary Mauritians, just as they were also authorized to take turns and spend brief "vacations" at a holiday camp set up for that purpose on the beach at Palmar, on the East side of the island.

The remaining members of the group were finally able to leave Mauritius on August 11, 1945 on the *S. S. Franconia* bound for Haifa. They appear to have been the first group of immigrants allowed into Palestine at the end of the war. Most remained there and eventually became Israeli citizens; some however went back to Austria and Czechoslovakia, a few others to the United States, Canada, Australia, and Argentina, and some later returned to visit the prison and the gravesite. In 1999, fifty former inmates came to participate in ceremonies of restoration and re-consecration at the gravesites, and the local *Amicale* along with the South African Jewish Board of Deputies and the United Jewish Appeal worked together at documenting the history of the Beau-Bassin years. But this World War II episode of Jewish life has remained relatively hidden from public memory. Understandably so, given the much more dramatic and tragic events of the Holocaust. As Aaron Zwergbaum writes in "Exile in Mauritius," this is a "singular, peculiar and rather exotic chapter of modern Jewish history" (191).

But this is also a crucial chapter of modern *Mauritian* history that has remained invisible to the country's citizens because the British colonial government had no interest in encouraging public scrutiny of the "classified" events that led to the Jews' exile on the island, and of the way the British had systematically foiled the refugees' efforts to be reunited with family in Palestine. After Independence in 1968, the events were all but completely forgotten: they had been but an incidental occurrence tied to a war that had been waged in a distant European theater, a mere footnote on a page of colonial history with no apparent or immediate significance for the new nation in development.

However, a Franco-Mauritian independent scholar, Geneviève

Pitot, who was living and working as a structural engineer in Germany in the 1980s and1990s, became aware of the full significance of that history and of the small role that her Francophone and Creolophone native island had played in the larger story of Holocaust survival. She spent the better part of the 1990s gathering as much information as she could. She is the only one to date to have published a painstakingly detailed account of the role of Mauritius in these intertwined histories of the 1940s. British policies in the Middle East had far-reaching impact across many Commonwealth territories: camps for war refugees of all ethnic and religious backgrounds sprouted from Australia to Uganda. Pitot's book, *The Mauritian Shekel: The Story of Jewish Detainees in Mauritius 1940–1945*, was finally published in an English translation in Mauritius in 1998, reprinted in the United States in 2000. To my knowledge, the French version still remains in manuscript form. It is the only history of these events that attempts to be comprehensive.[28]

Pitot, who died in 2002, was ten years old in 1941, and her school, the Mazérieux Elementary School in Curepipe (which I also attended in the mid-1950s) had benefited from the teaching and expertise of one of the camp's detainees, an artist known to the pupils simply as Madame Frank. Anna Antalie Frank (née Klein) was a Berliner who had received an exit visa in November 1939 from the Bolivian Consulate. Why she ended up in the group that was sent to Mauritius instead of being allowed to go to Bolivia is unclear. She taught art classes at the Mazérieux private school for almost a year, at a time when the curriculum only included the "basics," and the pupils had no art or music instruction. While I was growing up in Mauritius in the 1950s and 1960s, I learned about the Jewish "guests" of the island from my mother, Madeline Bérenger. She had been in her early twenties during the war, and was recruited in the nursing ranks of Women's Auxiliary Territorial Service. She used to tell me about the Sunday morning concerts by Jewish musicians that were transmitted live on the island's radio, the MBS or Mauritius Broadcasting Services. In the 1950s, she read avidly about the French Resistance movement and the Nuremberg trials which seemed to help her flesh out the little she had known about the historical context that led to the Jews' presence in Mauri-

---

28. The book was translated into German in 2008. Pamela de St. Antoine, "Book on Jewish Detainees in Mauritius Gets Audience in Germany," *Le Mauricien-Week-End*, "American Scene" section, March 2, 2008, http://www.lemauricien.org/weekend/080302/pam.htm.

tius, including the alarming rumors of mass extermination that had filtered through the Red Cross in 1943.

Anna Frank was one of the many detainees able to participate in various activities outside the prison walls. In their memoirs, both Deutsch and Zwergbaum relate the numerous contributions to the local economy and to the war effort on the part of individuals with special skills. These were the chemists who worked in soap factories; the tailors who sewed soldiers' uniforms and the artisans who made the uniform's metal belt buckles; the cobblers who made shoes (including one man who went to work for Isaac Birger at Bata and even became a manager at the shoe factory); and the engineers and mechanics who repaired Army and Navy vehicles. But that relative freedom of movement was suddenly curtailed on 7 August 1943, after a series of explosions sank Allied ships and British convoys near Mauritius. It was reported that German and Japanese submarines positioned in the Indian Ocean were getting dangerously close to the island. Restrictive security measures against the detainees were re-established due to the cloud of suspicion that the German-speaking Jews were under. Paranoia set in, and some local papers published false reports about presumed spying activities at the camp. Pitot's book, to date, is the one and only that finally sets the record straight. It provides an invaluable and balanced historiography of the political, social, and cultural contexts of those years, and it does so with scrupulous attention to the distortions and exaggerated claims that fueled negative rumors in and out of the camp.

SITES OF INTERSECTING MEMORIES: MONUMENTS AND DOCUMENTS

In 2005, sixty years after the Shoah, the United Nations General Assembly declared 27 January International Holocaust Remembrance Day. Journalists in Mauritius took note of that fact, and some have since called for a government-led effort to include relevant pedagogical material in the public schools. Writing in the Anglophone Hindu weekly *The Mauritius Times* on 25 January 2008, Tiberman Sajiwan Ramyead drew attention to the fact that the General Assembly urged member states "to develop educational programmes that will inculcate future generations with the lessons of the Holocaust in order to help to prevent future acts of genocide." At a time when the rhetoric of Holocaust denial was being fine-tuned by countries that are the economic partners and political interlocutors of the Mauritian government, Ramyead is to be commended for writing:

> It is hoped that the Mauritian government, as a Member State of the UN, will organise some sensitisation programme on the Holocaust; even on its website, which the young probably peruse more than the written press. The lessons learnt from this genocide are not altogether disconnected from our multi-ethnic realities.[29]

He urged the MBC to take part in such an initiative and he suggests that the national network include the 1961 American film *Jugement à Nuremberg* (in its dubbed French version—the most common format for Western movies screened in Francophone Mauritius) as part of its 27 January official programming.

He underscores the baffling national indifference to an important page of local history when he states:

> A few years ago, genealogy and the search for graves of earlier Indian immigrants took me to the Saint Martin cemetery, and there I stared in disbelief at 127 graves of Jews. A Jewish section in a cemetery in Mauritius! One's feelings during such moments are difficult to convey to those who have not experienced them.[30]

Having embarked on a project to reclaim the memory of his own immigrant community and how it had been subjected to colonial racism, Ramyead is brought face to face with, and feels complete empathy for, another group whose history of loss and victimization intersects with his own and even shares the same *lieu de mémoire* [site of memory]: a cemetery where the material presence of the dead is monumentalized. There, the affective charge of the past is triggered not by the presence of the nineteenth-century graves he expected to find, those of indentured laborers, the ancestors whose ethnic identity he shares. Instead, he is rendered speechless by the presence of Jewish headstones and finds himself unable to express emotions "difficult to convey to those who have not experienced them." He makes a "minor transnational" connection between two histories of oppression, and thus recognizes the need for solidarity rather then competition among victims. Having made that connection, he is able to find the words to argue in favor of a national pedagogy that would go beyond the local Mauritian

---

29. Tiberman Sajiwan Ramyead, "Prejudice and Pride," *The Mauritius Times* (January 25, 2008), http://www.mauritiustimes.com/250108ramyead.htm.
30. http://www.mauritiustimes.com/250108ramyead.htm.

politics of identity and communalism. His thought process exemplifies the multidirectional approach that "brings together that which is supposed to be kept apart."[31]

Appanah, too, develops an interest in the history of Jewish presence in Mauritius by way of a commitment to History writ large. In a 2007 interview about *Le dernier frère*, she explains:

> I have always wondered about the links between History and history. How our little daily lives could at a precise moment be turned upside down by something much bigger . . . I have always wanted to tell stories on a human scale. I am not a historian, but I find this very interesting. With regard to *Les rochers de Poudre d'Or*, I am a descendant of those Indian indentured laborers. And their history, one knows it without really knowing it. I have heard many anecdotes from that period. But for me, those remained rather ordinary. I wanted those characters to come to life in another sort of context.[32]

In November 2003, when asked about the history of indentured servitude in comparison to that of slavery, she refuses to "rank" the degree of suffering endured by discrete groups of people, and expresses her dismay about the seeming rivalry that such comparisons can lead to. The interviewer asks if *l'engagisme* [indenture] ought to be considered a "crime against humanity" the way slavery now is, and she replies:

> I refuse in every way any comparison with slavery. Sure, indenture followed in the same furrows traced by slavery, but it is not the same thing. Slaves were tied up like animals, Indians were not; Indians signed contracts—even if some of those were barely legal—but that left a record of their indenture, whereas slaves had no such thing; Indians could come with their families . . . slaves were literally stolen from their villages, sold, exchanged; Indians were paid, slaves were not. . . . Also, I have a lot of trouble with what I call the embrace of misfortune. There is something like a competition to determine whose ancestors were the most miserable, and some consider it a form of glory to know that they are the descendants of a people that has suffered more than others. Does that make us into more honest men and women?
> So, for me, nothing will change if indenture is recognized or not as a crime against humanity. I am not among those who fight for this recog-

---

31. Rothberg, 25.
32. http://livres.fluctuat.net/nathacha-appanah/interviews/2432-un-autre-horizon-mauricien.html.

nition. *I believe that today, in our world, there are many things that need attention now, and that we can effect change while there is still time. The present, that's what's important.*[33]

The past, then, is not as urgent as the present. But it is a vital reason for acting in the present and rejecting either the ethical paralysis linked to the uncertainties of memory and the ambiguities of language or the politically divisive forms of *ressentiment* that will endlessly defer closure when they become the problematic ground for comparative grievance claims and competitive victimology.[34]

Appanah emphasizes the importance of living in the now because, for her, the present moment with *its* trail of grief is what constitutes the ground of ethics. In other words, History matters because its traumatic impact on the lives of ordinary people can trigger the realization that personal or collective forms of suffering are connected cross-culturally but should neither be compared nor ranked, neither overstated nor glorified. History provides a context for grief, it is what creates the "condition of pain"[35] and the fortuitous moments that may lead to the awareness that we are always implicated in, if not always responsible for, the trauma suffered by others at the site of our common or mutual encounters. Thus, the reclamation of diverse histories, followed by the production of documents and narratives that can flesh out these histories, along with the public acknowledgment of that process are for Appanah the indispensable conditions of possibility of a future-oriented exchange.

But the question remains: when a literary narrative such as *Le dernier frère* is a site of engagement with trauma, repression, and re-memory, what is the status of its thematic insistence on notions of truth and *exactness*? And what are we to make of the text's structural resolution of the problem by means of an embedded story—the 1973 article—that contains patent falsehoods (e.g., the reference to the *S. S. Atlantic*), especially when references to other archival accounts (e.g.,

33. Appanah, Interview, http://www.indereunion.net/actu/NAM/intervnam.htm (emphasis added).
34. The 1985 UN Declaration on the rights of victims is useful in this regard, as are the essays included in the book edited by Schneider. United Nations. Office of the UN High Commissioner for Human Rights, "Declaration of Basic Principles of Justice for Victims of Crime and Abuse of Power," Resolution 40/34, November 25, 1985, http://www2.ohchr.org/english/law/victims.htm. *The Victim in International Perspective*, ed. Hans Joachim Schneider (Berlin: Walter de Gruyter & Co., 1982).
35. Paul Gilroy, *The Black Atlantic: Modernity and Double Consciousness* (Cambridge: Harvard University Press, 1993), 203.

those regarding the cyclone and the polio epidemic of 1945) are verifiable and historically completely accurate?

Raj explains that he feels responsible for David's deteriorating health and eventual death from malaria during their *fugue* [escape].[36] "David might still be alive today" (113), he says and later confesses: "I thought I was capable of freeing him from jail" (145). Raj does free David from captivity, as Moses did the Jews. But the children's journey provides but a brief moment of freedom in the now hurricane-torn forest. As he recalls the escape decades later, Raj struggles with both the scandalous historical and cultural silence about David's short life and his own feelings of illegitimacy as a survivor who continues through the years to be the sole beneficiary of a luminous encounter in which:

> David was my *shadow*, the echo of my slightest movements, a mirror that was by turns comforting and unbearable, so that it was *impossible for me to hide from my responsibility, my decisions*, down to the smallest, most minute and insignificant ones. (170)

David dies free because of the decision made by Raj to flee during the storm. The night before his death, David sings a plaintive Yiddish song that is a revelation for the narrator:

> his words . . . surrounded the forest and enveloped me, the little Raj. . . . The words . . . entered into me, found my heart and connected me to the world around me as if for the first time. (179)

Even if he does not understand the *words* of the song, Raj is deeply affected by its poignant melody. He realizes, in retrospect, that it is David who was in fact his, Raj's, savior. Their walk across the tropical landscape as well as David's untimely death echo several episodes of Bernardin de Saint-Pierre's *Paul et Virginie*, especially the death of its very Christian heroine.[37] Raj, who contracts polio, eventually makes a full recovery, thanks to his mother's constant ministrations and her indigenous knowledge of the properties of native plants.[38] But

---

36. Appanah, *Le dernier frère*, 147; 163; 182.
37. Jacques-Henri Bernardin de Saint-Pierre, *Paul et Virginie* (Paris: Garnier-Flammarion, 1966 [1787]).
38. The mother's indigenous knowledge and the place of alternative forms of healing are given a great deal of attention in the story. I cannot elaborate on this here; suffice it to say that this puts the novel in dialogue with yet another interesting global movement, the "IK movement" and its network of resource centers. D. Michael Warren, "The Role of the Global Network of Indigenous Knowledge Resource Centers in the Conservation of Cultural and Biological Diversity," in *On Biocultural Diversity: Linking Language, Knowledge, and the Environment*, ed. Luisa Maffi (Washington and London: Smithsonian Institution Press, 2001), 446–61.

there is the underlying hint that it is David's passing that enables Raj's return to a state of normalcy, and indeed, his renaissance to "the world around [him]."

In his narrative, Raj desperately wants to be able to convey as truthfully as possible David's *own* story, and he speculates about what his friend might have said and thought.[39] But he does not want to be put in the role of a ventriloquist. He wishes he could put David "at the center of this story" so that the Czech boy would have "the space to *speak* [*dire*] his sorrow and pain" (171; emphasis added) but the language difference increasingly becomes a source of frustration for both of them: "He would sometimes speak very fast and now I understand that he was holding on to his mother tongue, Yiddish, because that was all he had left" (172); and "sometimes, when David would try in vain to tell me something, he would get frustrated and his first language would come back into his mouth" (173). Raj's faith in the power of narrative thus gradually breaks down because a difference that had initially been overcome through the "neutral" medium of French is now insurmountable. The incommensurability of their individual experiences is thus brought up to the surface, but in the end, Raj's dissatisfaction with the numerous lacunae that he is unable to fill gives way to the conviction that David's story—such as he can document it—is one he must pass on to his son "so that he too may remember" (211).

Writing down the past accurately may be an impossible task, but the narrative space of *Le dernier frère*, like the small monuments on the site of the Saint-Martin cemetery that Raj visits with his son (13–16), brings back to life figures from that past that may provoke a fruitful engagement with the multidirectional possibilities of the present. Recall that Toni Morrison ends her novel *Beloved* with a meditation on memory by using a stylistic device that produces the repetition, in slightly altered form, of the phrase: "It was not a story to pass on."[40] In the preceding few pages of *Beloved*, however, the character Paul D explains that he wants to "talk more [and] make sense of the stories he had been hearing"[41] because, as he puts it, they make up "the pieces I am, she [Sethe] gather them and give them back to me in all the right order" (272–73). Listening to Sethe's stories, "He wants to put his story *next to* hers" (273). It seems to me that Appanah pro-

39. Appanah, *Le dernier frère*, 160–61.
40. Toni Morrison, *Beloved* (New York: Knopf, 1987), 275.
41. Morrison, 267.

ceeds the way Morrison does in *Beloved*: remembering for the sake of remembering is unwise (274), but it becomes productive when it motivates a search for meaning that spells out the relational and entangled experiences of seemingly discrete individuals or communities. Those whose proximities define them can then begin to weave narrative bonds with and *next to* each other, without subsuming one point of view to another, without developing the conviction that there might exist one single hegemonic or definitive narrative of, and perspective on, past events. Repression and re-memory thus alternately provide the difficult political ground for the articulation of a common future, personal or communal differences notwithstanding.

That all individuals have a claim on the representation of their partial and particular truths is one of the threads that is pursued here, but from a non-relativistic ideological stance: Jewish refugees and indentured migrants, coolies and slaves, their descendants and heirs, all may have to offer conflicting perspectives on the realities of their suffering, their sea voyages, deportations, enslavements, or internments. But the processes whereby they come to realize, like Appanah's Raj and Morrison's Paul D or like the journalist Ramyead, that the point is to understand proximity and cohabitation and to be able to put one's "story next to" those of others who have every right to their own narrative, then and only then can more peaceful, less violent, transnational or creolized encounters become possible, and indeed desirable. This appears to be the primary, laudable, and humanistic goal of Appanah's oeuvre. But by resolving narrative questions about truth and fiction by means of a "news" story that is not one, she risks undermining, in the end, the best contribution of her compelling novel, that is, the fundamental opacity of humans to one another, and of the past in the present.

Or perhaps the point is, ultimately, for the reader to question this so-called "document" and the "facts" it presents. But because the article, inserted only at the end, stands out typographically as different from, and alien to, the text of the novel, it is presented as information to be taken at face value by the reader. Indeed, the narrator reveals it to be the primary motive for his anxious exploration of the past. Structurally, it thus provides a form of certainty that is more limiting than satisfying. What I am suggesting is that this "document" blocks further reflection on the meaning of responsibility in a context where *one* point of view, presented as fact, is allowed to stand as the final and definitive "truth." Up to that moment, however, the adult Raj's anxieties about the past, and especially his childhood decision to *fugue*, present a convincing narrative working out of the author's own questionings in the first interview cited above: "what does one do when one comes face to face with History? You don't know it when it is happening."[42] Is "responsibility" a diffuse and imperfect concept because one's degree of implication in the lives of others turns on one's (in)ability precisely to grasp the *extent* to which one is inexorably and traumatically bound to another as to one's own "shadow?"[43] Cathy Caruth has argued that for Freud, "the traumatic nature of history means that events are only historical to the extent that they implicate others" (188) which is why repression and latency are constitutive of an "indissoluble, political bond" (188) that necessarily creates many forms of "entanglement" (182, 192). This bond, as Caruth theorizes it after Freud, is analogous, it seems to me, to what Édouard Glissant theorizes as *la Relation*,[44] and which he anchors back to the *point d'intrication*[45] or the entanglements of creolization.[46]

I have argued elsewhere that the crux of what I call *mé-tissage* (mixed-weave)[47] is not the blending or homogenizing of disparate stories into one single overarching narrative, but rather "the textual braiding,"[48] "the weaving of different strands of raw materials and threads of various colors into one piece of fabric"[49] so that individual strands retain their elemental singularity without becoming com-

42. http://livres.fluctuat.net/nathacha-appanah/interviews/2432-un-autre-horizon-mauricien.html.
43. Cathy Caruth, "Unclaimed Experience: Trauma and the Possibility of History," *Yale French Studies* 79 (1991): 170.
44. Édouard Glissant, *Poétique de la relation* (Paris: Seuil, 1990).
45. Glissant, *Le discours antillais* (Paris: Seuil, 1981), 36, translated as "entanglement" by J. Michael Dash, *Caribbean Discourse: Selected Essays* (Charlottesville: University Press of Virginia, 1989), 26.
46. Space does not allow me to elaborate on the broad psychoanalytical and political convergences and divergences among Glissant, Freud, and Caruth. To my knowledge, there exist no comparative discussions of Glissant's and Caruth's work. In my own (very brief) engagements with trauma theory, I have argued against the universalizing impulse in the field, and have pointed to the blind spots that result from insufficient attention to questions of bilingualism or multilingualism in contexts of "colonization by language." Lionnet, "Universalisms and Francophonies," *International Journal of Francophone Studies* 12/2–3 (2009: 203–221).
47. Lionnet, "*Métissage*, Emancipation, and Female Textuality," *Life/Lines: Theorizing Women's Autobiography*, ed. Bella Brodzki and Celeste Schenck (Ithaca: Cornell University Press, 1988), 260–78.
48. Lionnet, *Autobiographical Voices: Race, Language, and Self-Portraiture* (Ithaca: Cornell University Press, 1989), 157.
49. Ibid., 213.

pletely absorbed, and thus invisible, within the thick texture of the cultural, social, or historical patterns that make up the tangled knots of creolization. What is particularly persuasive about Appanah's narrative, then, is the narrator's desire to recount, however tentatively, what he can recall of the 1940s, and how this in turn can contribute to a global history of displacements. *Le dernier frère* suggests that memory, however flawed, is a function of interconnected sensory experiences (the smell of blood, the sound of Yiddish songs, the touch of healing hands, the blue of the sky and the green of the forest, etc.), of the conflicting accounts of these experiences, and of the moments of entanglement that give both surface and depth to a given field of perception. What is most poignant is that the narrator strives to articulate and, when appropriate, to alter his memories in ways that consistently do justice to their braided and multidirectional nature, just as either Paul D or Ramyead finds significance in the juxtapositions and proximities that emerge unexpectedly from their personal quests for meaning, whereas such quests might just as easily have led them to cultural fantasies of historical exclusiveness and purity.

For many diasporic Indians, the sea journey across the Indian Ocean—the *kala pani* or impure waters that "Hindus were supposed to refrain from crossing as it distanced them from the pure waters of the Ganges"[50]—is what anchors the sense of community. Many Indians in Mauritius, Reunion, Trinidad, Guadeloupe, Guyana or South Africa increasingly define themselves in relation to their respective histories of displacement and separation from "Mother India." Khal Torabully's coining of *coolitude* on the model of Césairian *negritude* serves to theorize "the Indian share of creolization,"[51] and thus to stress the hybrid historical and cultural experiences of coolies as opposed to endorsing a return to a "pure" culture of origin. Appanah (much like Torabully or Amitav Ghosh in his 2008 novel *Sea of Poppies*) is engaged in both describing and critiquing these new trends.[52] While acknowledging important differences, such as the fact that an Indian diasporic community may become either a "majority" (e.g. in Mauritius) or a "minority" (e.g. in Guadeloupe) in its new environment, Appanah repeatedly insists on the need to be open to creolization in a multiethnic country. Her contributions further widen her

50. Véronique Bragard, *Transoceanic Dialogues: Coolitude in Caribbean and Indian Ocean Literatures* (Brussels: Peter Lang, 2008), 71.
51. Ibid., 57.
52. Amitav Ghosh, *Sea of Poppies* (New York: Picador, 2009).

own as well as her compatriots' understanding of the various and converging histories of discrimination and injustice. As she delves into this journey through the hidden history of the Jews in Mauritius, and adds a new stone to the edifice of the long history of intertwined diasporas, she challenges survivors everywhere to acknowledge their shared responsibility to a common future, but to a future that is undeniably finite.

FRANÇOISE VERGÈS

Wandering Souls and Returning Ghosts: Writing the History of the Dispossessed

> ... It is hard to imagine all is lost
> Since the energy of ashes is still here
> And blows from time to time
> through the debris.
> —Aimé Césaire[1]

MONTAGES

When I first reflected on the question of *noeuds de mémoire*, a series of thoughts came to mind. I propose to approach this question from the so-called "South," which for me is not a geographical space but rather the historical site of the dispossessed: workers, peasants, the colonized, slaves, displaced people, refugees. Viewed from this "South," the history of enslavement, mass massacres, genocides, does not belong to the ethical and legal framework that has emerged from a consideration of the Shoah as a unique tragedy, with the metaphors and tropes that construct it as a crime against humanity *which is unparalleled*. When viewed from such a perspective, any event loses its inscription in history. It belongs to a world outside of humanity, to the register of metaphysics. The discourse of uniqueness situates the catastrophe of the Shoah on the plane of belief, rather than encouraging a plurality of readings of the disaster itself and of its critical examinations. This metaphysical approach inevitably leads to a hierarchy of historical violence. Rather, from the perspective of the South, a state of crisis such as the Shoah is not the exception but the rule and

---

1. Aimé Césaire, "Slowness" in *Lyric and Dramatic Poetry, 1946–82*, trans. Clayton Eshelman and Annette Smith (Charlottesville: University of Virginia Press, 1990), 15.

YFS 118/119, *Noeuds de mémoire*, ed. Rothberg, Sanyal, and Silverman, © 2010 by Yale University.

human-made catastrophes belong to the disorder of things, which is the history of human affairs.

Though I am aware of the limits of biography, it may be necessary to say that I am writing from multiple positions: as a cultural activist, a researcher, a project director, and a writer circulating between France and its overseas territories, and Africa and Asia. For years now, I have been working with social educators, associations, and teachers. I have experienced the difficulty of building a project from the bottom up, and have confronted hesitations, administrative obstacles, political conservatism, division among "natural" allies. All this has transformed my theoretical approach and made me wary of grand claims, suspicious of grand narratives, particularly of the narrative of emancipation as a total rupture, as an erasure of the past, as the dawn of a "new" world. Instead, emancipation is a long process in which any victory opens up a terrain for new struggles (see for instance, the abolition of slavery followed by struggles against new forms of economic exploitations and post-slavery colonialism). My experience of such conflicts, tensions, and solidarity and my research on diverse instances of struggle and their fields of contradiction make me wonder if the notion of *noeuds de mémoire* might not be misleading. The potential immobilization of history into a "knot" of fixed relations is real. The way in which memories perform a role in our lives is connected to the questions we raise at a certain moment, and the connection can be explained through a constellation of causes. Hence, the emergence of the memories of slavery and colonization in the French public space and the role these events have played in the public debate can be explained by a number of factors: the growing importance of the problematic of the Shoah (politics and morals, evil and politics), the role of the tribunal and the witness in politics; the role of grass-roots groups, the discontent of French youths whose parents came from the former colonies or the French overseas territories and who experienced racial and ethnic discrimination; and finally, the role that memory plays in the articulation of a discourse about injustice ("it is because of this past that I am discriminated against today").

In other words, the ways in which we use memories and histories are dynamic. Thus, although I know that the editors would not advocate the reification of memories into a fixed construct, I worry that the image of "knots" might lead us to consider a nexus of contradictory or overlapping discourses and representations as a fixed structure that needs unknotting. I suggest using the notion of "contacts of memories," a space where diverse memories enter into contact either by chance (those of refugees escaping wars and repression, or of migrants); or through the deliberate actions of groups or individuals (the memories of the Shoah and slavery, for instance). The contact between diverse currents of memory obeys a different logic, and answers to different interests. It marks a space of encounter, conflict, and exchange between speeches, representations, objects, and sounds that trigger and reactualize past events in ways that cannot be predicted. Such a notion opens up a site for the unexpected, that is, for dynamic history. Even if we observe a "knot of memories," that is, a series of reified, fixed speeches, representations, objects, and sounds that perform the same role of triggering and reactualizing past events, we can look at this knot as the expression of a political goal anchored in present interests, i.e., integrated in a dynamic political process. A "knot" can thus exist as a form of contact, a temporary moment where fixation is constructed to serve diverse interests. "Contacts of memories" describe the changing sites of encounters among memories. It allows us to observe not only how actors instrumentalize or create memories, but also how memory has become an active source of references for articulating present contradictions and emergences. Memory has entered the historical and political vocabulary and rather than bemoaning this fact, we can analyze how it is changing the ways in which struggles are deployed against injustices. The questions raised by the editors led me to operate a self-reflexive work on memory and to be more precise about the notions I use.

I consider a "contact de mémoire" to be the source of active contradictions, a challenge to monolinear national narratives, a zone of encounter and conflict between different layers of memory, all making claims for recognition and meaning. The current debate in France around a "war of memories" ("guerre des mémoires") implies that memories (of slavery, colonialism, wars, and so on) are peaceful constructions, that they are an expression of the human desire to be unique among others. But the fact that they are in conflict should not surprise us because they reflect conflicting interests. Psychoanalysis has made us aware of the importance of the small differences as well as the aspiration to be noticed, the importance of narcissism. Why would memory not be, like any other human activity, the terrain of conflicting interests? A "noeud de mémoire" evokes what could bring human beings together and what might forbid movement, therefore immobilizing them.

I also looked at the question of memory from different positions that, from my point of view, do coexist. It is partly the result of growing up on a small island, Reunion Island, barely situated on the maps but which, since the first years of permanent settlement, has been caught in world events: slavery, abolitionism, colonialism, French colonial empire, south-south migrations, end of colonial status, Cold War, communism, French politics, Indian Ocean politics, European economic regulations, and more recently the challenges of climate change, the emergence of regional world powers (India and China) in the Indian Ocean, and new cultural expressions. The diversity of processes of creolization in such a place make it impossible to ignore multiple layers of signification in, and alternate approaches to, history, as well as to what constitutes the self and the Other. I do not argue for an endless indeterminacy in the reading of history, but instead, I attempt to find the points of contact and conflict between memories and histories. As I try to remain open to emerging or unfamiliar expressions, my assumptions are continually challenged. If there is a theory by which I approach situations, it is the theory of human frailty, of human longing for the infinite, and for the (too often denied) need for others. Although the critique of Western Reason, of the Western belief in free will and in the individual's capacity to realize "himself," has been widely developed, that belief remains strong and hegemonic. One acknowledges the critique but continues to believe in Reason and free will. Thus, "history" is the history of progress or regression, of good or evil, rather than of human actions. However, I seek out the unexpected, the accident of history. I seek out the history of the "anonymous," of those without graves. To think about "noeuds de mémoire" in this context is to think about the history of the dispossessed, about those "without whom the earth would never be the earth," as Aimé Césaire wrote. The history of the dispossessed is the history of economic and psychic domination and of resistance against that domination. A hierarchy of events is therefore impossible. Rather, we may consider the modalities, finalities, time, location, routes, networks, zones of contact and conflict, and draw a cartography of crisscrossing events, one that cannot lead to a linear and coherent narrative but rather to hybrid memories that are dynamically reconfigured. Just as people formulate questions about their past from concerns about their present, memories follow the same dynamics. The "noeuds de mémoire" of the dispossessed are articulations of explanations about their present with explanations about their past.

I would like to argue for the notion of "contact de mémoires" as a source of active and dynamic contradictions through the memories of slavery, how they have played out in France, in Reunion Island, and in Togo. Writing about "contact de mémoires" requires one to remain open to the "small" events, to the singularities of experiences enmeshed in larger events of global importance. Writing the history of the dispossessed requires evoking a simultaneity of events to which the method of *montage* seems better suited. Montage suggests an encounter between what is intimate and what is foreign, it implies a shift in our gaze, it challenges preconceptions. It is a pedagogy of complexity, a warning against the temptation of easy and self-righteous judging. It rests on the understanding that our current multifarious position can no longer be apprehended through one discipline. It also rests on my own experience of traveling between asymmetrical languages and places, of always trying to understand the fabrication of the subaltern in a situated locale. It also means making the effort to understand the position of the oppressor, its fears and angers, the causes for its narcissistic wounds, and acknowledging its capacity for self-reflection. In this contribution, I construct such a montage by looking at slavery as a "contact de mémoires" in three different settings: hexagonal France, Reunion Island, and Togo.

WHOSE MEMORIES MATTER?

In the last two decades, race, slavery, and the colony have become hotly contested terrains in France. Intellectuals, historians, sociologists, elected officials, the ministers of Education, of Immigration, of overseas departments, and the president of France, have all contributed to the debate on memories of slavery and colonialism, their role and place among other central events (deportation of the French Jews, Vichy), and the writing of their history.[2] The petitions of eminent historians against "memorial laws"[3] and for vigilance about the

---

2. Witness the current debate on "national identity," which has allowed xenophobic voices to freely and anonymously express themselves on an official website. Colonial memory and immigration play an important role in the enterprise of "what it is to be French": see www.debatsuridentitenationale.fr.

3. Liberté pour l'histoire (www.lph-asso.fr), an association begun by historians such as Pierre Nora, Pierre Vidal-Naquet, Jean-Pierre Vernant, and Françoise Chandernagor in December 2005, stated as its objective the "defense of historians' freedom of expression against all kinds of political interventions and ideological pressures" and wrote a petition on this theme. In 2008, their petition received the support of numerous European and US historians of international reputation. Though their objective

"public use of history,"[4] the declarations of Nicolas Sarkozy (as a candidate for the French presidency) who coined the term "repentance" to counter demands for a rewriting of French national history that would explain why and how slavery and colonialism are central to French culture and politics, his policies once elected (the creation of a Ministry of Immigration, Integration and National Identity), the debate about ethnic discriminations in housing and work, the governmental project of a *Maison de l'Histoire de France*,[5] the debate around national identity launched in November 2009 by Eric Besson, Minister of Immigration, Integration and National Identity—all these elements show the points of contact and conflict among memories and histories that are currently at the heart of French public debate in the hexagon. The memories of slavery and colonialism constitute sources of reference for both sides of the debate, whether they acknowledge or diminish the importance of the colony as a formative cultural and political site. Declarations and speeches are examined through this lens,[6] but these declarations and speeches must concern the hexagon. What happens in "overseas" France is barely acknowledged.

Since history is said to "be constitutive of French national identity,"[7] questions such as who has the right to speak, to be included, which memories are legitimate, what are their routes and roots, which events are said to be central, are political questions. The relation between history and national identity has been closely associated with the debate on the "integration" of children of migrant workers in France. The objective could be summarized as "no more shame," no more retrospective blame, but a strong pride and a "new relation between the French and their history."[8] On March 31, 2009, upon taking up his position, Eric Besson was told by Nicolas Sarkozy and his prime

---

appears to be the support of research, it has been perceived as directed against the Law of May 21, 2001 that recognized the slave trade and slavery as "crimes against humanity" and whose application has been met with resistance.

4. Comité de vigilance face aux usages publics de l'histoire (http://cvuh.free.fr) is more involved than Liberté pour l'histoire in the debate about educational programs, textbooks, and the history of slavery and colonization.

5. www.ladocumentationfrancaise.fr/rapports-publics/09400029/index.shtml.

6. Witness the recent row around the declaration by Eric Raould, a conservative, who told the Prix Goncourt winner Marie N'Diaye not to make negative remarks about Nicolas Sarkozy, now that she was representing France with this award.

7. Christine Albanel, Minister of Culture, cited in "La Maison de l'histoire de France franchit un pas," www.nouvelobs.com, September 23, 2009.

8. Hervé Lemoine, author of the preliminary report on the project, cited in "Un musée de l'histoire de France: pour quoi faire?" www.lepoint.fr, January 13, 2009.

minister that "the promotion of our national identity must be at the heart of your action" and that his ministry would take part in the construction of the museum, "Maison de l'Histoire de France," which is destined to play a central role in the elaboration of "national memory."

The 2001 Law of May 21 that qualified the slave trade and slavery as "crimes against humanity"[9] was received with indifference by French public opinion and historians. The events of 2005 (riots, controversies, and so on) deeply transformed the discursive terrain as claims for rewriting colonial and postcolonial history became social claims seized by young rioters and associations. The response of the academic and political elites indicated fear that an unspoken but existing hierarchy between different events could be challenged. The memories and histories of the Shoah and colonial slavery were rapidly opposed: which one was a "crime against humanity" and which one did unjust and terrible damage but nonetheless did not entirely deserve to be called a "crime"? Olivier Pétré-Grenouilleau, whose book *Les traites négrières* (2005) became for the historians of *Liberté pour l'Histoire* the emblem of their resistance, put forward remarks that have supported commonly-held ideas. In an interview (June 12, 2005), he declared that the "Muslim empire started the slave trade," that slavery was abolished thanks to the work of the "essentially white and protestant abolitionists," and that the Law of May 21 induced a comparison with the Shoah that was impossible to maintain since the slave trade was not a "genocide."[10] The reduction of the judicial notion of "crime against humanity" to "genocide"[11] has

---

9. www.legifrance.gouv.fr, text of Law n°2001-434, May 21, 2001.

10. I do not discuss here the complaint of Antillean associations against Olivier Pétré-Grenouilleau's declarations in the name of the 2002 Law which was finally withdrawn, even though a close reading of the affair should be done one day to show the diversity of interests at stake.

11. The London Charter of the International Military Tribunal, which issued the decree that set down the laws and procedures by which the post-World War II Nuremberg trials would be conducted, defined "crimes against humanity" as: "Murder, extermination, enslavement, deportation, and other inhumane acts committed against any civilian population, before or during the war, or persecutions on political, racial or religious grounds in execution of or in connection with any crime within the jurisdiction of the Tribunal, whether or not in violation of the domestic law of the country where perpetrated." The "Rome Statute of the International Criminal Court Explanatory Memorandum" defined them as "particularly odious offences in that they constitute a serious attack on human dignity or grave humiliation or a degradation of one or more human beings." The Declaration of the Powers, on the Abolition of the Slave Trade, of February 8, 1815 (which also formed Act XV of the Final Act of the Congress of Vienna of the same year) included in its first sentence the concept of the "principles of humanity and universal morality" as justification for ending a trade that was "odious in its continuance."

served as a device to draw the boundary between slavery and the Shoah. The other argument that has found credence is time. Historian Henry Rousso's declaration is symptomatic of this position. For him, slavery is a "past which was foreign to 'us'" because it was "four centuries old" whereas the Shoah remained the sole and legitimate "memory erected as a universal symbol of the struggle against all forms of racism."[12]

"French history" is *European* history; the hexagon's borders were traced by the European wars of the sixteenth century. The imagined community that is "France" remains strangely narrow, expelling from the national body its "overseas parts," as well as "jungles" and "*quartiers*"[13] perceived as transplanted elements rejected by the national body because they contain(ed) "alien" matter. The geography of memories and histories is still firmly contained within these borders. This partly explains why even shameful events like Vichy and the French active complicity in the deportation of French Jews could eventually be discussed: they concern "France" whereas slavery concerns the "descendants of slaves" who do not live on French "historical territory." Slavery is kept within the racial borders of blackness (being "Black" marks one as being directly interested in slavery). The advocates of the republican myth continue to conceive of slavery as something that happened "over there." The containment of this event in the field of "memory" (subjective, fickle) masks its importance in the making of French modernity (an importance that did not escape the Haitian revolutionaries). French national history persists in its refusal to consider the centrality of the colony in the making of its identity; it is a chapter, important perhaps, but a chapter only. There is currently no real public debate on cultural memory in a transnational age, on the points of contact and conflict between the memories and legacies of genocide, slavery and colonialism.

The reduction of the French national narrative to European territory was concomitant with the end of its colonial empire and the transformation of French society.[14] The reinvention of France as innocent of colonial crimes was the price society was ready to pay in

12. Cited by Catherine Coquery-Vidrovitch, "À propos de l'histoire des traites négrières et, plus généralement, des positions contrastées des historiens," www.cvuh.free.fr/spip.php, Article 64, January 5, 2006.

13. "Jungle" is the name given to squats built by refugees around Calais as they try to cross the Channel, "quartiers," to the places where poorer social classes live.

14. See Kristin Ross, *Fast Cars, Clean Bodies: Decolonization and the Reordering of French Culture* (Cambridge, MA: MIT Press, 1995).

order to embrace the benefits of modernization. France could recreate itself without a colonial past. The *longue durée* of the colony could be forgotten. Stories about French generosity (abolition of slavery, schools and hospitals in the colonies) were kept.[15] The power exerted by the romantic narrative of revolutionary rupture on generations of French intellectuals has made it difficult for memories of the slave trade and slavery to become "interesting" facts. For generations of French intellectuals, the Algerian war of independence (in Algeria) has constituted *the* model of anticolonial struggle (though resistance to slavery was anticolonial struggle). In a dramaturgy that put together Algerian peasants, veiled women, young and heroic women, heroic French men, French torturers and their victims, displaced populations, conflicting memories, a coup d'état, nationalist fighters, internal and violent tensions within the nationalist movement, the violation of rights, transcontinental solidarity, and the fall of a Republic, France could play and replay a twisted, idealized version of decolonization. With slavery, the iconography is impoverished: there are too few moments of bloody revolt with the flag on the barricades, bodies falling, battle cries, in which the French can see themselves as primary protagonists. Slaves risked their lives and died for freedom but very few French subjects died for the abolition of slavery. The hegemony of a model of radical historical rupture inevitably marginalizes the memories and histories of the slave trade and colonial slavery. These lasted for centuries, putting into contact and conflict continents, systems of laws, cultural expressions, philosophies, theologies, and notions of sovereignty. A long, patient, and transcontinental struggle led to their abolition, practically four centuries after the first slave ship left England. And yet, what event other than slavery better resonates with our era of massive migrations, massive fabrication of disposable people, massive and growing inequalities, and the return of an economy of predation that rests again on the belief in infinite resources and the desire of the powerful to impose their rule?

A Eurocentric reading of history seeks to marginalize the memories of transcontinental solidarities. With regards to decolonization, it also reorganizes events through the narrative of liberal democracy. Thus, the role and impact of the Soviet Union and the international communist movement on movements of decolonization are slowly erased

---

15. See Todd Shepard, *The Invention of Decolonization* (Ithaca: Cornell University Press, 2006.)

(in postcolonial countries as well: witness the erasure of Nelson Mandela's past as a communist). The geopolitics of the Cold War and their legacies have produced subaltern memories. I am thinking of the Chagos Island,[16] where a population was expelled from its native land to give way to one of the most important US military bases in the world, Diego Garcia. The territorialization of memories and histories undermines the routes of exchange and concrete solidarity.

The geography of French "noeuds de mémoire" speaks of its still unchallenged borders. If "France" is contained within the hexagon, it is understandable that a hierarchy of memories dominates. European wounds and human-made catastrophes are then undoubtedly major events. However, hybrid memories exist. The routes of solidarity among the dispossessed trace another map of contact and conflict. Indeed, conflict occurs among the dispossessed, as we can see, for instance, in the color line that runs through history and sets feminists against slaves, trade unions against immigrants.

STORIES THAT CUT THROUGH OFFICIAL NARRATIVE

On October 31, 2009, at the Père Lafosse cemetery in Saint-Louis, Reunion Island, a thousand people gathered under a canopy and in the shade of trees. It is a small cemetery with graves bearing no names or dates, close to one of the last two sugar factories that remain active on the island. Père Lafosse was a French priest who came to Reunion Island in the eighteenth century and embraced the cause of the slaves. During the French Revolution, he denounced slavery and called for the application of the "Declaration of Rights of Man and the Citizen" to the colony, but was opposed by the local colonial power. Oral tradition says that slaves are buried in the cemetery and that Père Lafosse himself was buried there upon his death in 1820. For a time, the cemetery was abandoned, even though people came to perform rites to ancestors and to honor Père Lafosse. In the late 1980s, grass-roots groups and progressive priests worked with the city of Saint-Louis and the Regional Council to renovate the site. Local artists contributed to the renovation. Anonymous graves and the grave of Père Lafosse have be-

---

16. See David Vine, *Island of Shame: The Secret History of the U.S. Military Base on Diego Garcia* (Princeton, NJ: Princeton University Press, 2009) and Rosabelle Boswell, *Le malaise créole. Ethnic Identity in Mauritius* (London: Berghahn Books, 2006).

come places of pilgrimage, prayer, homage, and rites to ancestors; they are surrounded with flowers, candles, and objects of creolized rites (red ribbon, cigarettes, glasses of rum). The anthropologist Christiane Rakotolahy has remarked on the Malagasy spatial organization of the site. The history of the cemetery, its place in the oral tradition and in popular history, its role in vernacular practices and rituals explain why, on October 31, 2009, the scientific and cultural team of the *Maison des civilizations et de l'unité réunionnaise* (MCUR) chose it as the place to inaugurate a monument to all the ancestors buried without a marked grave, that is, to the hundreds of thousands of women, men, and children deported as slaves to Reunion Island.

The ceremony was organized around three moments: prayers and songs to the dead, a speech, and the unveiling of the monument. The moment of prayers was opened by Madame Baba, a 91-year-old woman who has been performing creolized Malagasy rites to enslaved ancestors for decades, first with her husband who died in 2005, then with her children. She gave a short speech before singing of her unknown ancestors. Following Madame Baba, Afro-Malagasy, Catholic, Buddhist, Hindu, and Muslim songs and prayers were heard. They called upon the mercy of God, of gods and goddesses, of spirits to appease the wandering souls that haunt the island. For two hours, the public listened to words of sorrow, mourning, grief, and hope. The singer Christine Salem arrived with a *kayamb*, an instrument that accompanies *maloya*, the music created by slaves and enriched by indentured workers on the sugar plantations. She spoke first. She had just learned that her father was denied last rites according to Catholic tradition because he was a communist. She made a connection between this refusal and the ways in which her enslaved ancestors had been denied last rites. She improvised a song in Creole and Malagasy. The monument was unveiled, a sober piece of gray and red granite, the local stone. People could read the text on the monument: "Hundreds of thousands of children, women and men were wrenched from their native land and enslaved on this island, from the end of the seventeenth century to the abolition of slavery in 1848. The Code Noir reduced them to the status of 'furniture.' Colonial slavery deprived them of a marked grave and erased all trace of their presence. Every human being has a right to memory. With this monument, we repair this oblivion. We celebrate their lives, their courage and what they left us." One by one, people put a flower on the monument. Some people came to me to tell me that they would come back later, once the crowd had thinned, to perform vernacular rites, to give the ancestors rum and cigarettes.

The following day, one of the daily newspapers wondered why so much trouble had gone into this ceremony: why a canopy, why so many speeches, why flowers?[17] On the Internet, the blog "Français de souche"[18] contested the idea that slaves were buried without a marked grave. It claimed that the Code Noir required that their owners bury them, that they were not to be left to the dogs, that it was a duty to bury them to avoid epidemics. Other voices concurred: it was time for slavery to be put behind us, time to move forward. The lack of empathy, the refusal to consider—just for once—the sorrow of those who were present at the ceremony, spoke of the contempt for a long history of slavery that had deeply changed the world and shaped the island.

During the October 31 ceremony at the Père Lafosse cemetery, a renowned Sufi visiting from Senegal spoke of the relations among human-made historical catastrophes—slavery, genocide against Native Americans, genocide against European Jews, genocide in Rwanda—and called for a common reflection on the connections among these events. They were all actions of destruction and crimes against humanity, he said; they all sought to transform human beings into refuse, into excess to annihilate, "things" to maim, torture, and kill. This was their point of connection. In other words, human-made historical catastrophes appear to share a line of thought: the dehumanization of another group. Denying the humanity of others justifies enslavement, deportation, destruction. Yet, despite the connection that dehumanization provides, is it possible to compare genocide and slavery? Or, to compare genocides that were the consequences of clearly defined plans and genocides that were the unexpected consequences of invasion, conquest, wars? How and where do these events connect? The history of the slave trade and slavery is still too often read through the theory of liberal and Marxist economy, whereas genocides or mass massacres are explained by a failure of morality and ethics. It is more difficult to confront, outside any moralistic approach, the logic of economic exploitation and progress that justifies forced labor and the fabrication of disposable people.

Slavery is in itself a space of "contact of memories" that assem-

---

17. JIR, November 1, 2009.
18. *Français de souche* is quite untranslatable in English. The expression was coined by the National Front and meant a "true" French person, with "authentic" roots.

bles different sites and layers of memory, different languages and expressions of shame, denial, mourning, and commemoration. It still resonates because it speaks of the transformation of a human being into pure animal force, into a disposable thing whose life and death cease to matter. What matters is the profit the trafficker and the owner can make and the pleasure of consumption. Slavery evokes human dependency on things that are immorally extracted or produced. Are we that foreign to this situation? People wanted to forget the cost of a pound of sugar. We are ready to forget the human cost of a gallon of oil. What I mean here is that a "contact of memory" is not just about history, it is about the way we live, what we accept and what we fight against. The memory of slavery in Reunion Island must remain a source for examining one's own complicity with exploitation and injustice. It is not a lesson in morals, but a lesson in politics.

In France and Reunion Island, it is not that the cultural expressions of memory and the history of slavery are fully ignored, but rather that there is a refusal to acknowledge slavery as a *common* and *worthy* legacy. Slavery is not part of "universal memory." The *longue durée* of European colonialism inscribes Reunion Island within different globalizations: first, the one produced by slavery, then by imperialism, and today by the different multipolarities created by current globalization. It is important to place the island within different temporalities and spaces, within different modernities: the time and space of the Indian Ocean world, of the slave trade and slavery, of imperialism, of anti-imperialism, of south-south exchanges and encounters. The cartography that is suggested is one of multiple roads and routes of memory, of Gujarati migrants, Malagasy slaves, French settlers, Tamil and Chinese indentured workers, among others. Current issues—economic, cultural, geopolitical—have brought up new questions: what does it mean to live on a small island in a maritime space deeply redrawn by emerging regional powers—South Africa, China, India—which use old routes and connections or invent new ones, in an ocean bordered by countries where the majority of Muslims in the world live today, that remains the main road for oil, and where wars are waged for the control of these routes? This complex situation suggests the existence of new sites of memories, of new *contacts* of memories.

Reunion Island is an intense zone of contact. It was uninhabited when the French decided they needed ports of call on their way to the riches of India. They took possession of two islands to the east of Madagascar which they named Bourbon (La Reunion) and Ile de France (Mauritius). Reunion Island had no native population. The society was created by slaves, colonial settlers, and migrants, brought or coming from Madagascar, Mozambique, Comoros Islands, France, Gujarat, Tamil Nadu, Bengal, Malaysia, Vietnam, South China. Waves of migration have contributed to the making of Reunion culture. They trace itineraries of contact through the Indiaoceanic world, of south-south migrations and routes of exchange and conflicts. Today, two out of three monotheisms—Christianity and Islam; one of the major religions—Hinduism; Buddhism; and Afro-Malagasy rites or ancestral worship ceremonies all coexist on an island of 2500 square kilometers. In each of these religions there is also a diversity of churches and practices, with Evangelism, Shiism, Sunnism, and Comorian rites. Interculturality is not some hearsay notion. *Métissage*, which elsewhere often implies binaries ("white/black") is considerably multiple and layered. There are an infinite number of combinations of interethnic mixing. In the same family sisters and brothers bear testimony to the game of the genetic luck of the draw, throwing out all forms of presupposition and all forms of determinism. On Reunion, the unexpected consequences of history constantly contradict the idea of linearity and determinism. Who would have foreseen the creation of Creole cultures out of colonial slavery? Who would have known that the first abolition of slavery in 1794 would be rejected by the slaves' owners and therefore not applied? Who would have foretold the importance of the conflict between the Reunionese Communist Party and a local conservative xenophobic movement in the transformation of the society in the post-1946 years (The colonial status ended on March 19, 1946)?

Creolization processes and practices show a cartography of crisscrossing trajectories that do not necessarily produce a nomadic identity, but an identity that recognizes the diversity of worlds, and moves through different territories. There is *no creolization without conflict* among differences and the movement toward cultural unity is itself affected by new differences. Creolization is about the experience of *being a foreigner*, hence about radically questioning the relations among roots, territory, and identity. It is the *territory of language*, rather than blood. Creolization allows a theory of the subject that is not contained within the limits of imperial and national sovereignty. It challenges the "truth" of identity. It suggests that loss is not necessarily a lack. It is about having to learn to share a territory with others, a territory one has not necessarily chosen as one's own.

Processes of creolization are also about contingencies, accidents of history. Gender, class, ethnicity affect the processes. Let me show this through three imagined examples based on fact:

- In 1798, a young man is captured in a village of what is today northern Mozambique. He is taken to a slave ship. He has been brutally separated from a familiar world and must make sense of many new things: chains, whip, hunger, solitude. Along the way, he meets other captives. One night, he is thrown into the belly of a ship. Fear and terror are his new companions. After a month, he disembarks on an island whose name he has never heard, whose language he does not understand. He is sold to a man who takes him to his house. He was a son, a brother, a husband, he is now a slave, an "object" according to the laws of his new land. Slowly, he learns a new language, new ways of living. He undergoes creolization, he becomes a Reunionese.

- In 1857, a young woman leaves south India for an island whose name she barely understands. She leaves a world of misery, she wants to believe the promises that the strangers who came to her village made: that she will find wealth, that she will be able to return when she wishes. On the ship, she has to protect herself from the sailors and the men who are her companions in the program of migration organized by the British and French colonial powers between their respective colonies. She arrives on an island and is right away quarantined in an isolated and overcrowded place, "Le Lazaret." She plants the seeds of sacred spices she has hidden in her hem, she recreates her rituals. She hides her caste, reconstructs herself. Finally, she is taken to her new "home," a plantation on the island. She reconstructs a life, she goes to the *koilou*, the Hindu temple, makes her offerings, cultivates her spices and cooks her curries. She learns a new language, she shares with her new neighbors their own food, participates in their festivals, invites them to her own. She undergoes creolization. She becomes a Reunionese.

- In 1910, a young couple leaves France to find fortune in the colony of Reunion. They soon find that work is hard despite the privilege the color of their skin affords them in a colony. They squat some land in the mountains—the rich land of the coast is the reserve of the wealthy—and cultivate vegetables, geraniums, vanilla. They lend their hands to a wealthy landlord when times are hard. They slowly learn Creole, they share with their poor neighbors, some of them of Malagasy, African, or of Indian descent, a harsh life but one that is also filled with festivities. They become Reunionese.

Anthropologists have shown that people in Reunion often circulate between practices and beliefs. They call this *intraculturality* to express the existence of multiple modalities at work in a singular expression. For instance, *narlgon* is a form of vernacular theater that came with Indian indentured workers but was transformed in Reunion. Contrary to *terrukkutu*, a well-known form of vernacular theater in Tamil Nadu, the actors of narlgon are not professional and women, not men, play the female roles. Two stories are favored that reflect local concerns and experiences. One is *Vanavarson*, which tells the story of exile of the *Pandava*, called *Barldon* in Reunion Island, and echoes the experience of exile of indentured workers. Another favorite story is the love story of Vali and Soubramaniel (or Muruga), which is a story of mixing, of love stronger than class or ethnic origin.

To trace the itineraries of ideas, women, men, gods, spices, goddesses, songs is to trace a pluralized history and memory of the dispossessed. Totalizing terms, such as "African slave," "Indian indentured worker," or "European settler," are deconstructed and a diversity of stories weaves a common history of multiplying presences. What emerges are the memories and histories of peoples who were and are still denied humanity in the inhuman field of brutal exploitation. In 1989, Alain Gauthier and Henri-Pierre Jeudy imagined a museum of holes of memory (*trous de mémoire*)[19] where a surface communicates with another surface without any temporality. "Contacts de mémoire" are not "trous de mémoire" but rather memories that are inscribed in time, context, and space. What method of writing will best preserve the intricacies, hesitations, failed opportunities, the memories of fear, complicity, betrayal, and hope that accompany any moment? To write about "contacts of memories" is to write without retouching photographs and rewriting biographies and histories, to allow for inconsistencies and human frailty, in other words, to be open to history.

A crossed history of the gestures, actions, and words of the dispossessed questions the ways in which global history is still written as the history of nations and countries. In a world where there is a growing fabrication of disposable people, where states and multinationals mock the common good and glorify egotistic satisfaction, interconnected histories of resistance demonstrate that there are grounds for fighting and that hope (not an empty word) is a political category. It took practically four centuries to abolish colonial slavery. It was a long

---

19. Alain Gauthier and Henri-Pierre Jeudy, "Trou de mémoire, image virale," *Communications* 49, "La mémoire et l'oubli" (1989): 143.

and difficult struggle. Slaves denounced the plots of insurrection; African kings sold their neighbors; Europeans looked elsewhere. Despite protests, Europe and its colonies and the United States continued to traffic in human beings. The addiction to spices and sugar, the addiction to brutality and power, the easy gains, the belief in "Whites'" superiority, the territorialization of suffering, the distinction between who matters and who does not, the complicities of the Law and of the Catholic Church contributed to keeping millions of Africans in bondage. The fabrication of disposability went along with the fabrication of assent. Is this really foreign to us?

BLACK DIVINITIES OF BRAZIL AND TOGO

For the last four years, the association ACOFIN (from the name of a Togolese musical instrument) has organized the Festival of Black Divinities. For the 2009 event, which took place from December 16 to 20, the theme was "Africa and Its Diaspora: An Eternal Alliance." Tête Wilson Bahun, ACOFIN's president, explained why he wanted to organize a ceremony of purification and reconciliation between people from Bahia, Brazil and the people of Togo: "The quest for African roots goes through Salvador de Bahia, which is called the 'Black Rome,' because it is the city that has best preserved African culture from the time of slavery." He traced a route of complex memories that ran between Togo and Brazil. More than two million Africans left the continent from Ouidah (Benin) and Aneho and Agbodrafo (Togo) and among those, slaves who had bought their freedom came back to the region and settled. They established a new social and cultural identity. Their descendants live in villages and cities in Ghana, Benin, and Togo.

The Festival brought together Africans whose ancestors had never been slaves, Africans whose ancestors had sold African captives, Africans whose ancestors had been slaves in Brazil but had come back as free men, and Brazilians who were descendants of slaves. The guests from Brazil were reincorporated within the African social community through cultural and social ceremonies where African priests perform rituals, and where dances and songs celebrated a shared past and present. In his speech, Mensah-Assiakoley V, the traditional king of Agbodrafo (where the purification ceremony was held) acknowledged the responsibility of Africans in the slave trade and asked for a common reflection on the complex legacies of slavery. His speech was a meditation on a "noeud de memoire" that concerned south-south routes of commerce, traffic, and exchanges. He did not situate his reflections within the framework of apology, reparation, and compensation that has dominated public debate in Europe following the thirty-year campaign by Jewish organizations against European states, banks, museums, and individuals. The debates about compensation for damages always raise the question of who will pay and who will make sure that compensation goes to the right people. The King suggested that we all had to accept the past by building new bridges and new forms of cooperation. Reparation was about reconstructing a connection while acknowledging difference (the goal was not to transform Brazilians into Togolese). Apology was about acknowledging African complicity in the slave trade and receiving Brazilians in a poor region of Togo as honored guests and members of a transcontinental family. Compensation was unfair: who would pay and what would it accomplish? Aimé Césaire shared this approach when he explained why he rejected the concept of reparation. He did not even like the term because it implied that "reparation is possible." Césaire declared, two years before his death: "I know Western people. They will say: 'So, my dear, how much? I give you half to pay for slave trade. OK? Done!' And then it will be done; they would have accomplished the reparation. In my view, it is irreparable."[20] During an exchange at the University of Lomé, the Brazilian anthropologist Milton Guran was very clear: why would the Brazilians, descendants of slaves, have to compensate Africans, even though their ancestors had been captured and sold by Africans to Europeans? The idea was absurd. The king, like Césaire and Guran, defended transcontinental solidarity between the dispossessed and policies of cooperation that would serve the dispossessed.

The Togolese who received the Brazilians and carried out rituals to reincorporate them into a social and cultural lineage, even if it was imaginary, rejected the metaphysical approach. They acknowledged that there is no scale of human suffering. They also acknowledged that the history of those who had been "lost," whose names had been forgotten but whose lives had been preserved through song, music, poetry, and ritual, belonged to the history of humanity. They "performed" memories that inhabit people, the intangible history not found in monuments, palaces, and castles. We must learn to live with this complex legacy, with a "contact de mémoires" that constantly

---

20. Françoise Vergès, *Nègre je suis, Nègre je resterai. Entretiens avec Aimé Césaire* (Paris: Albin Michel, 2006), 39; my translation.

questions our desire for a clean and linear narrative. In Togo, the word "slavery" evokes both routes of deportation and routes of solidarity and exchange that were built then and there. The encounter, even if fluid and momentary, contributed to the writing of a history of the dispossessed, leaving a diversity of memories among those who were present. This diversity had meaning, the meaning of a "contact de mémoires," a source for future references that would feed new cultural expressions and emergences.

Events that coalesce into memories of displacement, loss of language, brutality, and harsh working conditions build sites of memorial contact, memories of suffering, complicity, and resistance. They all belong to the long history of the colony, as the site of exception, and a regime of forced labor. The interconnected stories of human cargo, of the memories of fear, solitude, despair, vigor, human ingenuity, and resistance challenge linear history. Ruptures, accidents, unintended consequences, the crossed histories of gender, imperialism, and race formation question a linearity in the history of the dispossessed. Ordinary lives and ordinary labors construct a vocabulary that speaks of intricacies and affiliations. In this contribution I have explored slavery as a fluctuating and dynamic site of memorial contact, as a constant source of reference to describe the transformation of human beings into things that do not matter. Slavery runs through human history. It raises a philosophical and anthropological question: why do human beings enslave other human beings? As a system of exploitation, slavery speaks of brutality and cruelty, it violates social and cultural ties. It constructs a culture of fear and submission, of shame and contempt. Yet, its history is also full of daily gestures of solidarity, of transcontinental struggle in a diversity of fields: judicial, religious, philosophical, economic, cultural. As a "contact of memories," slavery goes beyond a defined historical moment and offers a space for the exploration of disposability, of the ways in which memories become transcontinental, dynamic, and contemporary.[21]

---

21. One might ask if slavery can be a "global" contact of memories? I will suggest that it can, if we consider slavery as the fabrication of disposable people. True, slavery comes in different forms and the experience of colonial slavery stands apart. Yet, the notion continues to serve as a powerful trope for protest and resistance against what one perceives as the ultimate insult to one's humanity: being trafficked and denied access to basic needs.

DAVID CARON

Tactful Encounters: AIDS, the Holocaust, and the Problematics of Bearing Witness

Many historical instances of mass death have been compared to others, but few comparisons have inspired as much anger as that which brings together AIDS and the Holocaust. It is tempting to dismiss this hostility. It may emanate from defenders of the absolute uniqueness of the Nazi genocide. Perhaps it is spouted by homophobes or racists who won't acknowledge that the early association of the disease with marginalized groups prevented governments and societies from reacting in a timely fashion. Dismissals may be warranted at times but they fail to account for what I believe is a more subtle feeling that runs through such vehemence—a fundamental fear of contact, not just between specific people and histories but contact as a mode of being with others in the world. To be sure, a frightening disease transmitted by a virus easily lends itself to the embodiment of certain cultural fears. This is especially so when, as was the case with AIDS, the epidemic was initially identified with people with whom contact was already shunned and who were perceived to be themselves defined by modes of contact (homosexuality, prostitution, immigration . . .) often feared as illegitimate and/or pathogenic in the first place. In that context, advocating multidirectional sharing may sound too much like sexual promiscuity, global migration, and junkie sociality not to give people pause. But we are, after all, talking about rhetorical and not actual contact here, so why the fear? Beyond the traumatic experience itself, what is it about certain modes of writing or speaking about it in a comparative mode that prompts rejection?

When Hervé Guibert compared his AIDS-ravaged body to that of an inmate in Auschwitz, or when he likened his physician to a Nazi doctor in a war movie, he was not the first witness to turn to the Holocaust in an attempt to make sense of the pandemic and of his own experience of it. In France, Alain Emmanuel Dreuilhe had already systematized the trope for matters of personal as well as collective survival, positing AIDS as a historical turning point in gay history and relying on the cultural memory of the Holocaust to help shape the relationship between disaster, community formation, and political legitimacy. To compare AIDS to the Holocaust—or rather, to bring out their structural similarities—served some communities well in the first decade or so of the epidemic. Indeed it wasn't long before the trope escaped the confines of literary testimonials and was summoned in order to politicize AIDS and energize activists fighting for their lives. Drawing from a well-known historical legacy of societal indifference and government complicity allowed AIDS activist groups, in particular ACT UP-Paris, to denounce inaction in the face of mass death striking specific communities. They even called for trials that they compared to the Nuremberg trials.[1] In some quarters, the reaction was fierce, especially in France, where ACT UP's combative rhetoric was often denounced by the mainstream press and some intellectuals as apocalyptic and no different from that used by the *Front National*. Like the FN, AIDS activists were accused of undermining the basic principles of contractual citizenship in favor of divisive identity politics.[2]

Certain visual tropes, however, did not encounter the same level of hostility. To draw parallels, explicitly or not, between emaciated patients and concentration camp inmates generated little mainstream outrage, and the media relied heavily on these tropes in the 1980s. As the atrocities committed in Bosnia in the 1990s would soon demonstrate once more, certain bodies automatically evoke the Holocaust in Western minds. But why such disparities in public reactions? As Douglas Crimp has shown in his reading of an early exhibition of photographs of people with AIDS, portraits purporting to bring out the supposed universality of human suffering ended up erasing the political and social dimensions of the epidemic and producing images so abstract and so removed from the vicissitudes of daily human lives that they paradoxically impeded all possibility of empathy with their sub-

---

1. Most of ACT UP's rhetorical use of the Holocaust can be found in its collective book *Le sida: combien de divisions?* (Paris: Dagorno, 1994).
2. For a detailed discussion of the homophobic undercurrent of these arguments, see my article "AIDS/Holocaust: Metaphor and French Universalism" *L'esprit créateur* 45/3 (2005): 63–73. I have studied the trope's mechanics of community formation in my book *My Father and I: The Marais and the Queerness of Community* (Ithaca: Cornell University Press, 2009).

jects.[3] In short, comparing AIDS to the Holocaust appeared acceptable inasmuch as it constructed a certain image of AIDS sufferers as politically passive, essentially other, and soon to be dead; it did not when it underscored the realities of social exclusion.

The condemnations often concerned the trivialization of the Holocaust, which was said to be the inevitable outcome of comparisons. The political success of these comparisons, however, depended on their ability to respect, not dilute, the power of the Holocaust to evoke exceptionality—and to do so precisely by latching another historical event onto it. But how can this seemingly contradictory connection occur? I believe that tact, when understood as a relational play of differences, works to make such connection possible by acknowledging proximity and distance at the same time. In other words, it is a form of deconstructive *contact* whose status as mediation does not rely on, and indeed undoes, the self-sameness of who and what it connects. Acknowledgment without knowledge (*reconnaître sans connaître*) is, I think, how tact offers us clues to grasp the multidirectional dynamics of community at play in the act of bearing witness. Mediation is what makes such dynamics possible because it acts both as a community's contours and as its interface, suggesting its inherent vulnerability to difference—its alterability. Tact, a mode of indirection in language, functions precisely as this sort of mediation.

In their first-person writings on the Holocaust and AIDS respectively, Hélène Berr and Hervé Guibert describe instances of tact in order to embed and model both the act of bearing witness in which their books are engaged and the reading practice that does their testimonies justice. When used as empathy, tact is concerned with relationality. And so is witnessing, which, like tact—and *with* tact—relies on a kind of effacement of the writing or speaking self—its *unmaking* into words—in order to leave room for others and make community. The indirection of tact is what allows AIDS and the Holocaust to be brought into proximity, if of an uneasy sort, and to form something like a community of the traumatic. But such a community is itself a traumatic community in that its founding commonality is always mediated by difference—the wordless shattering of the self—and not reassuringly fused in sameness. In that sense, to rely on the

3. Douglas Crimp's critique of Nicholas Nixon's 1988 photo exhibit at the MoMA can be found in "Portraits of People with AIDS," in *Discourses of Sexuality: From Aristotle to AIDS*, ed. Domna C. Stanton (Ann Arbor: University of Michigan Press, 1992): 362–88.

shared, *cultural* memory of the Holocaust, as so many AIDS activists and witnesses did, served more than the communal interests of those directly affected; it was also intended to produce a larger view of community as difference against the hierarchical and exclusionary distinctions that were responsible for the spread of the disease to begin with. In other words, the AIDS-Holocaust trope often sought to convey the idea that the epidemic was not caused by dangerous contact but, on the contrary, by the dangerous fear of it.

* * * * *

In François Truffaut's film *Baisers volés*,[4] a young Antoine Doisnel falls under the charm of Fabienne Tabard, a fabulous older woman, his employer's wife. One day Antoine is invited for lunch at the Tabards. After the meal and with the husband out of the way, Fabienne pours the coffee and sets out to play a record. In a low, husky voice, she asks the nervous young man, "Do you like music, Antoine?"; to which Antoine replies in a high-pitched voice, "Yes, sir." Overcome with embarrassment and gender confusion, he drops his cup and runs out. He arrives home later to find a card waiting for him. On it Fabienne has written:

> When I was in middle school, my teacher was explaining the difference between tact and politeness. A gentleman caller mistakenly opens a bathroom door and discovers a lady stark naked. He withdraws immediately, closes the door, and says: "Oh! pardon me, madam." That is politeness. The same gentleman, opening the same door, discovering the same lady stark naked, and telling her, "Oh! pardon me, sir," *that* is tact. (my translation)

Tact, not unlike grace and taste (its etymological kin), is often defined as a natural elegance of the mind, unteachable and elusive. You either possess it or you don't. (The teacher in the story does not *teach* what tact is; he or she uses an allegory, essentially relying on one trope to define another. Fabienne does the same thing.) Because it requires the ability to gauge social situations and discern their dynamics instantly, tact appears effortless. It gives the impression that it does not require thought and that, therefore, it is not a skill one could work to acquire like politeness or etiquette, the stuff of manuals. In reality, of course, tact is a construct and a mode of social policing linked to shame and embarrassment. It is often required in order to respond to

---

4. François Truffaut, *Baisers volés*. Prod. Les films du carosse, 1969.

situations—slips, mishaps, and a variety of failures and shortcomings—that isolate a person from the social. But if it is a measure of group membership, and therefore not available to all, then tact is really designed to establish social hierarchies and enforce something like class privilege—reframing social proximity as distance.

In *Réflexions sur la question juive* (*Anti-Semite and Jew*), Sartre observes that tact appears to fall outside the realm of reason the better to outline, and reinforce, a community's boundaries:

> To act with tact is to appreciate a situation at a glance, to embrace it as a whole, to feel it rather than to analyze it, but it is at the same time to direct one's conduct by reference to a multitude of indistinct principles, of which some concern vital values and others express ceremonies and traditions of politeness that are altogether irrational. Thus to act "with tact" implies that the doer of the act has adopted a certain conception of the world, one that is traditional, ritual, and synthetic; one for which *he can give no reason*. . . . [I]t takes on its whole meaning only in a strictly defined community with common ideas, mores, and customs. (124; original emphasis)[5]

It makes sense to conclude that this social mastery over others is available only to members of the classes that have the power to define what social values are and how they are transmitted. While tact seemingly escapes reason and thus cannot be taught, like taste and grace, it must be learned—and learned from proximity. But if tact delineates social groups, proximity can only occur within the same class. The perception of unteachability and elusiveness is a way to naturalize a certain social system, discipline people, and perpetuate the allegedly undisputable superiority of one group.

In Western modernity tact essentially pertains to the bourgeois ideal of discretion as propriety. (As I will discuss shortly, the word acquired its current meaning in the decades preceding the French Revolution.) Forms of tact can be found in other social classes, of course, such as lower-class men, among whom tact may be necessary to preserve masculinity or "face." But just like taste, the dominant, normative form of tact belongs to the class that is itself in the dominant position. In any case, it is no surprise that the body (and the contiguous notions of sex-gender, race-ethnicity, sexuality, and illness) should play an essential part in this. Tact is often required to avoid mention-

---

5. Jean-Paul Sartre, *Anti-Semite and Jew: An Exploration of the Etiology of Hate*, trans. George J. Becker (New York: Schocken Books, 1948).

ing bodily functions, for example. But the erasure of bodily functions or sexuality or race—their privatization—cannot be separated from the body itself and the actual people it belongs to. Propriety and property, it seems, are germane, and what connects them is a division: that of the public and the private. You inadvertently open a bathroom door, you breach a boundary, and embarrassment ensues.

Because tact brings together bodies and the class system, distributing the former according to the categories of the latter, it has served as a tool for social inclusion and exclusion, while its unteachability ensures that class boundaries are not breached inappropriately. The supposed tactlessness of the Jews, for example, which triggers Sartre's observations, has been a way to assign them a specific place in bourgeois society—the place of the misfit. In the meantime, non-Jewish bourgeois may recognize and appreciate each other's mastery of tact, confirming that they naturally belong together and have power over others. No matter how one sees it, tact is always tied to the question of community.

In general, one needs to exercise tact when one's interlocutor is, in one way or another, vulnerable, when that person has failed at something. A person in need of tactful treatment is, in a sense, broken—not *intact*. His or her integrity as an individual (that which cannot be divided or broken down) has come into question insofar as feeling embarrassed presupposes the ability to judge oneself, occupying two positions at once. The avowed purpose of tactfulness is to mask the individual's failure, metaphorically covering his or her nakedness if you will, and pretend that nothing happened. Oftentimes, however, tact singles *out* what it purports to ignore. Discretion, in all its senses, is something one exercises like power, and tact-as-policing ironically erases others by bringing out their singularity. It seeks to define its relation to others as distinction—an essentializing move linking the discreet and the discrete. Indeed, the tactor's *discernment* is a multipurpose quality pertaining as much to tact as it does to taste and that relies on all the semantic possibility of the word: the ability to identify, distinguish, separate, discriminate, judge.[6]

But the distribution of power is not clear-cut. If the tactee's embarrassment is an experience of alienation—envisioning oneself as a judging other—social embarrassment is also highly transmissible. The

---

6. To avoid repeating long and clumsy phrases, I took the liberty to forge the words "tactor" and "tactee" to name, respectively, the person who behaves with tact and the person who is treated with tact.

tactor may want to self-protect from the same shattering results and avoid experiencing the fragility of his or her power. In Fabienne's story, who was embarrassed exactly? The woman who failed to lock the door and whose body was exposed or the man who failed to knock and saw the body? Both, I imagine. And both go through a comparable process of doubling and an experience of alienation that temporarily dislocates them. The fact that tactor and tactee may *share* this unsettling feeling of failure opens up the possibility of understanding tact in certain situations not as distinction but as empathetic difference.

Tact may take many forms: euphemisms and understatements, parables and fabulation, silences, even deflecting speech by speaking to a third party rather than directly to the intended recipient of the tactful gesture; tact's indirection is what makes it difficult to define and imitate. But I am focusing here on the sort described in *Baisers volés*. Within Fabienne's fable, tact is itself a mode of failure—a willing failure of language ("Pardon me, sir" for "Pardon me, madam") that rewrites Antoine's unwilled lapse ("Yes, sir" for "Yes, madam"). In this case, tact is not located in the actual statement but in the conditions of its utterance. Another, more tragic example, can be found in Charlotte Delbo's *Mesure de nos jours*. It is a scene in which Charlotte and two comrades say goodbye to a dying friend in Auschwitz. Sylviane is unable to speak, and words seem all but pointless in the situation. Carmen tries: "Comment vas-tu, ma petite Sylviane? demanda Carmen, et cette question qui était fausse sonnait juste."[7] I quote in French because the last segment is difficult to translate. "Fausse" suggests falsity but also hypocrisy—the hypocrisy of tact— and "juste" implies not just accuracy but justice and fairness. "Fausse" and "juste" also evoke music, especially when used near the verb *sonner*. In classical music, dissonance is allowed, but only on condition that it be immediately resolved.[8] Carmen's question may be *fausse* but the contact it establishes with the dying friend is *juste*. The community at work here is a form of disaccord. I shall return to the question of music, but what is now clear is this: whereas tactlessness means saying the wrong thing, one is tactful when saying the right thing means saying the wrong thing *on purpose*. Or, sometimes, saying nothing at all.

* * * * *

7. Charlotte Delbo, *Mesure de nos jours* (Paris: Minuit, 1971), 145.
8. I thank David Powell for this.

Hélène Berr was a musician and a student of English literature at the Sorbonne during the Occupation. She was also Jewish. Between 1942 and 1944, she kept a diary that was published in France in 2008 and translated into English that same year.[9] Arrested, deported, Hélène Berr was murdered in Bergen Belsen. Like all diaries with tremendous literary value, hers is at once ordinary and extraordinary. I focus here on a few brief scenes that directly evoke the impact, on her and on those around her, of the yellow star she is forced to wear—a shock that makes the extraordinary intrude on the ordinary and redraws the contours of the speakable.

At first, Hélène wears the star with defiance, the only way she knows how to gather up the courage to go out in public. She stares at people; they look away, or not at all:

> I was very courageous all day long. I held my head high, and I stared at other people so hard that it made them avert their eyes. But it's difficult.
>
> In any case, most people don't even look. The awkwardest thing is to meet other people wearing it. This morning I went out with Maman. In the street two boys pointed at us [nous ont montrées du doigt] and said: "Eh? You seen that? Jew." Otherwise things went normally. . . . I went back to place de l'Étoile on the métro on my own. At Étoile I went back to the *Artisanat* to get my blouse, then I went to catch the 92. At the stop there was a young man and woman in the line, and I saw the girl point me out to her companion. Then they exchanged some remarks. (54)

Everything seems redefined, and encounters once seamlessly woven into the familiar fabric of everyday life now signify exclusion from it: the sight of fellow Jews, the impropriety of children, the complicity of young couples. And although no mention is made of this, even the word *Étoile* conveys how tainted Parisian life is in its very cityscape. A word that would have gone unnoticed not long before startles us now.

The following day, Hélène meets Molinié, a fellow student, at the Sorbonne. He behaves as if nothing is wrong and talks about normal student business. What would have been a normal conversation in regular circumstances and would not, in all likelihood, have made its way into a diary, has become a meaningful gesture that denies the casual-

---

9. Hélène Berr, *The Journal of Hélène Berr*, trans. David Bellos (New York: Weinstein Books, 2008).

ness it flaunts. The *ostensible absence* of gesture *is* the gesture. The ordinary, once unspoken *as such* if it is to retain its ordinariness, must now be underlined in order to oppose the extraordinary that is the yellow star; the extraordinary, once the source of endless speech (gloss, interpretation, conjectures . . .) must now remain unspoken:

> I got to the main courtyard of the Sorbonne on the stroke of 2:00. I thought I saw Molinié in the crowd, but as I wasn't sure it was him I went into the hall at the library. It was him; he came over to me. He spoke very kindly, but his eyes drifted away from my star. When he looked at me, he looked up [*au-dessus de ce niveau*], and our eyes seemed to be saying: "Don't take any notice." He'd just sat his second philosophy paper. (55–56)

The moral high ground (*au-dessus de ce niveau*) that Hélène and Molinié take by means of silence (or: the high ground that each one may take thanks to the other's tact) is compromised from the outset. What their eyes are saying is that what goes *ostensibly* unnoticed *is* noticed. The same goes with other students: "We talked about the exam, but I could feel that all their thoughts were on this badge [*insigne*]" (56). The word *insigne*, we know, implies remarkability.

Language use thus becomes displaced. What it states and what it conveys are not the same, and the studied casualness of a conversation simultaneously veils and unveils something phatic: the purpose is to make contact in the face of a political order that prohibits it:

> [M]y confidence got a boost at the Department. Obviously I created a stir when I came in, but as everyone there knows . . . no one was embarrassed. Monique Ducret, who is so sweet, was there, and she talked with me at length, deliberately—I know how she thinks; then the boy called Ibalin turned around . . . and gave a start when he saw, but made a show of coming over [*il s'est approché ostensiblement*] and joining the conversation (we were talking about music). It didn't matter what the subject was; the main thing was to display [*de faire comprendre*] the unspoken friendship that connects us. (57–58)

One could argue—and I will—that the topic does matter in this case, for the silent bond that ties these young people together, their "unspoken friendship," their tact, is a form of social music making. More on this soon.

Later in the diary—the year is now 1943—Hélène confronts a fundamental dilemma touching on the limits of tact as contact. Sometimes, one must tell. But can *one* tell without *individualizing* what is by definition a collective experience, without denying the experience in the process of representing it? At the Sorbonne again, Hélène faces this question with another student:

> Yesterday at the Sorbonne I had a talk with one of my very nice classmates, Mme Gibelin. There was an abyss of ignorance between us. However, I believe that if she knew, she would feel the same anguish as I do. That's why I was terribly wrong not to make a real effort to tell her everything, to shock her, to make her understand.... It's just that that brings you up against a serious problem: human nature is such that people only understand if you present immediate evidence, evidence which concerns *you*; they aren't upset by stories of other people, only about *your* personal fate. You only succeed in creating a little understanding by describing the misfortunes that have befallen you yourself. And then? I realize with disgust that I have become the center of interest, while the only thing that matters is the torture others are experiencing; it's a question of principle, it's the thousands of individual cases that make up this question; horrified, I see that the person I am talking to pities me (pity is much easier to get than understanding, for that requires the gift of one's whole being and a complete reconsideration of oneself [*une adhésion de tout son être, une révision totale de lui-même*]). (165–66)

What is problematic about the position known today as that of the native informant is that it sets up a context of utterance that seeks to deny the foundational relationality of the speaker and the recipient in favor of a strict separation of two distinct collectivities. It relies on the referential function of language and assumes a stable world outside the speakers. Put differently, Hélène is bringing out the fundamental difference between autobiography, as a form of individualizing and distancing, and bearing witness, a mode of relating and remaking the world that inscribes the self within the collective and the collective within the self. With this particular classmate, the community of tact —what I call contact—is not working because it does not entail a rethinking of the self as multidirectional, that is, as inherently plural.[10]

"How to escape this dilemma?" asks Hélène: "There are very few souls sufficiently generous and noble to face the issue itself [*la question en soi*], without seeing the person telling the tale as an individual case, and to see through that person the suffering of others." The

---

10. My thinking of the self as plural is informed by the works of Jean-Luc Nancy, especially his *Being Singular Plural*, trans. Robert D. Richardson and Anne E. O'Byrne (Stanford: Stanford University Press, 2000).

phrase *"la question en soi"* implies a depersonalization of the Holocaust and, therefore, the recognition of its collective dimension. Can we read it as "the question in oneself"? There is no indication that Berr intended to suggest this other meaning so directly, but she does evoke the fact that an ideal listener must be endowed with the ability to imagine him- or herself as other:

> Souls like that must be endowed with great intelligence, and also great *sensitivity*, because seeing is not sufficient; you have to be able to feel, you have to feel the anguish of a mother whose children have been taken away from her, the torture of a wife separated from her husband, the huge stock of courage that every deportee is going to need every day, and the physical suffering and misfortunes that he must endure. (166; my emphasis)

Whereas Mme Gibelin "reads" Hélène naively, not seeing the enormity of the situation, the ideal interlocutor appears endowed with an elusive sense of discernment and intelligence. This ability resembles reading because it is premised on figuration and on the understanding that the part—the individual—stands for a much larger whole. If a sympathetic but literal reading can be a form of denying ("seeing is not sufficient"), to recognize that there is a metonymy at work pluralizes the individual case by connecting it to others. The empathetic *feeling* Berr describes is the sign that contact has been established and that the awareness of internal pluralism, or self-otherness, has been transmitted to the interlocutor via the act of bearing witness. The blend of "intelligence" and "sensitivity" that brings together the intellectual and affective meanings of "understanding" is precisely what links witnessing and tact. Far from excluding Hélène as a token other —a Jew who stands for other Jews but would still stand apart from non-Jews—empathy brings otherness within the self, pluralizing the individual *en soi*.

Sartre recalls how people who were once forced to wear a yellow star in public often felt harmed by other people's marks of sympathy, charitable gestures that looked suspiciously self-serving and only made matters worse by objectifying them *as Jews*. Acknowledging that embarrassment goes both ways and speaking in the name of those Gentiles who recognized the paradox of ostensible sympathy, Sartre writes:

> In the end we came to understand all this so well that we turned our eyes away when we met a Jew wearing a star. We were ill at ease, em-

barrassed by our own glance, which, if it fell upon him, made him a Jew in spite of himself and in spite of ourselves. The supreme expression of sympathy and of friendship lay here in appearing to ignore, for whatever effort we made to reach to the *person*, it was always the *Jew* whom we encountered. (77; original emphasis)

And the body reappears, for this *Jew* is the one produced by racial anti-Semitism, whose strategy was to make emancipated Jews visible again in order to make them radically invisible by way of extermination. The yellow star is the mark of this re-embodiment. This definition of Jews as radical others is what Sartre seeks to reject here, yet his use of the first person plural seems at odds with his stated goal. Who is this "we" he speaks of in "we came to understand all this so well"? The community it outlines and which, by definition, does not include star-wearing Jews, seems endowed with, indeed defined by, a binding sense of discernment. Sartre seems unaware that what he is describing is the kind of magical tact he denounces a few pages later and that his "we" bears a disturbing resemblance to the one fantasized by anti-Semites.[11] This cannot be what he means.

Tactful silence is another kind of statement—*un silence qui en dit long*. And one of the things silence is saying in the situation Sartre describes is this: The tactor's glance, the glance by which one is able to feel the situation as a whole and exercise power, is itself altered, or *redirected*, by the other's embarrassment. What was intended to bring a feeling of naturalness and belonging becomes instead a source of discomfort, alienation, and discordance; or rather, it is revealed to have always been so. The key lay not in ignoring the situation but in "appearing to ignore" it, since to know when to look away presupposes that one has already seen and understood. True friendship may come at that price: embracing artifice, in this case, experiencing oneself as other—a form of distance from reality that may feel (or sound) *false* but is an effect of figuration.

Tact, whether as statement or absence of statement, is an experience of alienation by means of trope—less a figure of speech than a figure of thought perhaps, but based on figuration all the same: what it conveys is not what it states. If we understand Fabienne's note as a parable, then it doesn't just *tell* a story of tact, it *is* a tactful story. This,

---

11. For a critique of Sartre's ambiguity, see Susan R. Suleiman, "The Jew in Sartre's *Réflexions sur la question juive*: An Exercise in Historical Reading," in *The Jew in the Text: Modernity and the Construction of Identity*, ed. Linda Nochlin and Tamar Garb (London: Thames and Hudson, 1995): 201–18.

in short, is why tact isn't natural but cultural: like irony, it is an utterance effect and, therefore, occurs only in what Erving Goffman would call a situation of co-presence.[12] It may not be, however, a rhetorical tool of persuasion; that would imply reducing the possibility of noise, or interpretive errors. To make sure that one's tactful statement or act is "properly" understood as such would in fact be tactless. Tact should be understood as a poetic trope whose readability leaves room for multiple interpretations and maintains the tactee's agency and freedom *not* to see the tactor as tactful. In short, empathetic tact must contain the possibility of the tactor's own tactical erasure.[13] A Gentile tactfully pretending not to notice a yellow star runs the risk of being misread as indifferent or worse (assuming that in this context "indifferent" and "worse" are not the same thing). But that is the price to pay—except for the fact that tact-as-its-own-erasure falls precisely outside any dynamic of exchange. It is a present that is never present but that one cannot refuse without acknowledging it. While always situational, tact is what can never *present* itself as tact without self-destructing. (In that sense, it is a bit like the gift that ceases to be a gift the moment it creates an obligation, as Derrida has shown.[14]) In the absence of any stable object of knowledge, all that is left is empathy itself, that is, the pure play of relationality between the people involved—what I called acknowledgment. Tact-as-policing, however, seeks to silence others under the pretext of respecting their privacy. In that case, if saying the right thing still means saying the wrong thing, the "right thing" is enforcement of class privilege and the "wrong thing" is social exclusion.

* * * * *

Here's another example, from Hervé Guibert's AIDS memoir, *Le protocole compassionnel* [*The Compassion Protocol*]. One day, the narrator enters a neighborhood café where he has been a regular customer for years, often having a cup of coffee at the counter, even though the waiters have always seemed hostile, presumably because they are homophobic. Hervé, ill and frail, trips on the doorstep and falls to his knees, unable to muster enough strength to get back up on his feet.

---

12. *Encounters* (Indianapolis: Bobbs-Merrill, 1961).
13. "Tact" and "tactics" are not etymologically related.
14. See in particular *Glas* (Paris: Galilée, 1974), *Mémoires for Paul de Man* (New York: Columbia University Press 1986), and *Ulysse gramophone: Deux mots pour Joyce* (Paris: Galilée: 1987).

The other customers are staring at him: he has committed a literal *faux-pas*. He finds himself in an uncomfortable position (again, literally), and is making onlookers uncomfortable as well—a contamination that *is* the source of discomfort. Something happens then that he did not expect:

> *Not a single word was uttered,* and there was no need for me to ask for help, for one of the two waiters I had always thought to be an enemy came up to me, *took me in his arms* and put me on my feet again *as if it were the most natural thing in the world*. I avoided the other customers' eyes, and the man behind the counter simply asked: "Coffee, sir?" I feel deeply grateful towards those two waiters I'd never liked and who I thought detested me, for having reacted so spontaneously and with such delicacy, *without a single unnecessary word*. (translation modified; my emphasis)[15]

Notice that Hervé is the one looking away. As was the case with Berr, it is difficult—and probably unnecessary—to determine whether he is trying to shield himself from the gazes of others or treating their own discomfort with tact. Regarding the waiter's gesture, when Guibert writes "*as if* it were the most natural thing," he underscores a fundamental aspect of tact-as-policing: that it is *not* natural but must appear so in order to stay out of reach of those it singles out for exclusion. But in this particular scene, the waiters' tact testifies to their professionalism. Whether they actually hate Hervé or not doesn't matter. What *does* matter is that their professionalism allows the two men neither to enforce nor to erase their power over Hervé, but only to deflect it without singling him out. By doing so, they maintain their *difference* from him—they are waiters; he is a customer—but it is a difference that rests on the codependency of the two social positions. When the first waiter proceeded to *ease* Hervé back up, he may have wished to conjure away the latter's *dis-ease* and the customers' *malaise,* but Hervé perceived his professional distance as an act of community occurring within the delicate, ephemeral parameters of a specific situation.

Throughout the book, Hervé also praises the professionalism of some doctors and nurses and often does so by emphasizing their linguistic restraint. By contrast, he fires the well-meaning doctor who tells him, "I understand" (22), a tactless statement in this French mid-

---

15. Hervé Guibert, *The Compassion Protocol*, trans. James Kirkup (New York: George Braziller, 1994), 4.

dle-class context because it is read as condescending. He soon replaces him with one "who never utters one word more or less than is necessary" (my translation). The professional distance of the second doctor appears more beneficial to Hervé than the sincere but misguided sympathy of the first.

The corporeal nature of medical relationships reminds us that "tact" derives from the Latin *tangere*, to touch. Soon after telling us how the waiter took him in his arms, Hervé describes a similar, albeit more expected, gesture from his masseur: "I'm so knocked out after each session that my muscles no longer respond, and I always have to put my arms around the masseur's neck" (5). After describing their sessions as a shared struggle, he adds: "That was the contract we embarked upon every Wednesday afternoon, between three and six, *again* without uttering one unnecessary word [un mot de trop]" (6; my emphasis). The masseur's professionalism, as that of the waiters, links the studied withdrawal of language to a physical embrace, embodying the etymological link between the two and suggesting that tact, a sign of social dexterity, is always *contact*. What was made to appear *intangible* (that which cannot be touched) is in fact *contingent* (contextual, sometimes fortuitous, and a matter of contact: "contingency" and its cognates also derive from *tangere* and suggest a mutual dependency based on physical proximity). We thus begin to glimpse a form of relationality established by means of touch. Tactful community, it appears, rests on what in French is called *doigté* (the ability to *handle* delicate situations), whereas tact as a tool of social exclusion is a way to *montrer du doigt*.

The use of the word "tact" to describe social discernment and quick judgment begins to appear in the eighteenth century in the writings of Voltaire, Montesquieu, Diderot, and others. Until then, one of its dominant meanings, along with the older sense of "touch," was that of the German *Takt*, meaning beat or pulse, a musical term that referred to the organizing beat that the master of music would bang on the floor with a stick—what is known as "marking time."[16] At the same time as taste (whose etymological kinship with tact is still seen in *tâter* and the improvisational bricolage of *tâtonner*) saw its meaning shift from the strictly gustatory to encompass aesthetic judgment, tact went through a similar metaphorical turn. Moving from the cor-

---

16. Max van Manen, *The Tact of Teaching: The Meaning of Pedagogical Thoughtfulness* (Albany, NY: State University of New York Press, 1991).

poreal to the subjective, this shift pertains to the larger disembodiment and abstraction of Enlightenment's "Man" occurring in the period. Forms of togetherness involving sensing bodies that did things together (eating, playing music) moved away from *contingent* co-presence and made way for disembodied classes based on transcendent, universal Reason. One can, however, lure tact away from its police duties and reclaim it for the purposes of a radical undoing of the Cartesian mind-body dualism that underlies the metaphorical turns I describe. Those that tact excluded because they were allegedly unable to transcend and abstract their own bodies have much to gain.

This, I believe, is what we see in the writings of Delbo, Berr, and Guibert. There was, remember, Delbo's dissonant question to a dying comrade and Hélène and her friends talking about music to oppose the yellow star. With more levity, there was Fabienne's question: "Do you like music, Antoine?" There is also Guibert's following remark, encompassing nearly all the issues at stake. After having initially gone through a particularly painful fibroscopic exam, which he compared to torture, the narrator describes a second procedure in very different terms: "The alveolar lavage, unlike the first nightmarish fibroscopy, and despite the barbarity of the act itself, became, thanks to the delicacy and lightness of touch [*grâce au doigté et à la délicatesse*] of a young woman doctor and two nurses, almost a medical string quartet in which I was the fourth instrument playing in complicity with the other three" (62; translation modified). The barbarity he speaks of lies in the violent treatment by a person in authority of a human being reduced to being a body. In the contexts of catastrophic illness and genocide, this reduction of humans to their bodies *is* the barbarity from which all others stem, but it is one that finds its source in the rise of disembodied Reason as the basis for citizenship. Guibert uses words like *doigté* and *délicatesse* in such a way that it is impossible to determine if they are to be understood as literal or metaphorical, hence the difficulty of translating them. But that's the whole point. Being a homosexual dying of AIDS in the face of political indifference, not unlike being marked for racial extermination, makes it impossible to escape one's own embodiment. What we read in this passage is an assertion of community as a form of social music-making in the context of mass death. This is not, however, like the band of the Titanic, playing on as the ship sinks, or the orchestras established in the Nazi camps, and this cannot be confused with an aestheticizing gesture either, since that would require the expulsion of the body. Quite the contrary, the kinds of friendship we read here are glimpsed thanks to the re-embodiment of tact as *con-tact*, that is, a recognition that failures, shortcomings, and vulnerability are everyone's lot.

Le protocole compassionnel was Guibert's second book dealing with his illness and it followed the tremendous success of *A l'ami qui ne m'a pas sauvé la vie* [*To the Friend Who Did Not Save My Life*] a year earlier. Up to that point, Guibert was a fairly confidential writer whose readership consisted mostly of gay men. Now he had to face the thorny question of his relationship with a mainstream audience. Was a kind of community possible with them at all? How can his writing move away from the autobiographical and constitute instead an act of bearing witness? By placing the episode in the café early in a book he knows will be widely read, Guibert may have provided us with an allegory of reading, enjoining us to handle him as the waiters did. Given the fact that both sexuality and illness are considered private matters in dominant French culture, one is expected to handle them with discretion. When reading Guibert's book we should use tact but also avoid the erasure that is often the outcome of French universalism. If tact is a willing failure of language, a tactful mode of reading would be a way to share in the other's failure by foregrounding one's own—and one's own otherness, since otherness and failure are mutually defining as forms of alienation. In that sense, tact may be used as a basis for community—community *in* difference and community *as* difference.

This is why I have argued for tact as a trope for a form of relationality bringing proximity and distance together—which, naturally, is what all tropes do, since one does not substitute a thing for itself but for something *different*. As Ross Chambers tells us in his contribution to this volume, what cannot be compared cannot be known, because it cannot be recognized. This is the apparent paradox of troping as a means of acquiring knowledge: in order to know a thing, another thing must be substituted for it—or at least, such substitution must be possible. In other words, the only way to know what something is is to put it in *contact* with something it isn't. This other "thing" that the original object is not may very well be language itself, the words without whose mediation no knowledge is *conceivable* but that inevitably expose concepts to a perpetual process of alteration, to their alienation from pure reason. This inherent differentiality, or relationality, is what prevents knowledge from congealing into Cartesian categorization or, worse, Nazism, the absolute negation of the relationality of all things and people.

With the 1985 release of Claude Lanzmann's *Shoah*, a movie that paradoxically did not focus on France at all, the specificity of Jewish history during the Vichy years attained an unprecedented degree of recognition in a political culture long averse to so-called communitarian assertions. At the same period, the AIDS epidemic was reaching catastrophic levels and ravaging the gay community. The overlapping of these two different histories of mass death may have been an accidental encounter, but the fact that the memory of the Holocaust, with its role in rethinking the place of Jews *as Jews* in the nation, should have provided a model for gays was not. The memory of one collective disaster was soon enrolled in the fight against another, ongoing one. And things did not stop there. This rhetorical borrowing may have served tactical purposes but it also uncovered what the editors of this volume have called a *noeud de mémoire*: Jewish history and gay history had in fact long been entangled. In the wake of the gay community's newly acquired political legitimacy, the focus soon turned toward the fight for the official recognition of homosexual deportations under Nazi rule. That, too, created discomfort within the French Republic, and it did so in two ways: it put different histories in uneasy contact, as demonstrated by the violently homophobic reactions of some camp survivors against attempts to include wreaths with a pink triangle in official commemorations; but it also shed a light on the disturbing kinship between supposedly incompatible strategies for erasing differences.

There exist two main tendencies to homogenize: universalism, that disembodies before re-embodying through discourses of science; and right-wing totalitarianism, that re-embodies in order to disembody by way of murder. If knowledge is to resist both, it can only take the unstable form of approximations or nearness, which necessarily leaves stones unturned and particularities respected. But the particularities of others—their otherness—can only be respected by being touched: *acknowledged* if not fully *known*. One may, as many AIDS sufferers have done, invoke the memory of the Holocaust to help make sense of other historical catastrophes befalling other human communities *as communities* but one must do it *with tact*, for tact brings into thought and social relations the simultaneous dynamic of touch and distance that characterizes all tropes. And because AIDS, the Holocaust, and other catastrophes are not confined to the pages of books written by people now long gone, tact may serve as a general model for a poetic form of remembering history in the present, reading the social, and dealing with others—a form of contact with people one fails fully to comprehend. In that sense, tact's phatic function underscores its focus on contact rather than on the expression of accurate statements. Moving beyond the informational, the interpersonal, and the allegorical, the trope of tact may become a model of reading others that brings different historical "events" into a neighborly relation without erasing their difference—indeed by understanding difference as that which makes community possible—or, to keep with the music metaphor: as a kind of disaccord. The cultural memory of the Holocaust, then, is not denied but perpetuated in AIDS testimonies that, by appealing to past events, let themselves be haunted by them and bear witness to them. This could allow us to read history neither as a linear succession nor as a cyclical repetition of finished entities but, rather, as a multidirectional dynamic of proximity and concurrence: something that, like all encounters, only exists when shared.

III. Visual Traces

ELIZABETH EZRA

Cléo's Masks: Regimes of Objectification in the French New Wave

There is a moment early in Agnès Varda's 1962 film *Cléo de 5 à 7* when the film's eponymous heroine, a pop singer named Cléo, notices a display of tribal masks in a shop window while riding in a taxi through the streets of Paris.[1] This is an iconic moment in the film, highlighting the importance of masquerade in Cléo's narcissistic world of appearances. But this scene also indicates the extent to which representations of alterity and discourses of cultural self-fashioning are rooted in narratives of historical progress. Masks are icons of "the primitive," and their presence in chic boutiques and bourgeois homes reinforces implicit cultural assumptions about how far "now" is from "then," and "we" are from "them." These assumptions, however, are seriously undermined by the forms of racialized violence that erupted in the twentieth century. Removed from one context and deposited in another, exotic masks perform a double displacement: they represent the cultures and places from whence they come (and a larger global system of expropriation and uneven exchange), and they also suggest a temporal *décalage* of instances of dehumanizing violence, invoking what Max Silverman has called "composite memories."[2] As objects, masks in these films come alive with the episodes of human history they embody, but they also invoke the reverse process of objectification in which human beings are reduced to the status of objects in cultural and sexual commodification, a reduction that paved the way for the worst atrocities of the twentieth century, including systematic torture and genocide. At the same time, masks inhabit a metaphorical

---

1. Research for this project was generously funded by a grant from the Leverhulme Trust.
2. Max Silverman, "Interconnected Histories: Holocaust and Empire in the Cultural Imaginary," *French Studies* LXII/4 (2008): 417–28.

YFS 118/119, *Noeuds de mémoire*, ed. Rothberg, Sanyal, and Silverman, © 2010 by Yale University.

space of disguise, censorship, and displacement. In *Cléo* and other New Wave films, masks appear as overdetermined memorial palimpsests, signifying multiple layers of historical trauma as well as the repression of these traumas in a dialectic of exposure and concealment. This essay will examine this dialectic in a number of films, beginning with *Cléo*, and culminating in a discussion of Alain Resnais's *Muriel ou le temps d'un retour* (1963).

In one sense, the masks Cléo sees in passing can be viewed as a comment on Cléo's own mask-like persona, her performativity as both a singer in the public eye and as a woman embracing the trappings of femininity, complete with blonde wig, makeup, spike heels, and a dress with swishing skirt and tightly-cinched waist that emphasizes her hourglass figure, making her look like nothing so much as a dragqueen. The masks Cléo sees from the passing taxi are displayed in the shop window very much like the hats in the women's hat shop she visits earlier in the film, reinforcing the idea of what Joan Rivière called "womanliness as masquerade."[3] But the masks also evoke the racialized violence lurking not so much beneath the surface as on the surface, hidden in plain view among the exotic objects and accessories introduced into French cultural life with the rise of mass culture.

The stage had been set for the display of masks in fashionable homes and department store windows in 1926, with the appearance in French *Vogue* of Man Ray's photograph *Noire et blanche*, which juxtaposed a white European woman's face with that of a Baule-style mask from the Ivory Coast. The photo's publication in a magazine designed to promote the mass-market consumption of fashion marked the official domestication of exotic objects that had begun with Picasso's incorporation of African and Oceanic objects into his work in the first decades of the twentieth century. The increasing visibility and availability of objects such as masks and carvings inspired the vogue for primitivism among Cubists and other avant-garde artists in the interwar period and beyond (André Malraux mused about this dimension of Picasso's work in his 1974 book on the artist called *La tête d'obsidienne*, translated as *Picasso's Mask*). According to Wendy A. Grossman and Steven Manford, the appearance of Man Ray's photo-

---

3. Joan Rivière, "Womanliness as Masquerade," *International Journal of Psycho-Analysis* 10 (1929): 303–313. For further discussion of the role of gender in *Cléo*, see Sandy Flitterman-Lewis, *To Desire Differently: Feminism and the French Cinema* (New York: Columbia UP, 1996), 268–84, and Jill Forbes, "Gender and Space in Cléo de 5 à 7," *Studies in French Cinema* 2/2 (2001): 83–89.

graph in the fashion magazine "brought the 'vogue' for things African into the mainstream."[4] It is significant that the site of the masks' display in *Cléo de 5 à 7* is not a museum, or even a bohemian-bourgeois home, but a shop window. This positioning of the masks as an item of consumption points to the convergence of exoticism and consumer culture in France. Arising from encounters with other cultures occasioned to a great extent by trade in the sixteenth and seventeenth centuries, exoticism proliferated with the advent of the printing press and the emergence of what Benedict Anderson famously called "imagined communities,"[5] culminating in the rise of the culture industry in the twentieth century. The New Wave (1958–62) emerged roughly halfway through the "Trente glorieuses," the thirty-year period of economic prosperity and modernization that, as Kristin Ross has argued, was closely bound to colonial exploitation and racist exclusion.[6]

The French New Wave also coincided with the height of the Algerian War—yet, as Benjamin Stora notes, very few films were made about the war while it was taking place, and those that were made were banned until after the Evian Accords in 1962, and not released until 1963 (such as Godard's *Le petit soldat*, Robert Enrico's *La belle vie*, James Blue's *Les oliviers de la justice*, Paul Carpita's *Demain l'amour*, et Alain Resnais's *Muriel ou le temps d'un retour*).[7] Filmmakers had to find other ways to represent the war. The New Wave directors were, according to Stora, particularly adept at expressing the "political, ideological, and cultural deconstructions that were taking hold in society at the time."[8] These deconstructions insinuated themselves into many New Wave films, undermining assumptions about social and cultural hierarchies. Masks in particular resonate both as a physical presence and metaphorically as a means of disguise, or masquerade, suggesting the larger dynamic of disguise that New Wave directors used in order to represent unpalatable events both past and present. According to Elza Adamowicz, "The mask never merges with the body on which it is placed; it remains attached to the context from which it was taken. The mask, space of the ambiguous, figure of al-

    4. Wendy A. Grossman and Steven Manford, "Unmasking Man Ray's *Noire et blanche*," *American Art* 20/2 (Summer 2006): 137.
    5. Benedict Anderson, *Imagined Communities* (London: Verso, 1983).
    6. Kristin Ross, *Fast Cars, Clean Bodies: Decolonization and the Reordering of French Culture* (Cambridge, MA: MIT Press, 1996).
    7. Benjamin Stora, *Imaginaires de guerre* (Paris: La Découverte, 1997), 111.
    8. Stora, *La gangrène et l'oubli* (Paris: La Découverte, 1991), 40.

terity, is the site of the emergence of the other within the same."[9] In Godard's *A bout de souffle* (1959), which Benjamin Stora has called a "film-miroir" for the "Algerian generation," whose "hero," like France itself, advances toward its ineluctable destiny,[10] there is an extended scene in Patricia's room, in which small-time gangster Michel sits against a wall displaying a Picasso print of a man holding a mask ("L'ancienne et la nouvelle année," from 1953). Michel says, "You might as well tell the truth; people will think you're bluffing, and that's how you win." Masks, like the truth in a double bluff, appear to conceal something else, when in fact their secrets lie on the surface for all to see. In films made during this period, masks act as monuments bearing silent witness to the legacy of objectification that underwrites the reduction of people to their purely corporeal dimension—whether on the basis of "race" or gender—and the violation or elimination of those bodies that such reduction legitimates.

CLOSE-UP ON *CLÉO*

Cléo de 5 à 7 was made in 1961, as the Algerian War entered its final, bloody year. Seemingly shot in real time (seemingly, because the film is actually only 90 minutes long), the film appears to chart two hours in the life of a minor celebrity anxiously awaiting the results of a medical test. The only explicit reference to the war, apart from a news bulletin on the radio in the taxi that ferries Cléo around Paris, is in the form of Antoine, the French soldier on leave who renews the despairing Cléo's sense of hope and vitality as she struggles with life in the public eye and the prospect of her own mortality. Cléo's name itself, we are told, is short for Cléopatre, or Cleopatra, an association reinforced by the name Antoine, or Antony. The film abounds in references to non-French cultures. At a pivotal point in the film, Cléo pauses to look at herself in a mirror on the outside wall of a Chinese restaurant, her face surrounded by Chinese characters. In a voiceover interior monologue, she observes, "I'm not looking at anyone but myself. It's tiring." Although this statement is ambiguous taken out of

---

9. Elza Adamowicz, "'Un masque peut en masquer (ou démasquer) un autre': Le Masque et le Surréalisme," in *L'autre et le sacré. Surréalisme, cinéma, ethnologie*, ed. C.W. Thompson (Paris: L'Harmattan, 1995), 91.

10. Stora, *La gangrène et l'oubli*, 40.

context (the "it" in "it's tiring" could be interpreted in opposite ways: looking only at herself is tiring, or looking at others would be tiring), it actually refers to Cléo's newfound determination to emerge from her narcissistic shell and open herself up to the world around her. In one of her first acts of awareness of her surroundings after her turn away from her habitual self-absorption, Cléo enters a café where she hears two men discussing Algeria, followed by two other men discussing surrealism, while others debate the merits of Miró and Picasso. At another table, people discuss an acquaintance's trip to Africa. (These snatches of conversation, all referring to other cultures, recall the first time we see Cléo in a café, near the beginning of the film, when Cléo's minder Angèle tells a story about a man who travels to Egypt and Turkey.) Before meeting Antoine, Cléo inquires, in an apparent non-sequitur, whether an observatory that has been drawn to her attention in the Parc Montsouris is "from *The Arabian Nights*?" Finally, at the very end of the film, as a sign of her newly emergent interest in the outside world, Cléo announces that she would like to "know Lebanon." For Cléo, awareness of other people seems to be linked to an awareness of other peoples.

Varda briefly develops this dynamic of perception and difference in a playful film-within-the-film, which Cléo's friend Dorothée, an artist's model, shows her when they visit Dorothée's boyfriend at work. Shot in black-and-white and approximately three minutes in duration, *Les fiancés du Pont Mac Donald* features such New Wave regulars as Anna Karina, Jean-Luc Godard, and Jean-Claude Brialy. In this whimsical tale, Godard plays a young man whose world changes completely once he puts on a pair of dark glasses. His blonde girlfriend, called Anna, turns into a black woman, and an insignificant mishap becomes a fatal accident (complete with ambulance transformed into a hearse). Once the man removes the sunglasses, everything returns to normal and he cries, "It was because of my glasses that everything looked black." Blackness turns out to have been an illusion, a question literally of outlook. The short film's funereal imagery indicates that the color black is meant to be interpreted as a metaphor for affect (as in a dark mood), but in the context of the larger film's exoticist allusions, the short film's use of a black woman inevitably conjures up certain cultural associations. Judith Mayne has noted the short film's "unproblematized relation between black and white; indeed, the black remains as the unexamined projection of the white man's sunglasses, or the spectacle of a 'primitive' mask."[11] The black version of Anna is presented as a disguise covering the "real" Anna, who, within the diegetic universe of the short film, appears to have been wearing a kind of black mask. This notion of blackness as a mask or visual effect can be read as a kind of reversal of Frantz Fanon's 1952 *Peau noire, masques blancs*, which argues that colonial subjects of African descent internalize the worldview of their white oppressors. For Fanon, the white mask was a symbol of the attitudes and behaviors of a dominant (colonizing) culture that had been embraced by a dominated (colonized) culture. The performance of blackness, on the other hand (as epitomized by the wearing of blackface, for example) is a form of cultural tourism, a temporary borrowing or wearing of a mask—representing not "black" culture, but the system of domination that insists on polarizing what the terms "black" and "white" represent. In the short film, difference turns out to be a reflection of the lens through which one looks—in other words, subjective, and culturally conditioned. Cultural tourism commodifies "racial" identity, making of it something to be tried on like a hat in a shop, or displayed like an Oceanic mask in a European artist's living room or office.

Immediately following the scene in *Cléo de 5 à 7* in which Cléo is confronted with the masks in the shop window, she encounters art and architecture students engaging in the ritualistic behavior of the French tradition known as *bizutage*, or hazing, complete with disguises (we see an American Indian headdress, and some students' faces are painted, and some wear homemade masks and headgear). Varda is suggesting a parallel between the "primitive" masks and rituals and those of the Parisian students, in the manner of the *Exposition anticoloniale* staged by Surrealists and Communists during the *Exposition coloniale* of 1931, which presented Christian religious icons as domestic fetishes by displaying them alongside masks and sacred objects from cultures deemed "primitive." When one of the students, a young black man, presses his face to the window of Cléo's taxi, it is, according to Steven Ungar, "as though one of the masks she had just seen suddenly came to life."[12]

The masks in *Cléo* are shown in a brief but striking collage of

11. Judith Mayne, *The Woman at the Keyhole: Feminism and Women's Cinema* (Bloomington: Indiana UP, 1990), 202.
12. Steven Ungar, *Cléo de 5 à 7* (London and New York: BFI Film Classics/Palgrave Macmillan, 2008), 35.

close-ups, in such as way as to evoke the 1953 Alain Resnais and Chris Marker film *Les statues meurent aussi*, which itself mirrors the display of masks in ethnographic museums, often removed from their historical context.[13] This cultural commodification finds its parallel in the way in which Cléo herself is packaged and sold to the public as spectacle. As a star, Cléo herself is commodified, her humanity objectified in the mechanical reproduction and dissemination of her image. (Her commodified status is the inverse of the sculptures that her friend Dorothée poses for, which comprise a range of original representations of a single referent, rather than the multiple copies of Cléo's hit single.) Varda's film explicitly invokes this process of objectification through the use of close-up in the scene set in Cléo's apartment, in which she sings one of her songs, and her face, detached from its suddenly darkened surroundings, is bathed in a spotlight, illuminated show-biz style. Cléo's face is thus projected as that of a star performer, wearing the frozen mask of what Deleuze and Guattari call "visagéité" or "faciality."[14] In faciality, which is the effect produced by close-ups in films, the face is separated from what Deleuze identified as its three conventional functions: those of individuation (that which distinguishes or characterizes each person), socialization (the manifestation of a social role), and relation or communication (the assurance not only of "communication between two persons, but also, within a single person, the internal accord between one's character and one's role").[15] (Blackface would be an exaggerated form of faciality.) According to Ronald Bogue, "Rather than being a body part in a determinate spatio-temporal setting, or a marker of an identity, a role or a relation, the face in close-up is an autonomous object."[16] Like close-ups in the cinema, racial and sexual objectification appear to bring things and people closer to the subject who contemplates them, thus creating the illusion of intimacy, while in fact alienating their objects from the viewer.

13. See Martine Beugnet, "Du film d'art à l'art du film. *Les statues meurent aussi* de Chris Marker and Alain Resnais," *Cinémaction* 122 (2006): 39–47.
14. Gilles Deleuze and Félix Guattari, *Mille Plateaux: Capitalisme et Schizophrénie* (Paris: Les Éditions de Minuit, 1980): 205–34.
15. Gilles Deleuze, *Cinéma 1: L'image-mouvement* (Paris: Éditions de minuit. 1983): 141; 99; cited in Ronald Bogue, *Deleuze on Cinema* (New York: Routledge, 2003), 78.
16. Bogue, 78.

OVERLAPPING REGIMES OF OBJECTIFICATION

François Trauffaut plays on this objectifying function of the close-up in his 1962 *Jules et Jim*, through the use of a series of freeze frames, which highlight and intensify Catherine's self-conscious mugging. When she poses and pouts in freeze frame, Catherine's fixed, mask-like expressions exaggerate the expressivity that differentiates humans from other animals, to the point of reversal, so that they slip into the realm of the non-expressive inanimate. Adapting Michael Rothberg's "overlapping regimes of racialization," it is possible to speak of overlapping regimes of objectification, as Catherine's (like Cléo's) star turn through the use of close-up is inseparable from the performance of gender, and as the logic of sexism is shown to overlap with that of exoticism.[17] When Catherine and Jules are walking along the banks of the Seine, Jules asks Jim, in the presence of Catherine "Who wrote 'woman is natural, and therefore abominable?'" To which Jim replies, "It was Baudelaire, but he was referring to women from a particular world, and a particular society." Jules counters: "Not at all; he was talking about women in general."[18] Traits that Jim reserves for subaltern women, women "from a particular world, and a particular society"—far from "here," in other words, whether "here" is defined in terms of geographical location or social class—Jules would ascribe to all women. This alternation between "other" and "all" women reveals a similar objectifying dynamic at work in discourses of exoticism and sexism. Later in the film, Jim encounters a man in a bar who introduces his girlfriend as "hollow," "empty," "a thing," "a beautiful object," which would seem to describe the fossilized, flattened images projected by Catherine's reified facial expressions. At the end of the film, Catherine and Jim do become reduced to pure matter, in a striking sequence that shows their incinerated bodies being ground into ashes. This scene illustrates the logical conclusion of the decontextualizing objectification described and performed by the man in the bar, and invokes what Rothberg calls "multidirectional memory" in its unavoidable allusion to the Holocaust—an association made previously in Varda's early short film *L'Opéra-Mouffe* (1958) in a shot of a wall bearing the graffiti-scrawled slogan "Peace with free Algeria," next to a swastika.[19]

---

17. Michael Rothberg, *Multidirectional Memory: Remembering the Holocaust in the Age of Decolonization* (Stanford: Stanford UP, 2009), 258.
18. The quote is actually "La Femme est naturelle, c'est-à-dire abominable," from Baudelaire's *Mon coeur mis à nu*.
19. Rothberg. See also Ungar, 106–107.

These moments serve as *noeuds de mémoire*, which rupture narrative flow and compel us to consider the historical consequences of such objectifying acts. The overlapping regimes of objectification seem to invoke a concomitant temporal overlap, a palimpsest of cultural memories. This temporal layering is periodically invoked in New Wave films. In *Jules et Jim*, for example, it is no accident that Jules and Jim's interest in Catherine is predicated on their obsession with a so-called primitive sculpture, which they first see in a private slide show given by a friend, in a mixture of academicism and tourism. Like archeologist-explorers of the Indiana Jones variety (or perhaps like Truffaut's fellow filmmaker Godard, who studied ethnography at the Sorbonne), Jules and Jim travel to the Adriatic island where the sculpture is situated, in order to admire it firsthand. It is significant that the sculpture that so captivates Jules and Jim is located on an island in the Adriatic, to the west of Greece and to the east of Africa, midway on the ideological world map between the "primitive" and the classical, the exotic and the ancient. In his notes for an *Essai sur l'exotisme*, Victor Segalen proposed "exoticism in time" as a corollary to "exoticism in space."[20] Baudrillard, too, noted the analogy between historical and geographical displacement: "For modern man . . . , changing country or latitude is essentially equivalent to plunging into the past (as tourism well demonstrates)."[21] In New Wave films, representations of antiquity and exoticism at times overlap in a diffuse atmosphere of cultural *décalage*.

Some New Wave directors used antiquity to stand in for, or disguise, the unpalatable present of a colonial war. Just as *Jules et Jim's* World-War-I setting can be seen on one level as a displacement of the Algerian War, other New Wave films evoke the past in order to bypass, or more accurately, to point obliquely to, a present that cannot be acknowledged explicitly. Resnais's *L'année dernière à Marienbad* (1961), for example, whose ambiguous rape scenes have often been interpreted as an unambiguous metaphor for France's actions in Algeria, is a film that is overwhelmed by antiquity, in the form of neo-classical statues that grace the formal gardens in which the nameless

---

20. Victor Segalen, *Essai sur l'exotisme* (Paris: Le Livre de Poche, 1986 [1955]), 38. For an interesting analysis of Segalen's work and the larger context of exoticist thought in France, see Charles Forsdick, *Victor Segalen and the Aesthetics of Diversity* (Oxford: Oxford UP, 2000).

21. Jean Baudrillard, *The System of Objects*, trans. James Benedict (London: Verso, 2005), 79 n.4.

characters circulate. In fact, Resnais himself has insisted, somewhat enigmatically, that the film was a "documentary about a statue."[22] Lynne Higgins has pointed out that M's supposed "identification" of the statue as a representation of "Charles III," is actually a mystification, as no such historical personage existed. Higgins traces the web of associations generated by the false identification to Charles de Gaulle, who was often referred to as "Le Roi Charles" in jokes and cartoons of the period, and who of course played a major role in the decolonization of Algeria.[23] In foregrounding antiquity (and a false one, no less), Resnais is performing a double substitution, in which a temporal displacement stands in for a geographical one. However, this masking effect, far from obscuring its object, actually draws attention to it. A similar dynamic can be seen in Resnais's next film, Muriel ou le temps d'un retour.

MULTIDIRECTIONAL MEMORY IN MURIEL

In Muriel, as in Marienbad, allusions to earlier eras signal the processes of displacement that ostensibly enable us to "forget" more recent historical traumas, but which ultimately flag the multidirectional nature of cultural memory. In Muriel, the horrors of both the present (the Algerian War) and the recent past (the Second World War) are obscured beneath the banal surfaces of everyday life, as sexual and cultural objectification are pushed to their logical conclusion in the violation and murder of an Algerian woman.[24] Perhaps more than any other New Wave film, Muriel engages with the complexities of multidirectional memory and overlapping regimes of objectification by staging the temporal displacement of violence, revealing not so much a greater violence as the fact that one mask can sometimes conceal another.

Old and new are juxtaposed in the film's setting, in the gleaming glass, neon-lit city of Boulogne, erected on the ruins of those parts of the city destroyed in the Second World War. The film's narrative and visual emphasis on commodity culture (the buying and selling of antiques, the repeated shots of brightly lit shop windows groaning with

---

22. Cited in Lynne A. Higgins, New Novel, New Wave, New Politics (Lincoln: University of Nebraska Press, 1996), 101.
23. Higgins, 104–105.
24. Celia Britton has argued that, although the film does not establish unequivocally that Muriel was raped, the motif of violent penetration that permeates the film adds a dimension of sexual violation to Muriel's torture (44–46).

the latest consumer goods and gadgets) go beyond the symbolic articulation of effects. Resnais's depictions of interiors-as-exteriors (shop windows lit in such a way as to merge with the streets of Boulogne) suggest that the commodities that decorate the homes and streets of metropolitan France appear not as arbitrary signs, but as both symbols and artefacts of a system of social relations based on expropriation, uneven exchange, and, ultimately, objectification.

Hélène sells antiques out of her home, and her grown stepson Bernard, back from military service in Algeria, comments that because of all the to-ing and fro-ing of antiques in the apartment, he never knows which era he's going to wake up in. Hélène's apartment, with its chaotic jumble of antiques and layering of historical eras, is a microcosm of the city of Boulogne. Gaston Bounoure has noted the sense of displacement the characters experience: "The characters in *Muriel* . . . are displaced. They come from another time, and are searching for another place."[25] This perpetual state of displacement in which the characters find themselves is accompanied by their attempts to obliterate their own past. Alphonse, Hélène's former lover, claims falsely to have spent several years running a café in Algeria, and travels around with his young girlfriend, whom he introduces as his niece, neglecting to mention that he is actually married to another woman. Bernard claims to have a girlfriend named Muriel, but it emerges that Muriel is in fact (or may be) the name of a woman in Algeria whose torture Bernard witnessed and in which he appears to have participated. Emma Wilson has suggested that in *Muriel*, Resnais "does not so much echo physical mutilation . . . as intimate the psychological effects of torture on its victim."[26] If the familial and social entanglements articulate the psychological effects of colonial brutality, the form of the film itself, whose fragmented editing style Celia Britton has interpreted as a cinematic embodiment of Muriel's mutilation, mimics the structures of torture and dismemberment.[27] It is as though the film's form were mirroring the dynamic of displacement that haunts the narrative.

This sense of displacement is most acute in the context of Bernard's complicated relationship to his own past. In some ways, Bernard wishes to hold on to the past, and even carry it into the present (he keeps meticulous records of his wartime experiences, and when going

25. Gaston Bounoure, *Alain Resnais* (Paris: Seghers, 1974), 55.
26. Emma Wilson, *Alain Resnais* (Manchester: Manchester UP, 2006), 100.
27. Britton, "Broken images in Resnais's *Muriel*," *French Cultural Studies*, 1/1 (February 1990): 38.

to visit his girlfriend Marie-Do, he says that he is going to visit Muriel). At the same time, he is not forthcoming about disclosing his own desires and motives to others. As Lynne Higgins has noted, Bernard's face is often concealed or obscured, and he even wears a mask one evening at dinner—a pair of googly-eye glasses, for which his stepmother reprimands him—hinting at the broader function of the mask of censorship.[28] Exactly halfway through the film, Bernard shows a home movie he has shot composed of banal scenes from military life in Algeria, which he projects while recounting the story of Muriel's torture and death, which we never see. Naomi Greene calls the absence of scenes of torture in Bernard's film "[a] black hole at the center of *Muriel*," and interprets this absence as an indictment of France's repression of the war.[29] After showing the film, Bernard stands before the blank screen, illuminated (or interrogated) by the harsh light of the projector, the blank screen a possible reference to the "*carré blanc*," literally the blank space of censorship.[30] This *carré blanc* might also be likened to the gleaming plate glass shop windows to which Resnais returns so often in the film, and which, it may be argued, are monuments not to memory, but to forgetting—or at least, like screen memories, to attempts to forget that ultimately point to the events they are trying to suppress. In a similar way, the apparently innocuous, even jocular, images in Bernard's home movie finally reveal more than they disguise. Leo Bersani and Ulysse Dutoit have argued that the seemingly random scenes of military life in Algeria actually match up with the acts of torture being described, in a series of "correspondences":

> When . . . Bernard says that the five soldiers participated in the torture of Muriel, we see five canteens lying on the ground; a soldier raises his arm just as Bernard speaks of Muriel putting her hands over her eyes; the shape of the minarets we see evokes that of the flashlight Robert is said to have focused on Muriel; Bernard's reference to Muriel's swollen body looking as if it had been under water is followed by an image of a soldier diving into a pool.[31]

Although the banal images cover over and attempt to distract from the violence, they cannot seem to help replicating its form, as though

---

28. Higgins, 110.
29. Naomi Greene, *Landscapes of Loss: The National Past in Postwar French Cinema* (Princeton, Princeton UP, 1999), 49.
30. Higgins, 110.
31. Leo Bersani and Ulysse Dutoit, *Arts of Impoverishment* (Cambridge: Harvard UP, 1993), 195–96.

the violence had infected everyday life, seeping through the screen that would obscure it. These superficial images invite us to plumb the depths of the surface, to find what Hannah Arendt called "the banality of evil,"[32] and what Max Silverman has called the "everyday horror" that characterizes involuntary memories of historical trauma in post-Holocaust France.[33] The way in which the anodyne images from Bernard's home movie both illustrate and disguise the brutality that cannot be shown mirrors the way in which modern Boulogne paves over its wartime ruins: the "correspondences" of which Bersani and Dutoit speak are themselves multidirectional, reaching out to link (certainly analogically, if not causally) traumatic events from different eras. The pointed allusions to the Second World War in the shots of the ruined city cannot fail to invoke the Holocaust, especially in the wake of Resnais's explosive documentary *Nuit et brouillard* (1955), the text of whose narration was written by Jean Cayrol, the screenwriter of *Muriel*. Max Silverman has noted the earlier film's suggestion of associations between these historical traumas, writing that, for Resnais, "Algeria is the double of the concentrationary universe of the Holocaust."[34] Bernard's narration of his participation in Muriel's torture resonates with the voiceover in *Nuit et brouillard*, a film that also juxtaposes banal shots of everyday life with descriptions of the most horrific atrocities. Alastair Duncan has observed the echoes in *Muriel* of the Holocaust documentary, whose voice-over "exhorted its audience not to believe that the plague rampant in the concentration camps was limited to one time or one country and urged them to look around 'autour de nous.'"[35] In *Muriel*, we are again asked to look around us, at the trappings of modern consumer culture and daily life in postwar France, and beyond, to atrocities being committed on other continents or in other eras. As Bernard's home movie masks the violence of torture, the horrors of the Algerian War inevitably mask the horrors of the Holocaust—not as the "ultimate" horror finally revealed, but as a still-living cultural memory (one of the possible referents of the "retour" of the film's title) and reference point for sub-

---

32. Hannah Arendt, *Eichmann in Jerusalem: A Report on the Banality of Evil* (New York: Penguin Classics, 1994 [1963]).

33. Max Silverman, "Horror and the Everyday in Post-Holocaust France," *French Cultural Studies* 17/1 (2006): 5–18.

34. Silverman, "Horror and the Everyday . . . ," 14.

35. Alastair Duncan, "The problematic commemoration of war in the early films of Alain Resnais," in *Memory and Memorials: The Commemorative Century*, ed. William Kidd and Brian Murdoch (Aldershot: Ashgate, 2004), 217.

sequent acts of unfathomable brutality. If these incomparable historical traumas are unspeakable examples of barbarity, it is their very ineffability that brings them together, weaving them into a single, tongue-tied knot of memory.

In New Wave films, made in the lengthening shadow of the Holocaust and as the sun was setting on France's colonial empire, masks evoke the play of concealment and exposure that characterizes multidirectional memory. But they also evoke the legitimating symbolic violence of objectification, which entails the construction of a phantasmatic mask that is overlaid on all members of an identified group. Within these overlapping regimes of objectification, masks function as fetishes in the Freudian sense, diverting attention from the face by means of a facial substitute, which disavows the assumed absence of humanity beneath the mask.

BILL MARSHALL

Of Cones and Pyramids: Deleuzian Film Theory and Historical Memory

Three instances (two cinematic and one that I shall call proto-cinematic) illustrate both the stakes at play in, and the different forms taken by, relations of memory in postwar France. Near the beginning of *Passage du milieu/Middle Passage*, a drama documentary made in 2001 by the Martinican filmmaker Guy Deslauriers and co-scripted by Patrick Chamoiseau, the omniscient narrator, both individualized victim of the Atlantic slave trade and embodiment of all slaves and their descendants, invokes in now familiar language the analogy between that trade and Nazi genocide.[1] Notwithstanding the rich and complex potentiality located in the juxtaposed and mutually informing discussion of anti-Semitism and colonial racism that is explored by commentators such as Paul Gilroy and Michael Rothberg,[2] such a reference here may be characterized as an *ideological claim* made within some national or transnational public sphere via competing ethno-social memories. In the 2005 French action film *Banlieue 13*, directed by Pierre Morel with a script by Luc Besson and Bibi Naceri, two young French heroes, a policeman and a *"marginal,"* confront both criminal elements and a corrupt, futuristic French state that is plotting the physical elimination of the inhabitants of the eponymous urban dis-

---

1. In *Ecrire en pays dominé*, Chamoiseau recounts a dream of disembarking from a slave ship: "The holocaust of holocausts, a kind of Nazism before its time, forgotten by the consciousness of the West" (Paris: Gallimard-Folio, 1997), 133.
2. Paul Gilroy, *The Black Atlantic: Modernity and Double Consciousness* (London: Verso, 1993), especially Chapter Six, 187–223; Michael Rothberg, *Multidirectional Memory: Remembering the Holocaust in the Age of Decolonization* (Stanford: Stanford University Press, 2009). See also, for example, Celia Britton, "Exile, Incarceration and the Homeland: Jewish References in French Caribbean Novels," in *Comparing Postcolonial Diasporas*, ed. Michelle Keown, David Murphy, and James Procter (Basingstoke: Palgrave Macmillan, 2009), 149–67.

trict, which has been surrounded by a wall for years, its two million inhabitants left to rot. The historical memory that is invoked, by the police captain in one of the film's not-infrequent "political" discussions between the two men, is that of the Holocaust ("six million have already been killed on the grounds they weren't blond with blue eyes"). The opposition between republicanism and fascism constitutes a safe and tidy reference: this is the Warsaw ghetto (created by the Other) rather than the much more ambivalent memories of the colonial city or even apartheid (Fanon: "The town belonging to the colonized people, or at least the native town . . . is a place of ill fame, peopled by men of evil repute. They are born there, it matters little where or how; they die there, it matters not where, not how.")[3] This is a classic ideological operation in the Althusserian sense, as the contemporary French republican edifice is naturalized by an imaginary relation to the real, helped along by a dose of what Roland Barthes refers to as inoculation.[4]

PASSAGES OF NANTES

These memory interventions may be seen as operating at the molar level, in Deleuze and Guattari's terms; that is, bound up with large social and institutional entities—such as nations and their gender identities—and their apparent or provisional unities. An altogether more mysterious example is to be found in my third, "proto-cinematic" example, André Pieyre de Mandiargues's "Le Passage Pommeraye," published in 1946. Here the shopping arcade, built in 1843, that is one of the most famous sights/sites in the city of Nantes and whose construction on three levels lends itself to the "descent" featured in the tale, becomes the setting for a fantastic short story in which the narrator is enticed down and through the phantasmagoria of the passage by a mysterious female figure, only to be subjected to a horrible surgical operation in which he is transformed into un homme-caïman ("alligator man"). While the story can be categorized as a variation on surrealist depictions in the lineage of André Breton's writ-

---

3. Frantz Fanon, *The Wretched of the Earth*, trans. Constance Farrington (London: Penguin, 2001), 30; *Les damnés de la terre* (Paris: Maspero, 1968), 8.
4. "One immunizes the contents of the collective imagination by means of a small inoculation of acknowledged evil; one thus protects it against the risk of a generalized subversion," Roland Barthes, *Mythologies*, selected and translated by Annette Lavers (London: Paladin Books, 1973), 150; (Paris: Seuil, 1957), 238.

ings on Nantes and those of Louis Aragon on the passages of Paris, what concerns us here is the juxtaposition, or short circuit, inherent in the following description:

> We set off again along the quai de la Fosse. Strangely, right in the middle of the city, a heavy train passed along the quayside behind the metal railings along its edge that she and I walked along. It was a slow cattle train, and right beside us, from all the carriage's tiny windows, came the bellowing of cows being taken to the slaughter-house; that and the iron screeching of wheels on rails made a horrible sound after the silence of the passage and of the dozing city.[5]

Here, a nightmarish image echoes the impending horrible destiny of the narrator, but this is also clearly an image of deportation, a recent memory-image invoked a year after the end of World War II, and four years after the main round-ups that had afflicted the city's Jewish population. Moreover, it is metonymically linked with a more distant, half-suppressed memory, in the very quayside by the Loire—the quai de la Fosse, which is the destination of any descent through the Passage Pommeraye—from which slave ships left for Africa in the triangular Atlantic trade, and their sugar and other colonial products unloaded (indeed, the story contains a whole litany on sugar in the evocation of the objects in the Hidalgo *Farces et attrapes* shop window). Nantes was far and away the most important French slave-trading port from the late seventeenth to the early nineteenth century, over 45% of all such activity emanating from there. In recent years the city has been wrestling with the politics of memory of its participation in the slave trade.[6] However, these "molar" concerns are less important here than the more mysterious "molecular" processes at work, namely the lateral, proliferating, non-unifiable and indeed rhizomatic micro-linkages that seem to form here. The massive work of disavowal that characterized the city's memory of the slave trade throughout most of the twentieth century, and the story's surrealist fascination with the unconscious, including a hydraulic Freudian model based on (hetero)sexual drives, fantasies, fears, and interdictions, lends itself to an analysis of "Le Passage Pommeraye" that would emphasize the return of the repressed (the bourgeois shopping

---

5. André Pieyre de Mandiargues, *Le musée noir* (Paris: Robert Laffont, 1946), 98.
6. See for example my "Nantes's Atlantic Problem", in *Branding Cities: Cosmopolitanism, Parochialism, and Social Change*, ed. S.H. Donald, E. Kofman, and C. Kevin (London: Routledge, 2009), 123–36.

arcade was built, "hygienically," through the clearing of a disreputable district), and the processes of displacement and substitution characteristic of the cattle truck/slave ship metonymy. However, there seems to be no question of the latter here "screening" the former, or vice versa. We seem to be very much in the domain of "knots of memory," of non-totalizable, multidirectional, entangled images and imaginings of the past. How are these to be grasped? I have attempted elsewhere to use Slavoj Žižek's understanding of the Lacanian Real to see in this and other invocations of the Passage Pommeraye evidence of a traumatic kernel that the social order is unable to symbolize or account for.[7] But what I wish to explore in the rest of this article is, first, the supremely cinematic aspect of the Passage (as site and representation), and then the ways in which Gilles Deleuze's adaptation of Bergson's account of time and memory can help to address, at "molecular" levels such as this, images and instances of remembering.

For Giuliana Bruno, constructions such as the Passage Pommeraye form part of emerging ways of seeing in modernity:

> On the eve of cinema's invention, a network of architectural forms produced a new spatiovisuality. Such venues as arcades, railways, department stores, the pavilions of exhibition halls, glass houses and winter gardens incarnated the new geography of modernity. They were all sites of transit. Mobility—a form of cinematics—was the essence of these new architectures. By changing the relation between spatial perception and bodily motion, the new architectures of transit and travel culture prepared the ground for the invention of the moving image, the very epitome of modernity.[8]

In the cinema of Jacques Demy, the multiple, and already cinematic, connotations of the Passage Pommeraye often touch upon questions of time and memory. In his film *Lola* (1961), the first encounter between the eponymous heroine and her former lover Cassard takes place with deep focus shots of the passage stretching behind and above them, accompanying an effort to remember their last encounter more than a decade previously. In their final scene in the film, they are shown walking around the upper level, poised between virtual futures, with, in frame, the allegorical statues and the ephemeral advertising slogans

---

7. Chapter One, "Passages of Nantes," in Bill Marshall, *The French Atlantic: Travels in Culture and History* (Liverpool: Liverpool University Press, 2009), 24–58.

8. Giuliana Bruno, *Atlas of Emotion: Journeys in Art, Architecture, and Film* (London: Verso, 2002), 17.

and shop windows bespeaking differently embedded cultures of time. In *Les parapluies de Cherbourg* (1964), the camera travels around the same—empty—space in the passage as Cassard reminisces about his lost love. The setting and staging mean that these are much more than individual memories: Cassard's visit to the diamond-smuggling *coiffeur* in the Passage connotes instruments of torture (such as the curling tongs), along with the global and the colonial; *Les parapluies* is famously about the relations between the Algerian War and postwar modernization.[9] In Demy's *Une chambre en ville* (1982), a fatal visit to a television repair shop in the depths of the passage in 1950s Nantes points to, in Deleuze's terms, a contraction, a minimal circuit of exchange between the actual and the virtual. What does this mean?

BERGSON AND DELEUZE

In *Matière et mémoire* (1896), Henri Bergson sought to establish, in a fundamentally anti-Cartesian enterprise, the continuity between consciousness, matter, and time. Here, all matter is image, the universe is an aggregate of those images as they interact with one another. The human body, including brain and sensorium, is simply one of these images, acting and reacting within the interconnected web of images that is the universe and within the limits of its perception and capacity. The question of time and memory arises when we consider the relationship between perception and the fundamental splitting of time:

> every *attentive* perception truly involves a *reflexion*, in the etymological sense of the word, that is to say the projection, outside ourselves, of an actively created image, identical with, or similar to, the object on which it comes to mould itself. If, after having gazed at any object, we turn our eyes abruptly away, we obtain an "after image" of it: must we not suppose that this image existed already while we were looking?[10]

The arrow of time moves forward, and may be represented by a horizontal line: but at the same time, one might imagine a dotted line that falls away into the past. Each present moment, each "point"—or

---

9. See Bill Marshall and Sylvie Lindeperg, "Time, History and Memory in *Les parapluies de Cherbourg*," in *Musicals—Hollywood and Beyond*, ed. Bill Marshall and Robynn Stilwell (Exeter: Intellect Books, 2000), 98–106.

10. Henri Bergson, *Matter and Memory*, trans. Nancy Margaret Paul and W. Scott Palmer (London: George Allen & Co: 1913), 124–25.

"peak"—of the present, is accompanied by a simultaneous falling away into the past, "a present that passes" that joins the archive of the past, "the past that is preserved." Bergson's first figure illustrates this:

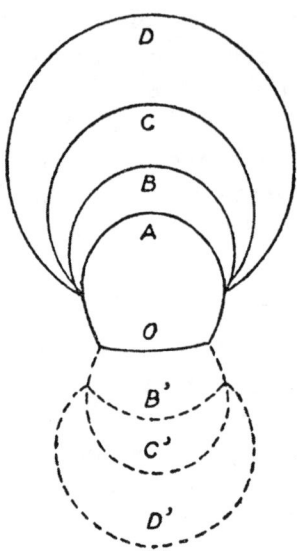

Here, O is the object perceived; A to D (but they could go on) are circles of memory beginning with the nearest to immediate perception (and with it therefore the consecutive memory which covers the object/image), and the ever increasing circles of memory which are called upon to elaborate details, connotations, and so on. In turn, circles B', C', D' (but they could go on), represent the modifications in perception brought about by this circuit. We are here in a domain of perpetual motion, of a self-fulfilling circuit powering the different possible levels of attention, from automatic/habitual to the most complex forms of reflection. This is the opposite of perception, knowledge, thought, and memory seen as a series of additions in linear, quantitative fashion piling up reflections and leaving the object behind, in the manner of some zero-sum game. The *virtual* image or images coexist with the *actual* perception of an object.

Bergson's other famous diagram, elaborated upon by Deleuze, suggests cosmic conclusions that may be drawn from the previous:

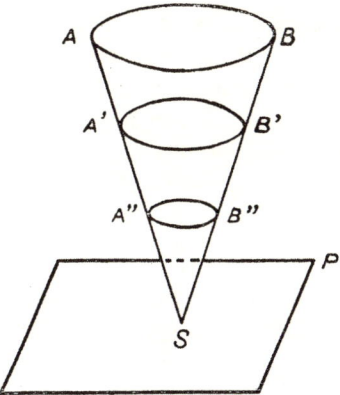

This inverse cone represents S as the contracted point of the present moment, the "sensory-motor" self constantly moving forward in time on P—the plane of reality that is how we perceive the images of the world—as the presents pass and fall into the non-chronological archive of the past which stretches towards the ever receding base A-B. The circuits represented by A'-B' and so on represent layers or regions (Deleuze calls them *"nappes"*/"sheets") within non-chronological time that are the virtual source of memory-images.

In *Cinéma 1: L'image-mouvement* (1984) and especially *Cinéma 2: L'image-temps* (1985), Deleuze uses these Bergsonian insights to inform and develop a more sustained understanding of the relationship between the actual and the virtual, and its application to different forms of filmmaking: the "movement-image" corresponds to the sensory-motor schema of S, as above, and its indirect representation of time in action and other images (*Banlieue 13* would be a classic example of this) that are thus analogous to the way mechanisms and interval-mapping spatial devices such as a clockface (fail to) represent time; whereas the "time-image" directly represents time by accessing the relations between the actual and virtual as they play themselves out across the non-chronological sheets of the variations on A-B:

> what would enter into relation would be the real and the imaginary, the physical and the mental, the objective and the subjective, description and narration, *the actual and the virtual*. . . . The essential point, in any event, is that the two related terms differ in nature, and yet

"run after each other," refer to each other, reflect each other, without it being possible to say which is first, and tend *ultimately* to become confused by slipping into the same point of indiscernibility. A zone of recollections, dreams, or thoughts corresponds to a particular aspect of the thing: each time it is a plane or a circuit, so that the thing passes through an infinite number of planes or circuits that corresponds to its own "layers" or its aspects. A different, virtual mental image would correspond to a different description, and vice versa: a different circuit.[11]

This notion of indiscernibility is key to Deleuze's reworking of Bergson, for it prioritizes what in a sense is a "failure" of OA in Figure 1, a failure to match perception in space with the memory-image that would grant identity and meaning. Deleuze's notion of the "crystal-image" makes visible the workings—and splittings—of (non-chronological) time by rendering indiscernible what is "real" or "imagined/remembered." We are not therefore dealing with memory-images or even dream-images that are in some ways either "useful" to a consciousness or that the latter endows with a fleeting, even capricious significance: crystal-images have nothing to do with flashbacks or dream sequences in film, which are conducted from a clear notion of a "present" "real" and even inform our understanding of it. The crystal-image represents a to-ing and fro-ing between the dilation that is the vast archive of the past, and the tiniest circuit of exchange between the present moment and its virtual image:

> Just as we perceive things in the place where they are, and have to place ourselves among things in order to perceive them, we go to look for recollection in the place where it is, we have to place ourselves with a leap into the past in general, into these purely virtual images which have been constantly preserved through time.... The crystal-image has these two aspects: internal limit of all the relative circuits, but also outer-most, variable and reshapable envelope, at the edges of the world, beyond even [movements] of world. (*The Time-Image*, 78)

Deleuze therefore provides a distinct perspective on the question of multidirectional memory. Before returning to Demy and further cinematic examples, let us pause to consider three ways in which Deleuze's theory might account for certain manifestations of multidi-

---

11. Gilles Deleuze, *Cinema 2: The Time-Image*, trans. Hugh Tomlinson and Robert Galeta (London: Continuum Books, 2005), 44.

rectional memory, how it might challenge this notion, and how it might itself be challenged:

- The past is out there, in the same way, effectively, as is the whole of space ("The virtual image [pure recollection] is not a psychological state or a consciousness: it exists outside of consciousness, in time, and we should have no more difficulty in admitting the virtual insistence of pure recollections in time than we do for the actual existence of non-perceived objects in space") (*The Time-Image*, 77–78). Despite the liberal appropriations of (an early) Bergson, duration and subjectivity are outside us, not inside us: "Time is not the interior in us, but just the opposite, the interior in which we are, in which we move, live and change" (*The Time-Image*, 80). These formulations emphasize the interconnectedness of memories, all memories, within a world memory (*mémoire-monde*): in Bergsonian theory, it makes no sense to talk of interiority and exteriority. The question of what mechanisms decide what circuits of the virtual archive are accessed and by whom, for what ends, and in what contexts, is here suspended as far as the molar level is concerned (for example, in the public sphere of French national narrative-building). At the molecular level, however, there is clearly an urgency to investigate the connection between memory and history.

- The past is non-chronological. Time travel science fiction usually makes the mistake of presenting time and the past as a river, or a tunnel, into which we can jump at selected points: 1066, 1789, the sinking of the Titanic, last year.[12] Alain Resnais's *Je t'aime je t'aime* (1968) gives the lie to this approach, as its protagonist, the subject of a time travel experiment, finds himself trapped and jumping about in non-linear, non-chronological time. In addition, the present itself is split between a present that passes and is conserved, the ever moving point that is the present moment, and the future. These formulations lend themselves to an enriching of the practices of individual (always to be understood as social) and collective memory to be found in acts of creation, multidirectionality pushed as far as chronological reversals and unexpected juxtapositions: "the relation between present and past can be contemporaneous, opposed, or layered as contiguous strata in any combina-

---

12. I say this despite some attempt in recent *Doctor Who* stories to present something more complex: see Damian Sutton and David Martin-Jones, *Deleuze Reframed* (London: I.B.Tauris, 2008), especially Chapter 6, "Time (and) Travel in Television," 107–121.

tion."[13] Again, the question is posed: what of agency and praxis, or rather what relationship between creative practice or reading of this kind and the wider public sphere?

- Non-chronology is closely linked to indiscernibility. But here I would wish to emphasize the micro-circuit of exchange in the crystal-image between the point of the present and its virtual shadow as it falls back into, and is conserved, in the past, along with the whole of memory, history, and beyond. This micro-circuit is what Deleuze describes as "The little crystalline seed and the vast crystallizable universe: everything is included in the capacity for expansion of the collection [*ensemble*] constituted by the seed and the universe" (*The Time-Image*, 78). In this article we are definitely in the domain of the molecular, but that grain or seed is eloquent of vaster circuits of historical or other meaning.

These ideas thus shed fresh light on the works of both Demy and the apparently non-cinematic but, following Bruno, proto-cinematic text by Pieyre de Mandiargues. In the depths of the passage, in the aquatic lairs that are the *coiffeur*'s or TV shop, or in the domain of the monstrous, a minimal circuit of exchange is happening, in which the contraction of the present, the point of the present, is the place from which the virtual sheets of the past are being accessed. What is more, the musical element of the films—the dialogue of both *Les parapluies de Cherbourg* and *Une chambre en ville* is entirely sung, *Lola* was originally conceived as a musical—means that the characters, and the world of the film, are swept along in a generalized movement, generating "pure" optic and sound situations which for Deleuze represent an enhanced attentiveness:

> We find both levels: on one hand sensory-motor situations defined by the city, its classes, the relations, actions and passions of the characters. But, in another way, and at a deeper level, the city merges with what provides the set in it, Pommeraye passage; and the sung action becomes a movement of city and classes, where the characters pass without recognizing each other, or on the contrary find each other, take up opposite positions, unite, stir each other up [*se brassent*] and separate in a purely optical and sound situation which traces an implied dream about them, "charmed circle," or real "enchantment." (*The Time-Image*, 64–65)

13. D.N. Rodowick, *Gilles Deleuze's Time Machine* (Durham, NC: Duke University Press, 1997), 100.

DELEUZE AND RESNAIS

For our purposes, within Deleuze's pantheon of "time-image" directors, it is the cinema of Alain Resnais that provides the most interesting examples of a multidirectional memory that embraces a crystalline attitude to non-chronological time while engaging profoundly with questions of memory and politics across different individual film texts: *Nuit et brouillard* (1955; the Holocaust); *Hiroshima mon amour* (1959; the atomic bomb and Occupied France); *Muriel, ou le temps d'un retour* (1963; the Algerian War and World War II); *La guerre est finie* (1966; the Spanish Civil War). To these could be added the Deleuzian themes to be found in the musical films *On connaît la chanson* (1997) and *Pas sur la bouche* (2003); the simultaneous possible and contingent worlds of *Smoking* and *No Smoking* (1993); even the fantasy sequences of *Providence* (1977), in which the images of prisoners rounded up in a stadium, so derided by the author-narrator Clive Langham (John Gielgud) as a "de rigueur fear symbol," speak of the actualization of sheets of the past associated both with the Vel d'hiv in Paris, where Jews were infamously gathered in July 1942, and the more recent Chilean coup d'état of September 1973.

Within this *oeuvre*, I would like to concentrate on *Stavisky . . .* (1974), a work relatively underestimated by Deleuze and other commentators. In this film, the theme of anti-Semitism is to the fore, and, apart from the period theatrical adaptations *Mélo* (1986) and *Pas sur la bouche* (2003), it is the only film by Resnais that is set in a historical past: a "costume drama" or "heritage movie," but with a very distinct flavor. Deleuze wrote of its "strangeness" (*The Time-Image*, 121), in that the film, unlike other works by Resnais, might be seen to construct a "fixed point" from which memory-images are accessed, rather than an indiscernibility between the actual and the virtual.

Stavisky . . . (some commentators forget the suspension points, but they crucially connote the undecidability about identity and truth in the film) recounts, over a central six-month period between July 1933 and January 1934, the final events in the life of Serge Alexandre, alias Stavisky (Jean-Paul Belmondo), a flamboyant Jewish swindler and impresario. The collapse of his financial empire, which was based on lies and fraudulent bonds, implicated a whole political class, brought down a left-of-center republican government, and provoked bloody riots in Paris on 6 February 1934 which heralded the further rise of the far Right and fascist *Ligues*, as well as the ultimately short-lived republican defense represented by the Popular Front. Discussion of the film forms part of Naomi Greene's project of emphasizing the importance of Resnais's *oeuvre* for an understanding of the vexed questions of *national French* memory in the wake of the Occupation and the Algerian War. Dudley Andrew and Steven Ungar have written of the "multiple perspectives and temporalities of the film,"[14] its "harmonics of historiography" (22), and, hinting at a Deleuzian vocabulary, its approach to the "archive" of the past: "The protean Stavisky . . . becomes for Resnais a marvelous magnet attracting disparate fragments from various archives" (39). Indeed, for Bergson and Deleuze metaphors of magnetism and attraction, rather than hydraulics of displacement and repression, are among the ways in which the relationship between the "sheets of the past" in the vast archive of "pure memory" (*souvenir pur*), and the "memory-image" that is then consciously or unconsciously—in dream, reverie, imagination—actualized, can be understood (*The Time-Image*, 118–19).

The sequence in *Stavisky . . .* that introduces the main character encapsulates Resnais's two favorite procedures for exploring memory, and here they function in a very "multidirectional" way. The first is the tracking shot, which here moves vertically down the facade of the Claridge Hotel in Paris. There is a whole intertextuality to the use of the tracking shot in Resnais's films, including of course the shots of present-day Auschwitz in *Nuit et brouillard,* and of the endless rows of books in the documentary about the Bibliothèque nationale, *Toute la mémoire du monde* (1956). The tracking shot is never about "a" memory, it is not a "memory-image" plucked from the non-chronological virtual archive of the past; rather, it is an exploration of the processes of thought and consciousness which source that archive. It explores mental landscapes, creating continua as well as fragmentation, strata, and warps. Resnais's second technique is that of rapid, seemingly unmotivated—what Deleuze terms "irrational"—cuts between Stavisky's actions and the arrival of the exiled Trotsky in the south of France. (Resnais's film *Muriel* also provides striking examples of this technique.) The two techniques—tracking shot and rapid cut—come together in the first appearance of Stavisky himself as he descends with his assistant in a cylindrical glass lift cabin. Indeed, this early sequence is saturated with "crystalline" images such as this, in-

---

14. Dudley Andrew and Steven Ungar, *Popular Front Paris and the Poetics of Culture* (Cambridge, MA: Harvard University Press, 2005), 16.

cluding chandeliers and revolving doors, as well as that of Baron Raoul's (Charles Boyer) visit to Biarritz; later, the glass cabin of Stavisky's office, the close-ups of precious gems, and a proliferation of mirrors will generate similar connotations and functions. On one level, the descent in the lift or the multiplication of images of Stavisky/Belmondo as he emerges from a mirror-lined bathroom, can be read as a comment on the (literally) superficial image-making involved in the confidence tricks, media culture, and empty capital and exchange value associated with his activities. But the relation of these bizarre entrances/ emergences to time and memory, as we have seen, is that Stavisky is seen to emerge, not just from some celebrity, god-like "elsewhere," but from an "else-when": he emerges from the past (just as the very first shot of the film positions the camera so that the motor car carrying Trotsky's assistants approaches/emerges from an empty road), and this emergence is presented in all its crystalline complexity. Indeed, he emerges from the dead, as further illustrated by the *réplique* about ghosts from Giraudoux's *Intermezzo* he offers to the German Jewish refugee actor Erna Wolfgang (Silvia Badescu) auditioning at his "Théâtre de l'Empire." Deleuze explains in a section of *The Time-Image* how memory is a membrane, connecting the "dedans"/"inside" of the past that is "always already there" with the "dehors"/"outside" that is "always to come," of the present layers of reality of the world. It is death that forms the absolute horizon of both these polarities. The "Lazarean" hero in Resnais is here linked to a post-concentration camp aesthetic:

> He passed through a clinical death, he was born from an apparent death, he returns from the dead. Auschwitz or Hiroshima, Guernica or the Algerian War.... beyond all the sheets of memory, there is this lapping [*clapotement*] which stirs them, this death from the inside which forms an absolute, and from which he who has been able to escape it is reborn. (*The Time-Image*, 200)

In *Stavisky*..., that death "from the inside" is framed by the "death from the outside," which is Stavisky's suicide (or murder).

The question that may be asked, however, is what is the "fixed point" that the film constructs? At one level, Stavisky's death in January 1934 (the "death from the outside") is the point around which the other time frames coalesce: the events of the second half of 1933, the parliamentary enquiry in April 1934 that occupies a greater and greater place as the film progresses, but also Stavisky's arrest in 1926, and also, potentially, as we shall see, his childhood. However, for whom, situated when, do these characters emerge from the past? April 1934 is just one more position on a sheet of time in the archive of the past. In a "normal" costume or heritage movie, what Homi Bhabha calls the enunciative gap between the pedagogical (the—national—past as origin) and the performative (the present as the constant elaboration of the national narrative)[15] is often drawn toward a (never complete) closure by the knowledge the audience has of an intervening event. Examples of the latter include the French Revolution and its "modern" aftermath for *Ridicule* (Patrice Leconte, 1990), or the sexual freedoms of the 1960s, and, to an extent, the feminism of the 1970s that *would have enabled* a "modern" heterosexual couple to form and endure, as in, say, *Titanic* (James Cameron, 1996). A stitching of the gap between past and present thus occurs. In *Stavisky . . .* , no such position is possible, for several reasons. Most simply, in 1974 a consensual historical memory of the previous forty years in France has certainly not coalesced, despite the hegemonic efforts of Gaullism. (The year of course marks a pinnacle of polarization in French politics, with the extremely close results of the Giscard/Mitterrand presidential race.) More importantly, the "intervening event" is that of catastrophe, not least Vichy, Occupation, and the Holocaust: Andrew and Ungar describe the 1941 exhibition "The Jew and France" organized by the Institut d'Études des Questions Juives, which drew 200,000 spectators and which included a photo of Stavisky in the section on scandals and the universal participation of Jews in them.[16] But the lack of a "fixed point" is not only about an unresolved national past, for the film goes well beyond the national in its depiction of Trotsky, and of course in the role of the Francophone Spanish scriptwriter Jorge Semprún (whose first and third novels, *Le grand voyage* of 1963 and *La deuxième mort de Ramón Mercader* of 1969, discuss respectively the Holocaust and the death of Trotsky). *Stavisky . . .* is also about a *mémoire-monde*.

PYRAMIDS

The workings of this "world memory," and the crisis of the "fixed point," can be explored via the most mysterious image in the film,

---

15. Homi Bhabha, "DissemiNation: Time, Narrative, and the Margins of the Modern Nation," in *Nation and Narration*, ed. Bhabha (London: Routledge, 1990), 291–322.
16. *Popular Front Paris*, 44.

that of a pyramid structure found in the parc Monceau in Paris. Its first appearance occurs 23 minutes into the film, when Stavisky's psychiatrist (Michel Lonsdale), in seeking to "explain" his friend, declares, "we must imagine his dreams," and even "dream of him." There is a cut to classic Resnais tracking shots of the parc Monceau lake, the Lycée Condorcet where Stavisky studied, and the facades of the seventeenth arrondissement where he grew up. A forward tracking shot approaches the pyramid, and then there is a cut to a woman in shadow—who *emerges* into the foreground—whom the psychiatrist believes to be Stavisky's sexual initiator. Stavisky himself then bursts in and declares, "but not at all." The second occurrence is after Stavisky's death, when similar shots of the pyramid accompany Baron Raoul's voiceover discussion of Stavisky's secrets to which his now imprisoned wife (Anny Duperey) may be privy, and how his death is that of "our epoch" and indeed announces all our deaths.

The pyramid in the parc Monceau was constructed, along with the rest of the park, between 1769 and 1773 under the orders of Philippe d'Orléans, duc de Chartres, who was also a freemason, holding the title of Grand Master. The freemasons believed that their origins lay in the construction of the pyramids in Egypt. Resnais exploits the infinite connotations of the image: a (possible) memory-image of Stavisky's childhood that is sought, and seen to be sought, by the tracking shot, on a sheet of the past; death (both "from the inside" and "from the outside"); differently embedded layers, constructions, and juxtapositions of the past, which are exemplified by the bizarre and extraordinary park itself, which also contains, for example, a bust of Chopin, and is heavily marked by the upheavals of both the Revolution and Haussmannization. It is possible to go further: coincidentally, André Pieyre de Mandiargues chooses the pyramid for another fantastic tale in the *Musée noir* collection, "L'homme du parc Monceau," in which a man with the power to elongate his body enters the edifice and is led through a trap-door through depths marked by exotic, orientalist, phallic, and vaginal imagery into some kind of extraordinary sexual union.[17]

The pyramid in *Stavisky . . .* can thus be compared with the sled

17. *Musée noir*, 105–125. Without pushing the multidirectional theme outlandishly far, it is nonetheless transversally suggestive—and we are here in the domain of connotation rather than denotation—that enslaved Jews contributed to the building of the pyramids. See Paul Gilroy's discussion of Edward Wilmot Blyden as a Caribbean man confronting the Pyramids: *The Black Atlantic*, 208–211.

"Rosebud" in *Citizen Kane* (Orson Welles, 1941) (a film that bears many resemblances to Resnais's cinema), but with the difference that it is not a "fixed point," and it therefore *fails* to explain anything about the eponymous protagonist, moreover opening up a crisis of chronology and discernibility. The pyramid, a crystal one at that, was the image used by Leibniz in his *Theodicy* (1710) to illustrate the *hierarchy* of "incompossible" (compatible + impossible, unable to exist if the other exists) worlds that culminates in the apex that is the best of all possible:

> The halls rose in a pyramid, becoming even more beautiful as one mounted towards the apex, and representing more beautiful worlds. Finally they reached the highest one which completed the pyramid, and which was the most beautiful of all: for the pyramid had a beginning, but one could not see its end; it had an apex, but no base; it went on increasing to infinity. That is (as the Goddess explained) because amongst an endless number of possible worlds there is the best of all, else would God not have determined to create any; but there is not any one which has not also less perfect worlds below it: that is why the pyramid goes on descending to infinity.[18]

In *The Time-Image*, Deleuze adapts this model, superimposing it however on Bergson's cone and on Borges's famous notion of the labyrinth as found in the short story "The Garden of Forking Paths" (1941): "This is Borges's reply to Leibniz: the straight line as force of time, as labyrinth of time, is also the line which forks and keeps on forking, passing through *incompossible presents*, returning to *not-necessarily true pasts*" (*The Time-Image*, 127). This idea—suggesting what we would now call parallel universes—has been extensively developed in relation to national identity and cinema by David Martin-Jones:

> Each bifurcation of the pathway through the labyrinth leads to two "incompossible presents," two possible, and possibly contradictory outcomes to any one situation. However, in the labyrinth this is not a paradox, as the potential for both outcomes always exists virtually, and both are always both played out (albeit in different parallel universes), in their respective actual manifestations. Moreover, the past becomes "not-necessarily true" for at least one outcome, thereby destroying the notion of a single, linear time. Rather than a direct causal chain of devel-

---

18. G.W. Leibniz, *Theodicy: Essays on the Goodness of God, the Freedom of Man and the Origin of Evil*, trans. E.M. Huggard: http://www.gutenberg.org/etext/17147, released 2005.

opment there is the emergence, with each fork in the path of labyrinthine time, of multiple virtual pasts. These fluctuate in and out of existence depending upon how they are realigned in the present.[19]

We have here a clue to what Deleuzian film theory might bring to a politics of multidirectional memory, including its relation to French national narratives. Laura U. Marks has noted how Walter Benjamin criticized Bergson's denial of the historical determination of his own philosophy, which was a reaction after all to "the inhospitable, blinding age of big-scale industrialism."[20] She argues that Deleuze's notion of the time-image needs Benjamin's notion of ritual, of "the association of images with history, of individual with community experience," to form part of the "shock" that peels away accretions of habit and official memory "to create a flow of experience": this she finds in examples of "hybrid" cinema.[21] On the other hand, Benjamin's emphasis on death, or the fact that his angel of history turns its back to the future as it gazes on the historical catastrophe piling up,[22] seems as apparently devoid of a notion of historical praxis as Deleuze's theory.

The relationship between Deleuze (and Guattari's) notions of the molecular and the molar is often, if not usually, elusive. But this discussion of the time-image and of a profoundly historical film such as *Stavisky...* demonstrates three possibly invigorating ways forward for textual study of multidirectional memory, and they are not without cultural-political import. The first is the Nietzschean take on Bergson: the eternal return means that it is difference that returns rather than the same; the archive of the past contains undecidable alternatives, the present forks into a multiplicity of possible worlds. The *mémoire-monde* of *Stavisky...* contains all the possible pasts and futures, as hinted at rather simplistically by Trotsky's admirer (if no Stavisky scandal, no fall of the Third Republic, no expulsion of Trotsky from France, etc.), so, paradoxically for a film set in the past, the future is seen to be open. As David Rodowick puts it, "The direct image of time presents the inventiveness of time: the possibility of

---

19. David Martin-Jones, *Deleuze, Cinema and National Identity: Narrative Time in National Contexts* (Edinburgh: Edinburgh University Press, 2006), 24.
20. Walter Benjamin, "On Some Motifs in Baudelaire," in *Illuminations*, trans. Harry Zohn (London: Fontana, 1970), 159.
21. Laura U. Marks, "A Deleuzian Politics of Hybrid Cinema," *Screen* 35/3 (Autumn 1994), 244–64 (258).
22. "Theses on the Philosophy of History," in *Illuminations*, 259–60.

the appearance of the new and unforeseen, a possibility renewed at each moment of time."[23] *Stavisky* . . . beautifully captures this forking path with a shot through a car's back window as lingering but increasingly separated gazes are exchanged between Stavisky, the would-be indiscernible and assimilationist Jew, and Erna, the anti-Nazi militant Jew who is now part of Trotsky's circle. Secondly, another Nietzschean emphasis proclaims "the powers of the false," in that the splitting of time puts truth in crisis; this is not an easy relativism, but a challenge to truth claims based on fixed and finished ideas of the nation, and of history. (Here the figure of Stavisky as the *faussaire* or con man is crucial.) And thirdly, the time-image forces a reinvigoration of Bergson's "attentive" (as opposed to habitual or clichéd) "recollection" and "recognition" so that, far from the zero-sum "addition of distinct objects on the same plane" that characterizes everyday perception of people or objects we "know" and that are prolonged in action because we retain "from the thing only what interests us," we may envisage a form of perception that creates new circuits and connections of memory. The contortions and short circuits found, for example, in our initial examination of the Passage Pommeraye and its representations, in the curling tongs in Demy or the cattle truck in Pieyre de Mandiargues, which connote both the Holocaust and the slave trade/colonialism, are illustrations of this attentive perception, by artist and reader/spectator, at work. This is the melding interplay of mental and physical cartographies and landscapes so fundamental to Bergson and Deleuze: "successive planes and independent circuits, cancelling each other out, contradicting each other, joining up with each other, forking, will simultaneously constitute the layers of one and the same physical reality, and the levels of one and the same mental reality, memory or spirit" (*The Time-Image*, 42–44). These interplays emphasize the unfixed and unfinished potential of French identities, and instead invoke a France, or Frances, to come.

---

23. *Deleuze's Time Machine*, 128.

LIBBY SAXTON

Horror by Analogy: Paradigmatic Aesthetics in Nicolas Klotz and Elisabeth Perceval's *La question humaine*

Nicolas Klotz and Elisabeth Perceval's singularly unsettling film *La question humaine* (2007) provocatively indicts neoliberal capitalism through analogy with National Socialism. The controversy the film ignited among sections of its international audience centered on its linking of multinational corporations and industrial genocide. *La question humaine* was accused of relativizing the horrors of Nazism by comparing it with capitalism. The cinema historian and critic Ariel Schweitzer warns of this danger in a letter to Klotz: "In my view, capitalism is not Nazism and, in thus relating them, we miss what capitalism really is and, worse still, we risk banalizing Nazism."[1] Less attention has been paid to the further analogies drawn between the death camps and other sites of racially inflected and biopolitical violence that are glimpsed, albeit fleetingly, on the screen. The memory of the genocide of the Jews becomes intertwined in sound and image with recollections of other state attempts to dominate or reshape populations, ranging from European colonialism, to Hitler's euthanasia program and Himmler's *Lebensborn* project, to the persecution of postcolonial immigrant minorities in France and Franco-British practices of border surveillance. In plotting links between these phenomena, *La question humaine* challenges the entrenched popular perception of the Nazi genocide as an incomparable event, disconnected from the rest of modern history. The film consciously intervenes in debates about the perils of downplaying, or "universalizing," the unique features of the Holocaust and the legitimacy of comparative perspectives.

---

1. Ariel Schweitzer cited in Antoine de Baecque, "L'histoire qui revient: la forme cinématographique de l'histoire dans *Caché* et *La question humaine*," *Annales. Histoire, sciences sociales* 63/6 (December 2008): 1293.

YFS 118/119, *Noeuds de mémoire*, ed. Rothberg, Sanyal, and Silverman, © 2010 by Yale University.

This article argues that the multiple analogies proposed in *La question humaine* serve not to destroy, but to provoke reflection on historical specificity, as much as on continuity. The allegation that the film trivializes the Holocaust overlooks the disjunctions foregrounded by its intricate palimpsestic structure and conveniently closes down the discomfiting questions it poses to the present. What do the disparate forms of violence referenced in the film have in common and what distinguishes them? How can we acknowledge the singularity of one without displacing the memory of others? And what aesthetic forms can express their interconnectedness without lapsing into reductive equations? *La question humaine* engages in dialogue with a range of leftist philosophical, sociological, and historical studies of modernity, totalitarianism, and genocide.[2] One of the innovative aspects of the film, I want to suggest, is that it juxtaposes three divergent conceptions of the camp—as death factory, as quasi-colonial enclave, and as biopolitical space where power encounters pure life—each of which marks its specificity differently.

La question humaine is the third film in a trilogy directed by Klotz and written by Perceval which aims to expose the hidden violence of neoliberal economic policies. These policies deprive the protagonists of *Paria* (2000) and *La blessure* (2004) of homes or asylum from violence overseas. Borrowing a title and a plot from a novel by François Emmanuel (2000), *La question humaine* shifts from the margins to the center and peers beneath the antiseptic veneer of the corporate world, while cross-referencing the histories of exclusion chronicled in *Paria* and, especially, in *La blessure*. All three films work to counteract the dehumanizing effects of capitalist ideology and dominant modes of representation both by rendering mechanisms of marginalization visible and by troubling conventional cinematic grammar. What makes the third distinctive is its aesthetic of layering or superimposition which fosters interaction between present and past without erasing their distinctions.

2. The production archives for the film include copies of the following texts: Zygmunt Bauman, *Modernity and the Holocaust* (Cambridge: Polity, 1989); Philippe Lacoue-Labarthe and Jean-Luc Nancy, *Le mythe nazi* (La Tour d'Aigues: Éditions de l'Aube, 1991); Lacoue-Labarthe, *La fiction du politique: Heidegger, l'art et la politique* (Paris: Christian Bourgois, 1988); Giorgio Agamben, *Remnants of Auschwitz: The Witness and the Archive*, trans. Daniel Heller-Roazen (New York: Zone Books, 1999); Alain Brossat, *L'épreuve du désastre: le XXe siècle et les camps* (Paris: Albin Michel, 1996); Enzo Traverso, *The Origins of Nazi Violence*, trans. Janet Lloyd (New York; London: The New Press, 2003).

Klotz asserts that his aim in *La question humaine* was to "film the word without being imprisoned by a meaning"—to film its "verticality."[3] What Klotz calls "verticality," or polyvalence, is a property not only of the dialogue and the written texts that infiltrate the narrative, but also, I would suggest, of the film's visuals, in which the contours of the present trigger memories of past horrors. Patrick ffrench has coined the term "paradigmatic montage" to describe the propensity of still images of imprisonment, destruction, and death in Chris Marker's *La jetée* (1962) to "remember" both real and imagined images of historical events. ffrench explains: "the *montage* of *La jetée* is effected not only syntagmatically, in terms of the horizontal sequence of images, but also paradigmatically, in terms of their imagined superimposition on a vertical level on images of the historical real."[4] In this account, "montage" retains its generic meaning of "assembly" and signifies a process not of editing but of *mise-en-scène*, through which images of post-apocalyptic Paris in *La jetée*, for example, may "recall" scenes of devastation at Hiroshima. In *La question humaine*, a film more conspicuously preoccupied with the legitimacy of transhistorical comparisons, "horizontal" or syntagmatic motion is recurrently interrupted by "vertical" or paradigmatic projections and echoes across time and space. This aesthetic of imaginary superimposition, I argue, brings analogies to light while troubling any straightforward logic of equivalence by foregrounding paradigmatic relations marked by contrast and difference.

THE FACTORY AND THE CAMP

Reviewers have tended to approach *La question humaine* as a paranoid corporate thriller, which casts its central protagonist and narrator, Simon Kessler (Mathieu Amalric), in the role of corporate superego. A psychologist employed in the Paris branch of a multinational corporation named SC Farb, Kessler has been co-implicated in a round of redundancies as author of a refined set of "selection criteria." Charged by associate director Karl Rose (Jean-Pierre Kalfon) with the delicate task of reporting on the increasingly erratic actions of CEO

---

3. Nicolas Klotz in Emmanuel Burdeau, "Magie noire," *Cahiers du cinéma* 623 (May 2007): 20. Translations from French are my own, except where published translations are cited.
4. Patrick ffrench, "The Memory of the Image in Chris Marker's *La jetée*," *French Studies* LIX/1 (January 2005): 36.

Mathias Jüst (Michael Lonsdale), Kessler sets out to investigate his boss's behaviour but ends up examining his own. *La question humaine* combines thriller trappings with motifs borrowed from the horror movie and the German literary genre known as *Väterliteratur* ("literature of the fathers," accounts narrated from the perspective of children of Holocaust perpetrators), including bloodstained fathers, lost children, and mental illness.[5] In spite of these affiliations with narrative genres, however, the syntagmatic unfolding of the plot is disrupted by sounds and images that draw attention to the paradigmatic axis of meaning.

The dialogue and *mise-en-scène* are scattered with references to Nazism which coalesce around the memory of the mass murder of the Jews. Kessler discovers anonymous letters that attempt to implicate Jüst's abusive father, Theodor, a member of a police battalion involved in massacres of Jews in Poland and Byelorussia, in the development of genocidal technology. The first letter contains a facsimile of one of the most notorious documents to have survived the Nazis' endeavor to conceal their attempt to destroy the Jews. Dated 5 June 1942, marked "top secret" and signed "Jüst," the report makes recommendations for improving the efficiency of gas vans following trials at Chelmno, the Nazis' first extermination camp. Historians have seen this memorandum as epitomizing the harmless-sounding code devised by the Nazis to camouflage mass murder.[6] What the author neglects to mention is that the *Ladung* (cargo) or *Stücke* (pieces) to be *verarbeitet* (processed) are human beings. Paradigmatic relations are foregrounded as the document's ostensibly innocuous bureaucratic jargon evokes in the viewer's imagination the horrors it disavows. In subsequent letters, fragments of present-day technical memoranda are superimposed over the report to create palimpsestic formations that place Nazi and neoliberal euphemisms in relationships of substitutability. Via code words such as "restructuring," "selection," "specialist," and "modification," the seemingly neutral technical phraseology of Kessler's nar-

---

5. See Erin McGlothlin, *Second-Generation Holocaust Literature: Legacies of Survival and Perpetration* (Woodbridge: Camden House, 2006) for analysis of the *Väterliteratur* genre.
6. Eugen Kogon, Hermann Langbein, and Adalbert Rückerl describe the report as "couched in an extreme form of Nazi double-talk, a monstrously inhuman language" in *Nazi Mass Murder: A Documentary History of the Use of Poison Gas*, ed. Kogon, Langbein, and Rückerl, trans. Mary Scott and Caroline Lloyd-Morris (New Haven: Yale University Press, 1993), 55.

ration gradually becomes charged with judeocidal connotations. As if to confirm these suspicions, "SC Farb" is reminiscent of "IG Farben," the chemical manufacturing conglomerate infamous for its role in operations at Auschwitz.

The paradigmatic *rapprochement* of capitalism and Nazism is accomplished not only through language games but also through historically charged iconography. Just as, in the anonymous letters, one text infiltrates and contaminates another, so too, in the *mise-en-scène*, separate images appear to have been superimposed over each other. Klotz and Perceval transpose what Kessler, in Emmanuel's novel, calls the letter-writer's "montage" into a cinematic register.[7] Images of contemporary industrial and bureaucratic spaces are awash with motifs that call to mind the distinctively modern architecture, technology, and administration of the "Final Solution." The narrative is punctuated by protracted long shots of factory chimneys spewing smoke. Summoning memories of the opening sequence of Michelangelo Antonioni's *Il deserto rosso* (*Red Desert*, 1964), a painterly montage of foggy, polluted views of an industrial plant in Ravenna, these self-consciously generic images emblematize the ambivalence of modernity: the mutual co-implication of civilization and barbarity, production and destruction, the factory and the camp. This emblematic function is amplified in a shot of a column of smoke that excludes the smokestack from the frame, removing its subject from a recognizable historical and geographical context. Other images strengthen the association between the premises of SC Farb and the camp. Billowing day and night from Kessler's nostrils, smoke also permeates interior spaces, and ashtrays are one of the few props that decorate the offices. For the *Cinéaste* reviewer, the film's grey-blue tint evokes "the Prussian blue residue of the Nazis' Zyklon B gas."[8] An overhead shot of a scientific laboratory cements this bond with the chemistry of genocide.

The specific lexicon and image repertoire discussed thus far suggest that *La question humaine* buys into a well-rehearsed account of the Holocaust that identifies its roots in industrial capitalism, modern forms of science, technology and bureaucracy, and the culture of instrumental reason. One of the most influential proponents of this view of the Holocaust is Zygmunt Bauman, whose sociological study *Modernity and the Holocaust* (1989) has recently been described as "a

---

7. François Emmanuel, *La question humaine* (Paris: Stock, 2000), 61.
8. Megan Ratner, "Heartbeat Detector," *Cinéaste* 33/3 (Summer 2008): 56.

type of conscious theoretical subtext of *La question humaine*."⁹ Bauman's book aims to demolish the still prevalent assumption that the extermination camps constituted an aberration, malfunction, or antithesis of modern civilization by showing how its constitutive features—its rationality, technology, and habit of "divesting the use and deployment of violence from moral calculus"—made the Holocaust possible.¹⁰ This analysis would seem to foreshadow the anonymous letters in *La question humaine*. In highlighting affinities between the jargon used to administer the "Final Solution" and the redundancies at SC Farb, these collages echo Bauman's critique of modern bureaucracy's propensity to dehumanize its objects. Similarly, the genocidal resonances of the images of factories appear to converge with the sociologist's view of the extermination camp as an assembly line for the mass production of corpses.

As we shall see, however, *La question humaine* negotiates the problem of the historical specificity of the Holocaust differently from Bauman. Bauman attempts to pre-empt the charge that his reasoning distorts this specificity by arguing that the "Final Solution" is simultaneously unique and normal: "it stands unique against the quotidianity of modern society because it brings together some ordinary factors of modernity which are normally kept apart" (Bauman, 94). On the one hand, the film marks the event's singularity more forcefully than Bauman by alluding to an influential conception of the genocide as uniquely resistant to representation. On the other, while a Baumanian reading illuminates the analogy between the factory and the camp, it cannot account for other imaginary on-screen superimpositions that point to alternative views of historical continuity and disjunction. Although Bauman touches briefly on the connections between the Nazis' exercise in "social engineering" and quasi-scientific theories about the inferiority of African races, he devotes more attention to the specific features of anti-Semitism (69). Furthermore, he draws a clear distinction between postcolonial manifestations of heterophobia and the kind of racism that leads to "the Holocaust-like organized crime" (81). *La question humaine* probes the limits of Bauman's account by exploring both the representability of the Holocaust and its capacity to render other histories of persecution audible and visible in the public sphere.

9. De Baecque, "L'histoire qui revient," 1290.
10. Bauman, *Modernity and the Holocaust*, 28.

THE CAMP AND THE COLONY

Shortly before the meeting between Kessler and Rose that provides the catalyst for the main plot-line, a brief close-up of an African mask intrudes into the narrative. Rather than elucidating the significance of this artefact, the next shot shows Kessler in the waiting room outside Rose's office. Since there is no action in this shot, our attention is directed to the décor. In contrast to the visual motifs discussed above, the interior design aesthetic of the bureaucratic spaces in SC Farb connotes historical amnesia.[11] The management suites are decorated in minimalist and functional style; bare walls in a range of textures and sombre tones feature prominently, while windows are blinded, diffusing the daylight, and glass doors lead merely to other, similar rooms. The only ornamental prop in the waiting room is a vase of ivory lilies, which, as we watch, is replaced by an assistant with a fresher vase, as if to disavow the blooms' transience. In the subsequent shot, however, Kessler and Rose appear seated in the latter's office beneath a row of masks that stands out against the pared-down décor. During the characters' second rendezvous later in the film, Kessler is out of focus in the foreground, while the artworks appear in sharp definition in the background, grazed by Rose's pacing shadow. Parts of these conversations are captured in shot/counter-shots, which frame Rose in turn with a mask and a bouquet of lilies.

The composition and editing of these shots thus compels reflection on the significance of the sculptures, which simultaneously draw our attention and disrupt our perception by troubling the distinction between figure and ground. Most obviously, they exacerbate our suspicion that the main protagonists, Kessler included, are each engaged in forms of masquerade. Even though Kessler eventually "unmasks" the anonymous collagist, an employee of SC Farb who was sacked when the branch was downsized, we learn that "Arie" Neumann (Lou Castel) has changed his first name, so that doubts remain about his identity. Looking beyond this literal interpretation of the masks' meanings to their cultural connotations, Antoine de Baecque views them as materializations of the occult energies that infuse the film: "The work is bewitched by a spell, a curse, like one of Jacques Tourneur's films, in particular *Cat People* or *I Walked with a Zombie*,

---

11. This effect of dehistoricization is achieved by the collaborative efforts of production designer Antoine Platteau and cinematographer Josée Deshaies.

films that are haunted by obscure forces."[12] Klotz rewatched Tourneur's *Night of the Demon* (1957) and Fritz Lang's *Dr Mabuse, der Spieler* (*Dr Mabuse, the Gambler*, 1922) (along with films by Charlie Chaplin, Jean-Luc Godard, and Philippe Garrel) in preparation for making *La question humaine*.[13] Tourneur's influence may be felt in Klotz's use of light, shadow, and darkness to evoke a threat that remains unseen. The generic affinity with horror is reinforced by the casting of Edith Scob, an actress best known for her role as the mask-wearing Christine Génessier in Georges Franju's *Les yeux sans visage* (1960), as Jüst's wife Lucy. By means of these cinephilic allusions to the fantastic and paranormal, *La question humaine* taps into the mythology of Nazi occultism that has been promulgated in popular culture since the 1940s.[14] But it also reminds us that speculation about the mystical roots of Nazism may distract from analysis of its political origins. I would suggest that the masks might also call to French minds a film in which horror is glimpsed through historical consciousness rather than a response to the supernatural. In Alain Resnais's and Marker's short documentary *Les statues meurent aussi* (1953), images of masks and other African artworks are overlaid with a commentary by Marker lamenting the damaging consequences of the West's acquisition of African cultural artefacts and, by implication, of colonialism. In this light, Rose's sculptures may be seen as heralding the return of the histories of racialized violence repressed by neoliberal ideology. Reduced to exotic wallpaper, they remind us that the rise of industrial capitalism in Europe went hand in hand with the pillaging of Africa.

Moreover, Rose's taste for African art opens up a new historical perspective on the Nazi genocide within the film. Jüst alleges to Kessler that the associate director was one of the *Lebensborn* children bred and stolen on Himmler's orders from occupied territories in the East to create a "master race" of Nordic appearance. Although this insinuation is never confirmed, the connection established by the *mise-en-scène* between Rose, the masks, and the white lilies, a flower historically associated in Western art with the purity of the Virgin Mary, functions as an *aide-mémoire* that both Nazi eugenics and European

12. De Baecque, "L'histoire qui revient," 1298.
13. See Klotz, "Ne pas perdre la parole: spectres contre spectres (2)," *Lignes* 26 (May 2008).
14. For discussion of this, mythology see Nicholas Goodrick-Clarke, *The Occult Roots of Nazism: The Ariosophists of Austria and Germany 1890–1935* (Wellingborough: Acquarian, 1985).

imperialism appealed to "scientific" theories of biological racism. This reminder is reinforced by the visual rhyme between Rose's masks and the classical Greek bust in Jüst's office, the only other piece of sculpture in the film. Both appear fleetingly in the background of dialogue scenes but are prioritized by shot composition (during one exchange, the bust is positioned center frame and glimpsed through the gap between Jüst's and Kessler's bodies in the foreground). In *Le mythe nazi* (1991), an essay read by Klotz during the pre-production phase, Philippe Lacoue-Labarthe and Jean-Luc Nancy analyze the exemplary status accorded to the ancient Greeks in Nazi self-mythologization. Yet whereas these authors emphasize the specificity of National Socialism, the film's pairing of the bust with the masks reminds us that the colonial "civilizing mission" also found succor in idealized classical aesthetics. These disembodied heads imply a continuity between the sites of colonial massacres and the Nazi camps as twin crime scenes of modern Europe's "civilizing" adventures.

The thesis that the seeds of Nazi violence were planted in the "fertile soil" of African colonial possessions is advanced in *The Origins of Totalitarianism* (1951) by Hannah Arendt.[15] In a chapter particularly pertinent to Klotz and Perceval's critique of administrative procedures, Arendt identifies bureaucracy and racism as twin principles of foreign domination (185–221). Arendt's argument is taken up by Enzo Traverso in *The Origins of Nazi Violence,* one of the film's source texts, which shows how Nazi anti-Semitism was rooted in "a theory and practice of the extermination of 'inferior races' to which all the imperial Western powers subscribed."[16] A reading of *La question humaine* that takes its cue from Traverso, then, might cast Rose, the rumoured *Lebensborn* child, as a neocolonial administrator. Under the gaze of the African masks, the Nazi camp is momentarily transformed in memory from a Fordist production line into a site of colonial conquest. As inconspicuous background details, the masks hint at analogies between the colony and the camp without eliding their differences. Such an interpretation, however, cannot account for a third set of superimpositions presented in the film, which extrapolate beyond the genealogies traced by Arendt and Traverso to capture reflections of what Klotz calls the Shoah's "fossil light" in postcolonial encounters.[17]

15. Hannah Arendt, *The Origins of Totalitarianism* (London: André Deutsch, 1986), 206.
16. Traverso, *The Origins of Nazi Violence,* 54.
17. Klotz in Burdeau, "Magie noire," 21.

THE EXTERMINATION SITE AND THE SPACE OF EXCEPTION

Halfway through the film, in a scene that might have been excerpted from *La blessure*, we witness police marching into a café and forcefully extracting and searching men from Paris's ethnic minority communities. This is one of numerous digressive sequences that interrupt the forward motion of Kessler's investigation and are suspended uncertainly between present and past, reality and dream, memory and hallucination. Kessler's appearance at the end of the scene, snatching a sideways glance as he hurries past the raid, provides only a contingent link to the main plot. Filmed at close range with an unsteady handheld camera, the images possess a documentary-style intimacy that dissociates them from the fiction and obviates the need for narrative justification. Rather, they signify paradigmatically by tapping into memories of other police raids on the streets of Paris. The scene may cue recollections of the brutal round-ups of FLN supporters during the Franco-Algerian war. This association is strengthened by the thematic parallels between *La question humaine* and *Caché* (Michael Haneke, 2005), a film that refers to the massacre of October 17, 1961. Michael Rothberg has charted how perceptions of this incident have been shaped by memories of Vichy.[18] In keeping with this multidirectional logic, the café sequence also taps into memories of the roundups of Jewish citizens during the Nazi Occupation, a connection fortified by its reprisal of words and images associated elsewhere in the film with Judeocide. The *gendarmes*' tactics resonate with references to the "selection criteria" developed by Kessler to evaluate employee performance. In addition, the enforced line-up against the shopfronts rhymes with the testimony of a witness to a massacre of Jews in Miedzyrzec, recounted to Kessler third-hand via Jüst and his secretary and former lover, Lynn Sanderson (Valérie Dréville). Recognizing Jüst's father as one of the executioners a decade after the war, the witness remembers seeing women and children lying by a cemetery wall. Just after Kessler reads out the memorandum from 1942, we hear this mediated memory rephrased again in the lyrics of one of the dissonant, melancholy musical pieces composed by Syd Matters for the soundtrack: "all the kids against the wall."

This association between state-sponsored violence against post-

---

18. Michael Rothberg, *Multidirectional Memory: Remembering the Holocaust in the Age of Decolonization* (Stanford: Stanford University Press, 2009), 227–308.

colonial immigrant groups and against the Jews is consolidated when a second historical document invades the diegesis. Pacing his apartment, Kessler tries to decipher a letter from Neumann in which sentences from a corporate psychology manual are infiltrated by others from an unidentified source, producing a palimpsestic formation that implicitly accuses him of fascism. In the next shot he sits facing away from the camera, while his voice provides continuity across the cut, leading the viewer initially to infer that he is still reading the letter. Instead, we hear an extract from a newspaper report applauding the efficiency of new electronic security technologies designed to stem illegal immigration by detecting breathing and heartbeats inside heavy-goods vehicles. Contamination across the cut between the article and the letter attunes our ear to chilling echoes of the 1942 memorandum. References to lorries, carbon dioxide.and life-detecting devices evoke the architecture and technology of industrial genocide. Similarly, the reduction of human beings variously to mere statistics ("230 have been arrested"), inanimate objects ("undesirable elements"), or biological functions ("breathing," "heartbeats") is reminiscent of the linguistic tactics of the Nazi report.

Even De Baecque, who is politically sympathetic to the *"critical memory* of the Shoah" constructed by *La question humaine*, remarks that its cross-references to the persecution of immigrant minorities are "questionable."[19] However, the densely-layered intertextual resonances of this scene point to an internal incoherency in the film rather than a crass logic of equation. In an interview, Perceval explains that the newspaper text was based on an actual article published in 2006 in *Le Figaro* to which she was alerted by a reference in Eric Hazan's *LQR: la propagande du quotidien* (2006).[20] An *exposé* of the domesticating and controlling function of the degraded language of neo-liberalism, Hazan's text plays on the title of Viktor Klemperer's *LTI* (1947). Klemperer observes that the *Lingua Tertii Imperii* (Language of the Third Reich) was a "breeding-ground" for Nazi thought processes and notes, in a multidirectional move, the colonial resonances of National Socialist terms such as *Strafexpedition* (punitive expedition).[21] Other (inter)texts are brought to mind by the second

19. De Baecque, "L'histoire qui revient," 1292.
20. Elisabeth Perceval in "Entretien avec Nicolas Klotz et Elisabeth Perceval," Press kit: *Quinzaine des realisateurs/Directors' Fortnight* (Cannes, 2007): 7.
21. Viktor Klemperer, *The Language of the Third Reich: LTI, Lingua Tertii Imperii: A Philologist's Notebook*, trans. Martin Brady (London: Athlone, 2000), 2, 39.

security device mentioned in the report. It seems apt that the film's English-language title, *Heartbeat Detector*, privileges a glancing allusion to surveillance practices in which the British state is named as complicit. The "heartbeat detector" recalls Jean-Luc Nancy's autobiographical account of a heart transplant in *L'intrus* (2000), which draws an implicit analogy between the intrusion of a foreign body into his own and the circulation of people among social "bodies." The primary inspiration for *La blessure* (as well as Claire Denis's short film *Vers Nancy* (2002) and feature-length *L'intrus* (2004)), Nancy's text also foreshadows *La question humaine*'s exploration of racialized language in drawing attention to the bio-scientific metaphors that permeate discussions of foreignness.

A footnote toward the end of *L'intrus* acknowledges Nancy's debt to Giorgio Agamben's thinking on the relationship between *bios* and *zoe*, pointing to another analysis of politics and the body whose influence is felt in *La question humaine*.[22] While Klotz and Perceval's production archives contain a copy of *Remnants of Auschwitz* (1999), the discussion of the "sacred man" in the first volume of Agamben's trilogy is more pertinent to the film's paradigmatic association of technologies of immigration control and extermination. In *Homo sacer* (1995), Agamben argues that Michel Foucault's discussion of biopolitics and Arendt's analysis of totalitarian power may be seen to converge when viewed through the "focal lens" of the concept of "bare life."[23] Charting the entry of biological life into the juridico-political order of the nation-state, Agamben proposes that the possibility of bare life is opened up by the state of exception, which is materialized in the camp, where prisoners were stripped of all rights and life and law "enter into a threshold of indistinction" (174). In Agamben's account, the camp, as "the pure, absolute, and impassable biopolitical space," replaces the city as "the hidden paradigm of the political space of modernity, whose metamorphoses and disguises we will have to learn to recognize" (123). Among the apparently harmless spaces that replicate the juridico-political structure of the camp, Agamben lists the "*zones d'attentes* in French international airports in which foreigners asking for refugee status are detained" (174).

22. Jean-Luc Nancy, *L'intrus* (Paris: Galilée, 2000), 43.
23. Giorgio Agamben, *Homo Sacer: Sovereign Power and Bare Life*, trans. Daniel Heller-Roazen (Stanford: Stanford University Press, 1995), 120.

It might be tempting to trace a straight line from *Homo sacer* to *La blessure*, which depicts the brutal treatment of a group of asylum seekers in the limbo spaces of Roissy airport. A close look at *La question humaine*, however, reveals an interrogative, as opposed to straightforwardly illustrative, stance toward Agamben's argument. Several aspects of the film are indeed susceptible to an Agambenian reading. As a machine that enables state power quite literally to penetrate the body, the "heartbeat detector" would seem to emblematize the inclusion of biological life in the political realm and perhaps to constitute the ultimate biopolitical weapon. Furthermore, in hinting at parallels between this device and the gas van, the film appears to support Agamben's claim that the "spaces of exception" inhabited by refugees should be recognized as camps. Regarding the film as a whole, the emphasis placed on embodied sensory experience and its regulation in a series of scenes involving music and dance (features of the film to which I do not have space to do justice here) further compels a biopolitical analysis. Such a perspective is at odds, however, with the film's repertoire of Holocaust-related imagery and vocabulary, which revolves around the act of genocide. In connecting the machinery of extermination and border-policing, the film points to a fundamental disjunction between the topographies of the Holocaust mapped out by Bauman in *Modernity and the Holocaust* and by Agamben in *Homo sacer*. Whereas Bauman's subject is the manufacture of death, Agamben's is the production of (bare) life. While Agamben mentions Auschwitz and the extermination process, his argument is focused on the legal and political structures that govern life prior to death in the "no-man's land" of the camp (the "most extreme figure" of which is the so-called *Muselmann*) (Agamben, 159; 184). This is surely why Agamben makes no allusion to Chelmno, the location of the trials detailed in the 1942 memorandum, or to the Operation Reinhard camps at Belzec, Sobibor, and Treblinka, where most prisoners were marched straight to their deaths. In *La question humaine*, then, the implicit association of the gas van and the "heartbeat detector"—the sites of extermination and exception —does not add up to a coherent political vision. Rather, this imaginary superimposition holds competing views of the camp and its paradigmatic function and figure in tension with each other, thereby implicating the spectator in the analytical thought process initiated, but not completed, by the film.

FROM UNICITY TO SPECIFICITY

The privileged position accorded in *La question humaine* to the secret report from 1942 places it in conscious dialogue with *Shoah* (1985), a film made by one of the most forceful advocates of the notion that the Holocaust is unique and that its meanings cannot be exhausted by a historical account. Claude Lanzmann writes: "Between the conditions that permitted extermination and the extermination itself—the *fact* of the extermination—there is a break in continuity, a hiatus, an abyss."[24] As Lanzmann reads out Jüst's memorandum in a sequence shot in the *Ruhrgebiet* and located exactly in the middle of *Shoah*, the camera zooms in on a brand name embossed on a travelling lorry: "Saurer," the van manufacturer mentioned in the report. Lanzmann's hunt for traces of the genocide in the industrial landscapes of the present thus provides supporting documentary evidence for the analogy between Nazism and capitalism formulated in fictional terms by Klotz and Perceval. Like *Shoah*, *La question humaine* avoids a relativizing conflation of past and present by withholding direct images of the genocide. Significantly, the only sequence that appears to reconstruct the Nazi era, featuring women sorting clothes, armed guards, and barking dogs, is retrospectively revealed to be a fragment of one of Kessler's nightmares. This aligns the film with an important intellectual and aesthetic tradition that views the Holocaust as unsusceptible to representation. In both *Shoah* and *La question humaine*, the Chelmno gas vans are located at the core of a program of genocide that cannot be visualized directly.

However, whereas *Shoah* is exclusively concerned with the Judeocide, *La question humaine* reminds us that the gas van's ancestry can be retraced to the secret program of euthanasia sanctioned by Hitler in 1939, when it was developed to put to death those said to be incurably sick. Perceval's screenplay omits the explicit references in Emmanuel's novel to "Tiergarten-4," the Nazi code name for the euthanasia program. Nevertheless, Kessler's voice introduces the 1942 report over a prolonged shot of the façade of a psychiatric hospital where he visits Jüst. Nurses tend to patients and scrub a veranda in one of several representations in the film of processes of bodily care and cleaning. This seemingly innocuous imagery is ambivalent and

---

24. Claude Lanzmann, "From the Holocaust to 'Holocaust,'" in *Claude Lanzmann's* Shoah: *Key Essays*, ed. Stuart Liebman (Oxford; New York: Oxford University Press, 2007), 34.

multidirectional; it evokes the corrupted ethics of care for the health of the *Volkskörper* (racial corpus) and the associated corporeal metaphors (disease, cure, hygiene, purification) that underpinned not only Hitler's anti-Semitism but also his support for euthanasia. The film's preoccupation with illness, bloodlines, and notions of heredity implicitly connects the fate of the Jews with others who fell into the juridical category of *lebensunwertes Leben* (life "unworthy of being lived," or bereft of value, an expression borrowed by the Nazis, as Agamben reminds us, from a pamphlet from 1920 advocating euthanasia).[25] So while *La question humaine* pays homage to Lanzmann's achievement in *Shoah*, its allusions to the concept of *lebensunwertes Leben* and to colonial and postcolonial violence question the legitimacy of bracketing the Judeocide as (in John Llewelyn's words) a "uniquely unique *sui generis* rupture."[26] In layering the document from 1942 over images of a medical establishment, however, the film simultaneously reiterates its distance from Agamben's account of the camp as the "hidden matrix" of modern politics, which is more hospitable to comparative approaches (Agamben, 166). For Agamben, the Nazis' anti-Semitic legislation can only be grasped in the wider context of the laws concerning the category of *lebensunwertes Leben*; it is this broad category that "corresponds to the bare life of the *homo sacer*" (139). While acknowledging the origins of the genocide in the euthanasia program, *La question humaine* marks the distinctions between the two more clearly than Agamben by using a report on the "Final Solution" as its narrative lynchpin.

The main aim of this article has been to show that the chains of paradigmatic associations constructed in *La question humaine* do not relativize the singularity of the Nazi genocide but foster dynamic, mutually transformative interactions between separate histories. Klotz and Perceval's vertical montage reminds us that the paradigmatic axis of meaning is governed by a logic not of homogenization but of substitution and differentiation. The film's silence about whether or not Kessler himself is Jewish (a question answered in Emmanuel's novel) is symptomatic of its refusal to conflate the experiences of the Jews with those of other minority groups. While influenced by seminal theoretical writings on the camps, the film also holds ideas that elude its in-

---

25. See Agamben, *Homo Sacer*, 136–43, for discussion of this expression.
26. John Llewelyn, "sELection," in *Postmodernism and the Holocaust*, ed. Alan Milchman and Alan Rosenberg (Amsterdam: Rodopi, 1998), 201.

tertexts. To Bauman and Traverso it poses questions about the postcolonial resonances of the Holocaust; to Agamben it enquires about the relationship between the dead and the "living dead" and the biopolitical features of colonialism. By juxtaposing these thinkers' distinctive views of the camp without synthesizing them into a totalizing perspective of its own, the film prompts us to reconsider what was singular about the genocide and suggests that its specificity can only be grasped when it is viewed in the context of the rest of modern history.

The closing sequence of the film reiterates its dual concern with analogy and difference. A performance by Neumann's string quartet reminds Kessler of a scene from his nightmare about the Quatuor Farb, the company ensemble that Kessler has used as a pretext for approaching Jüst and that recalls the orchestras of prisoner-musicians compelled to play in the camps. As the dream unfolds, narrated by Kessler in voice-over, the screen turns black. Kessler now paints a verbal portrait of a "black mass of entangled corpses" that juxtaposes euphemisms from the 1942 memorandum with the words they avoid: "urine, vomit, blood, sweat, saliva, *Flüssigkeit* [liquid], . . . all these bodies, *Stücke* [pieces], rolling on top of each other. . . ." Perceval has explained that this monologue was informed by her reading of testimonies of members of the Auschwitz *Sonderkommandos*, units of mainly Jewish prisoners who were forced to work in the gas chambers and crematoria.[27] The film's reluctance to visualize this scene also implies awareness of discussions among Lanzmann, Jean-Luc Godard, and Georges Didi-Huberman about the value of real and hypothetical Nazi-era images of the gas chambers and cremation pits.[28] But as Kessler recites the names of the dead, Perceval inserts new first names into the list of Jewish ones in Emmanuel's novel, including Robert (Antelme), Armand (Gatti) and Miguel (de Unamuno or Hernández). Layered over a dark screen that acknowledges the intangibility of its horror, this palimpsestic litany encapsulates the film's attempt to articulate the specificity of the genocide of the Jews not in conflict, but through dialogue, with other histories of political violence.

---

27. Private conversation between Elisabeth Perceval and the author (March 2008).
28. For an overview of these debates, see chapter 2, "The Missing Reel and the Unimaged Real: Godard/Lanzmann," in my *Haunted Images: Film, Ethics, Testimony and the Holocaust* (London: Wallflower, 2008), 46–67.

MAX SILVERMAN

Memory Traces: Patrick Chamoiseau and Rodolphe Hammadi's *Guyane: Traces-mémoires du bagne*

The short collaborative work *Guyane: Traces-mémoires du bagne* (hereafter *Guyane*) by the Martinican writer Patrick Chamoiseau and the German-Algerian photographer Rodolphe Hammadi opens with a commentary on the way in which the History and Memory of colonialism (with their capital letters) are written by the colonizers. Monuments and documents testify to the victors' point of view. But, asks Chamoiseau, how might one write things differently, so that the histories and memories (with their small letters) that official narratives have erased can be heard?

Produced as part of a series of photo-texts for the *Caisse nationale des monuments historiques et des sites* documenting France's major heritage sites, this slight book on the French penal colony in French Guiana (founded in 1852 for the transportation and imprisonment of French convicts and political prisoners and eventually closed in 1946)[1] is not only a critical response to the official writing of history but also a riposte to the republican story of national memory recounted in Pierre Nora's vast project *Les lieux de mémoire*.[2] Chamoiseau explicitly replaces "lieux de mémoire" with the notion of "traces-mémoires" or memory-traces (16).[3] Citing his Martinican compatriot

---

1. The penal colony consisted of the three islands known as the Île du Salut off the coast of French Guiana (Île Royale, Île Saint-Joseph, and the most famous Île du diable, or Devil's Island) and the mainland town of Korou. It was known as one of the most notorious prison camps in the world because of its harsh and disease-infested conditions. For a fuller discussion of the colony in one of the few articles devoted solely to *Guyane*, see Andy Stafford, "Patrick Chamoiseau and Rodolphe Hammadi in the penal colony. Photo-text and memory-traces," *Postcolonial Studies* 11/1 (2008), 27–38.
2. Pierre Nora, *Les lieux de mémoire* (Paris: Gallimard. 3 volumes: 1984, 1986, 1992).
3. Patrick Chamoiseau and Rodolphe Hammadi, *Guyane: Traces-mémoires du bagne* (Paris : Caisse nationale des monuments historiques et des sites, 1994). All trans-

Édouard Glissant on writing an alternative history "from below" (15), Chamoiseau defines the scope of his project with Hammadi as follows:

> In the Americas of the plantations (be it in Guiana, in the foothills of the continental plate, or the arc of the Antilles), to visualize the trajectories of the diverse peoples who found themselves there, we must reinvent the notion of the monument and deconstruct the notion of heritage. Beneath the written History of colonialism, we must find the trace of histories. Beneath the haughty Memory of forts and edifices, we must find the unfamiliar places where the lives of these collectivities took shape. (15)

Hence, from the opening of the text, Europe is related to the Americas, and the victim populations of Guiana are related to other victim populations of colonial rule—"Amerindians, slaves, Africans, Hindus, immigrants from Syria, Lebanon, China . . . " (13). Chamoiseau also draws on his own origins as a native of Martinique, and on its colonial history. Yet the challenge to monolinear, "monumental" national history not only opens up forgotten channels between metropolitan France and colonized peoples, but also among different sites of transportation, imprisonment, and dehumanization. Through text and image, Chamoiseau and Hammadi transform the narrowly-circumscribed surface of the ruins of the penal colony into a complex network of echoes and reverberations across space and time.

THE SHAPES AND SOUNDS OF THE MEMORY-TRACE

What poetics of text and image do Chamoiseau and Hammadi employ in *Guyane* to convert the linear and monovalent narrative of the monument into the hybrid and multivalent vision of the memory-trace? Ruins testify to the impermanence rather than to the fixity of place, to the discontinuities rather than to the linearity of time. They are, by their very nature, a sign of transformation and transience. Similar to but different from the buildings they once were, ruins are always haunted by a past; they are present but also bear witness to an absence. In the here and now but in the process of sinking into oblivion, they inhabit an in-between state, between past and present, presence and absence, visibility and invisibility. In this sense, ruins are uncanny:

---

lations from the text are my own. Page references will appear as numbers in parentheses in the text.

still recognizable though freed from the constraints of familiarity and use-value because of the ravages of time, they are strange and unknowable.[4] The bars, bolts, nails, locks, doors and walls which were once functional now "transform into new meanings" (37). Hence, "the *Trace-mémoires* is born from the erosion and chaotic destruction of buildings, materials and meanings" (42).[5] In surrealist fashion, defamiliarized objects become a kaleidoscope of color, shape, shade, and sound whose fluidity shatters the spatio-temporal constraints of the present of the penal colony.

The ruins therefore already inhabit a spatio-temporal no-man's land between here and there, now and then, the familiar and the unfamiliar.[6] Ruins allow the echoes of the memory-trace to reverberate from the fixity of the monument: "The Memory-Traces of the penal colony are broken, diffuse, scattered. We cannot approach them in the way we would approach the facade of a Cistercian abbey or a romanesque church" (21–22). Geometrical design partakes of the rigidity of the monument, and of the monolinearity of Western narrative (22), while the strange shapes of the ruins occupy a hinterland between coherence and chaos:

> everything comes back to elementary forms and the resonances of
> these elementary forms: squares, circles, triangles, straight and

---

4. In her excellent book on memory in Chamoiseau's work, Maeve McCusker suggests that hidden places of memory have this ghostly quality throughout his writings: "These places have a peculiarly spectral and uncanny quality in Chamoiseau's work, at once familiar and unfamiliar, representing what Freud would describe as that which 'ought to remain hidden but which has come to light.'" Maeve McCusker, *Patrick Chamoiseau: Recovering Memory* (Liverpool: Liverpool University Press, 2007), 103. See also 142–149 for a more detailed discussion of the uncanny in Chamoiseau's work.

5. Chamoiseau switches between different terms for the memory-traces, sometimes putting "trace" and "memory" in the singular, sometimes in the plural. However, his preferred usage is to mix singular and plural, upper and lower-case. In this instance, for example, "trace" is singular and with upper-case "T" while "memory" is plural with lower-case "m." I will keep the French for this particular usage and will discuss its significance in the final section of the essay.

6. Dylan Trigg affirms the spatio-temporal ambiguities of the ruins in his phenomenological study of memory and the sites of trauma: "At the outset, we discover that the ruin is both polymorphous and temporally dynamic. That is, unlike the 'felicitous' space that characterizes Bachelard's domestic enclosure, allowing time and space to coincide as unitary phenomenon, the formal features of the ruin are situated in an ambiguous zone, whereby what remains is defined by what is absent. With this ambiguity, the identity of place loses its certainty.... Instead of monumentalizing what remains, the ruin brings about a non-memory, a puncturing in spatio-temporal presence." Dylan Trigg, "The Place of Trauma: Memory, Hauntings, and the Temporality of Ruins," *Memory Studies* 2/1 (2009): 95.

curved lines, trapeziums, and their infinite connections. The functional rubs shoulders with the abstract, the familiar with the unfamiliar, immediate sense with hidden meanings. This is a primeval broth, a chaotic harmony whose only constant remains the emotion of the memory of the penal colony. The wear and tear born from abandonment ties together [noue] this assemblage according to the imperceptible—yet sovereign—aesthetic of an interior necessity. (41–42)

The aesthetic principle at work in "the resonances" of "elementary forms" is a dynamic tension between shape and meaning. The memory-trace is a "noeud de mémoire" because of its capacity to trigger diverse memories and connect disparate detail.[7]

Hammadi's photos are part of the same (fundamentally modernist) aesthetic construction of the memory-trace. Oblique angles, odd juxtapositions between foregrounds and backgrounds disturbing perspective, views framed in such a way that the object of perception dissolves into a play of shape and shading, blur the clarity of distinction between "different" spaces, volumes, and shapes, and splinter the meaning of the image. Here, as in the passage above, the aesthetic of the memory-trace is fundamentally one of deconstruction and reconstruction founded on the loosening of old connections and the creation of new ones ("The wear and tear born from abandonment ties together [noue] this assemblage according to the imperceptible—yet sovereign—aesthetic of an interior necessity."] "Knotting" is indeed Chamoiseau's metaphor of choice to describe the aesthetic device of making connections between disparate objects—"moss connects everything" ("la mousse *noue* le tout") (25); "knotted ironwork" ("un *noeud* de feraille") (27); "The walls have knotted ancient pacts with enormous roots" ("Les murs ont *noué* de vieux pactes avec d'énormes racines") (39) (see also 24, 31, 37)—while Hammadi's photos similarly transform the site into a series of abstract "assemblages" of shape, line, and color.

By transforming the ruins into knots of meaning, text and image connect the material remains with the human forms that once inhabited this site:

> Flesh knows how to erode stone. At Saint-Laurent, or on the islands, you have to see the signs of erosion. These broken or curved

---

7. Chamoiseau has often defined the notion of memory-traces elsewhere (see for example, *Ecrire en pays dominé*, Paris: Gallimard, 1997). McCusker discusses his use of "trace" and "traceé" in relation to memory in *Patrick Chamoiseau: Recovering Memory* (chapter 4, "Memory materialized: traces of the past," 101–127).

steps, the darkness more pronounced around openings, this particular patina that bears witness to an everyday gesture. Flesh has become a sculptor and a painter. The rubbing (the encounter) between man and stone, man and iron, was subtle. We must look at the rounded corners, assess the ferocity of these gates still intact and on which who knows how many bodies were shattered. On the paths, we have to imagine this rectilinear center that seems to remember the disciplined trudge of silent and anxious prisoners. (32)

The memory-trace is thus formed from the connections made (or imagined) between the shapes and sounds of the ruins and the inmates, and also between the visitors to the site (writer, photographer, and the readers and viewers of their work) and the lives of others before them. In the photos, we are invited to imagine the ruins haunted by humanity, the visible haunted by the invisible, to create a play of presence and absence. In the text, the associations between different linguistic fields (the human and the material) create the same in-between state: "the skin of the walls" (37), "the iron cried" (38), "Sometimes, prosthetic limbs of ironwork are embedded in the living skin of the walls" (41).

Chamoiseau and Hammadi dissolve the fixed meanings of word and image in the same way that the ruins have transformed the shape, stature and design of the original buildings. The transformation of the fixed monument into the memory-trace is therefore the poetic transformation of word and image into the echoes, resonances, and reverberations of memory:

> *Transportation camp.* It is written above. Camp. Transportation. In silhouette behind these terms are rules, statutes, an order of suffering, a track leading to death or breaking-point. What does it matter what they mean. The two coupled words are like carved inscriptions. This is not a naming, rather a flicker of memories. (25)

> Doors that are no longer doors, hinges unsure of their identity, windows that breathe, walls that enclose nothing, ironwork suddenly rendered strange ... We must forget these words and find others. All these apparent meanings are suddenly thrown into an anxious state, primary meanings disaggregated, a sort of unraveling of signification incited by the wandering nature of my advance and my spirit. I am open to sensation. (44)

Chamoiseau calls on artists of all sorts to bring the memory-traces to life and travel beyond the frontiers of entrenched meaning (44). This is, then, a poetic journey among the ruins of the penal colony. Echoes and evocations are provoked by the resonances established in the encounter with the deserted ruins of the camp, writer and photographer broaching their subject not through the tourist gaze but with the sensibility of the wandering poet: "And here I am among the memory-Traces of the penal colony of Guiana, not as a visitor but as a wanderer, not as a *flâneur* but as one who digresses" (43). The Baudelairean spirit guiding this "wandering'" and "digression" is key to conjuring up other worlds, so that the bland surface of the present opens out on a kaleidoscopic canvas of space-time superimposition that Chamoiseau calls "sedimented memories" (25). As Chamoiseau says in the last lines of the text "Here, the conservationist will belong to the tribe of poets. And conservation will be a poetics" (45).[8]

CAMPS AND COLONIES

The poetic evocation of "sedimented memories" in *Guyane* suggests that the memory-trace is an over-determined site in which the singularity of the moment is invaded by the complex layering of history. Although Chamoiseau warns of the dangers of historical writing as such—"It would be better not to write the history of the penal colony but to attempt, instead, to apprehend the murmurs of the memory-Traces" (23–24)—history returns in the murmurs of the memory-traces themselves. But this history is not the singular, monolinear and reductive History (with the capital 'H'), bolstered by its monuments (as the opening of the book has forewarned), but pluralized and hybridized by the memory-traces. The resonances of the past in the present—"the resonances come from everywhere, from the color, the matter, the stone, the iron, the shade, the flashes of light" (42)—are the raw material of the poet-cum-historian, that is, he or she who knows how to evoke the sound, the color, and the shapes of the memory-trace within which real history lies, in the sense of a Benjaminian constellation.[9] (Jean-Luc Godard's description of his own method in *His-*

---

8. The influence of Baudelaire is particularly evident in Chamoiseau's depiction of the ambiguous position of the poet, caught between preservation and the ravages of time, sifting the "confused bric-a-brac" for traces of those exiled and crushed by history (*Le cygne*).

9. "It is not that what is past casts its light on what is present, or what is present its light on what is past; rather, image is that wherein what has been comes together in a flash with the now to form a constellation." Walter Benjamin, *The Arcades Project*, ed. Rolf Tiedemann, trans. Howard Eiland and Kevin McLaughlin (Cambridge, Mass.: Belknap Press of Harvard University Press, 1999), 463.

toire(s) du cinéma is strikingly similar to that employed by Chamoiseau and Hammadi here: "with words/sounds/stones and colors/so that the space constructed might last/beyond time.")[10]

The aesthetic structure of the memory-trace, whose meanings are "constantly evolving, with diverse ramifications" (17), is therefore a condensation, or palimpsestic sedimentation, of other historical moments of transportation, imprisonment and dehumanization:

> But today's memory-Traces not only bear witness to the history of the penal-colony.... They have accumulated, over time, indefinable memories. They have associated long, moss-grown sighs with the vitality of the forest which today seems to knot them into a jewel-case. The building becomes ruin and the ruin becomes open-memories according to a spontaneous movement produced by an invisible accumulation. (23–24)

This "invisible accumulation" is the result of layers of superimposed resonances and evocations, rather like the language of a symbolist poem. It is true (as we have seen) that Chamoiseau links the inmates of the penal colony with other victims of oppression and will also compare the lives of the inmates with those of slaves in Louisiana (39). But these direct references to other times and places are rare. Instead, echoes, evocations, doublings, and hauntings of other spaces and times are triggered by the similarities between different moments arising from the (Proustian) encounter with the deserted ruins of the penal colony.

The treatment of Alfred Dreyfus on Devil's Island is indicative of this approach. The first two of Hammadi's photos are of the cell in which Dreyfus was imprisoned at the turn of the twentieth century for treason (47–49), and the final photo is of a tower known as the "tour Dreyfus" (114). But there is no mention of Dreyfus in the text, the most famous prisoner ever to be held on Devil's Island. His presence, and with it the history of anti-Semitism, is evoked rather than mentioned explicitly so that the ghost of one form of racialized violence overlaps with that of others in this space, a shadow of the past ("shadow" is a word that recurs throughout the text and is an integral part of the image-constellations) mingling with the other shadows formed by the crumbling buildings.

However, it is the echoes of other camps of horror that have also left their mark on the material remains of certain sites that are evoked

---

10. Jean-Luc Godard, *Histoire(s) du cinéma* (Paris: Gallimard, 1998), 177.

most vividly by the memory-traces of the penal colony: "These buildings were places of imprisonment, spaces of security, camps in the woods, artisans' workshops, sheds, ovens, animal parks, hospitals, administrative services" (18); "Camp. Transportation . . . an order of suffering, a track leading to death" (25). These references to transportation, tracks leading to death, camps and ovens (and the bizarre assortment of everyday objects and activities and those connected with horror referred to above) inevitably (and palimpsestically) overlay this space and time with the memory of the Nazi concentrationary universe half a century earlier. The "wandering" journey undertaken by writer and photographer in the remains of the penal colony in French Guiana, and the exploration of traces of memory in this site, cannot but recall the two major explorations of sites of horrific racialized violence in postwar French culture, Alain Resnais's *Night and Fog* (1955) and Claude Lanzmann's *Shoah* (1985).

It is Resnais's film (made in collaboration with the poet Jean Cayrol, who wrote the narrated text, and Hans Eissler, who wrote the musical score) that is so vividly recalled by Chamoiseau and Hammadi in *Guyane*. So, for example, the description of "the stale smell of sour soup" (27) echoes the image of an inmate sipping a weak broth in *Night and Fog* that is accompanied by the comment "the soup was diuretic"; "lime or coal-fired ovens" (28) recall the Nazi ovens for the incineration of bodies; the "nails which clawed the walls" (28) echo the description by Cayrol at Auschwitz of a "ceiling furrowed by nails"; "a mad grass stubbornly sprouting from the stone" (32) echoes Cayrol's description of "a strange grass (that) has grown up and covered the ground" or, at the end of *Night and Fog*, the description of "the faithful grass [that] has returned on the parade ground around the blocks."[11] The prisoners of the penal-colony are described by Chamoiseau as follows: "the burning fever of their look. As if the last energy of the will to live had attached itself to the fragile freedom of their eyes." And, to remove any doubt about the reference being made, he adds "We have already seen this in other camps of despair" (30), conjuring up the image in *Night and Fog* of an inmate at Auschwitz staring out from his bunk, another of inmates looking out wide-eyed across the barbed wire, and the narrator's comment that "Finally, all the prisoners resemble each other. They align themselves on the time-

---

11. Jean Cayrol, *Nuit et brouillard: Commentaire* (Paris: Fayard, 1997), 27, 38, 18 and 42 respectively.

less model of dying with open eyes."[12] Other descriptions will similarly evoke the Nazi concentrationary universe—"a haggard-looking mass, numbered, pouring out in confused ranks in their striped uniform—the whole of humanity dehumanized" (31); "The numbers are confused with drawings, with scratches, with the blackened moss: they cover the skin of the wall with a worrying tattoo. No man's name, no address: simply numbers" (35); "night in the barracks" (37), "the fearful night" (40)—so that memories of French penitentiary practice, French colonialism, and the Nazi camps are overlaid to create an image-constellation of meaning.

The repetition of the marching of boots recorded by Chamoiseau— "I hear the regular step of boots" (29), "this rectilinear center that seems to remember the disciplined trudge of silent and anxious prisoners" (32)—not only recalls the same image in *Night and Fog* but also evokes, in a similar way, the Benjaminian "double ground" or superimposition of different times provoked by the tread (both sound and trace) of feet.[13] Yet, as Chamoiseau notes, repetition and difference are always in an anxious relationship: "When we retrace our steps, meanings are not the same, lights and shades are modified, other details appear, other points are highlighted, other smells and other sensations arise from the colors; everything is alive and stimulates the spirit" (42). Chamoiseau's following image of footsteps in the present captures perfectly the complex, knotted, and delicate relationship between the different elements involved in the memory-trace, and especially between recall, preservation, and effacement: "And the tread is so loud that the steps, their middle caved in for a long time, seem to give way once more under the hesitating foot" (41). Hence, although walking now on the same earth that was trodden by the prisoners in the past ("And the ground bears witness to them: the earth, the stone, the cement have been friends to hordes of wrecked humanity," 36), in the same way that the film crew's footsteps retrace the steps of the inmates at Auschwitz-Birkenau in *Night and Fog*, the relationship between past and present, and us and them, occupies a space between sameness and difference. Just as *Night and Fog* refers allegorically to another site of racialized violence (the Algerian war of independence), but without collapsing one scene of horror into the other, so the mem-

12. Ibid, 33.
13. "In the asphalt over which (the flâneur) passes, his steps awaken a surprising resonance. The gaslight that streams down on the paving stones throws an equivocal light on this double ground." Walter Benjamin, *The Arcades Project*, 416.

ory-traces of the penal colony establish an uncanny space of repetition and difference, connecting but not collapsing the two concentrationary systems of French Guiana and Nazi Germany.

Hammadi's photos also recall distinctive features of Resnais's film in the portrayal of the camp. A majority of the images are shot through window-frames, ironwork, barred doors, open doors and other framings (47, 52, 55, 58–59, 63, 65, 73, 84, 87–89, 108–109) to create a tension between inside the buildings of the camp and the lush vegetation of the outside world. One's eye is held between the here and now of the camp and the light and shade, colors and shapes of elsewhere. The classic opening of *Night and Fog* plays precisely on shifting perspectives across the barbed wire at Auschwitz and a tension between the camp and the surrounding countryside, horror and the everyday.[14] In other photos, it is not the tension in perspective between here and there, inside and outside that disturbs our vision but, on the contrary, no perspective at all so that proximity to the object makes us lose any purchase on what it is. The interior of dilapidated cells is simply an intertwining of wood and wall, shape, shade, and color, more an abstract design or collage than anything familiar (62, 68–69). This, too, is a device employed by Resnais as, for example, a darkened screen only becomes recognizable as a mound of hair as the camera slowly withdraws and takes its distance, or, conversely, when the camera, panning around the gas chamber, focuses in on a corner of wall and ceiling to highlight the nail marks left by frantic victims. Just as Cayrol warns us that we need to know how to read the abstract inscription left by nail-marks on the ceiling as a sign, so the unfamiliar shapes of Hammadi's photos incite us to read the remains as complex signs.

Sliding perspectives, uncertain positioning, the questioning eye, and the transformation of the familiar into the unfamiliar are all techniques employed by Resnais in the filming of the concentration camps and adopted in this text by Hammadi to record the penal colony. The quest for the human traces and inscriptions left on the material remains of the colony discussed by Chamoiseau in the text, which is itself a fundamental aspect of *Night and Fog* (not least in the example of the scratch marks on the ceiling), are vividly displayed in the photos (54, 62, 112, 113). In part, they humanize these places of dehu-

---

14. See my "Horror and the Everyday in Post-Holocaust France: *Nuit et brouillard* and Concentrationary Art," *French Cultural Studies* 17/1 (2006): 5–18.

manization. Elsewhere, the words written above doors and gates ("cells," 52; "blockhaus," 82–83; "library," 86; "court-room," 88; "punishment area," 89) are the dehumanizing inscriptions that Chamoiseau, following Cayrol, ironically critiques as concentrationary language. The ambiguities of human inscription are captured movingly in Hammadi's photos; the memory-trace recalls both humanity and its denial. Nowhere is this more apparent than in the photo of the entrance to the camp where the words "Camp de la transportation" are written above the archway (98–99). Chamoiseau discusses the yawning gap between the words and the reality they designate (see above), but it is only Hammadi's photo that reminds us of the mocking words "Arbeit macht frei" over the entrance to Auschwitz.

Finally, Chamoiseau's description of the murals painted over a period of eight years by one of the prisoners in the church Saint-Joseph d'Iracoubo as "a noble cry" (40) recalls "the endless cry" of suffering which closes *Night and Fog*, and Chamoiseau's image of a ruined wall transformed into "a worrying stele" (43) evokes the final image of Resnais's film. Text and image overlay one camp with another, one site of terror with another, and highlight the interconnections inherent in cultural memory. In her profound book on space in the works of Patrick Chamoiseau, Lorna Milne discusses parallels between traumatic memory related to the Holocaust and to the history of Martinique.[15] However, the memory-traces explored in the penal colony in Guiana do not so much relate one trauma to another (which implies their separate and relative status) as connect and overlay them in a complex network of meaning. The memory-traces are, in Paul Gilroy's words, "between camps" rather than within them.[16]

THE REMAINS OF THE DAY

In her fascinating discussion of fascism and representation, the philosopher Gillian Rose criticizes the different techniques we employ (consciously and unconsciously) to distance ourselves from responsibility for acts of horrific violence. Using the metaphor of stages of the day, she suggests that if the beginnings of the day announce brave new worlds of human perfection (fascism and communism), and

---

15. Lorna Milne, *Patrick Chamoiseau: Espaces d'une écriture antillaise* (Amsterdam and New York: Rodopi, 2006), 44–49.
16. Paul Gilroy, *Between Camps: Culture, Nation and the Allure of Race* (London: Routledge, 2000/2004).

the middle of the day sees us reflecting on the catastrophe of these unfulfilled promises ("the broken middle," as Rose calls it), then it is only at the remains of the day that we can look back at "the ruins of the morning's hope, the actuality of the broken middles") to assess the day not as external observers of a damaged history but in terms of our fraught and complex relationship with that history, and with representation itself.[17] Rose argues that Kazuo Ishiguro's 1989 novel *The Remains of the Day* (and the 1993 Merchant Ivory film version) is just such a mature reflection as it does not represent fascism by leaving our own integrity intact (in the manner of a film like Steven Spielberg's *Schindler's List*, for example) or denounce representation entirely (in the manner of pronouncements by Claude Lanzamnn on representations of the Holocaust), but engages with representation to expose us to our own complicity with and response to the fascism represented. Rose suggests that being at the remains of the day—after the false dawns of utopian ideologies and the "broken middles" of sanctimonious critique—entails an awareness of the ambiguities of our compromised position as a basis for all action.

I propose that *Guyane* also shows us at the remains of the day. The wandering journey undertaken by Chamoiseau and Hammadi through the remains of the penal colony is undoubtedly a challenge to the haughty ideals of the colonial project and to the History written and monuments erected to inscribe it in fact. But the awakening of memory-traces by writer and photographer in the ruins of this utopian project does not simply expose the folly of power from the position of the self-righteous victim who has been written out of History. In Rose's terms, this would leave us still at the middle of the day, our sentimentality left intact as we look back, voyeuristically, at the ruins of empire-building.[18] The "sedimented memory" of the memory-traces leaves us at the

---

17. Gillian Rose, *Mourning Becomes the Law: Philosophy and Representation* (Cambridge: Cambridge University Press, 1996). See Chapter 2, "Beginnings of the Day: Fascism and Representation" (41–62), 42.

18. Defining our paradoxical situation as caught between the poles of "the representation of Fascism and the fascism of representation," Rose critiques simplistic portrayals of the opposition between oppressors and oppressed: "The representation of Fascism and the fascism of representation does not work with the opposition between the agent of imperial domination and the oppressed other. It points out that 'the other' is also an agent, enraged and invested; while the idea of the monolithic, imperialist agent amounts to the consolidation and reification of power, the dilemma of which is thereby disowned. The representation of Fascism and the fascism of representation does not oppose the idea of totalising power to the degrading of its others, nor does it propose cul-

remains of the day because it denies us any such vantage point or privileged perspective outside the knots of memory within which we ourselves are located. By transforming the site of the ruins into a haunted space, the memory-trace conjoins past and present, here and there, today's observers and former actors, in such a way as to preclude voyeuristic distance. In the "ambiguous zone" of the ruins, binary distinctions dissolve into a more complex space. The monument and the memory-trace are not opposites; the memory-trace is, instead, the paradoxical in-between state in which the autonomy, power, and self-presence of the monument are doubled by their own connectedness, vulnerability, and absence. Hammadi's photos capture this paradox perfectly as they show both the solidity and evanescence of buildings, the porous relationship between culture and nature as the luxurious vegetation reclaims the site of the colony, the ambiguous positions of inside and outside as the angles and perspectives fracture clear delineations and distinctions. Chamoiseau describes the mix of humanity and inhumanity of the penal colony in oxymoronic terms (and using a vocabulary which once again recalls the concentration camps) as "a hallucinating concentration of what makes up Man: a combustion of light and shade, of light in shade and shade which illuminates" (19).

At the remains of the day, distinctions are blurred and opposites confused. "The prisoner and the prison-guard are linked together in the same gasp in which the overwhelming desire to survive and the all-embracing nature of the power to punish have mired both in the same rot" (29–30). The reality of this space is one of collusion ("In the transportation camp . . . we should stop in the shadows, and wait for this testimony of a morbid collusion between the prisoner and the shadow," 33), complicity ("I confess that the shadow was complicitous and the light was not always so," 34) and contamination (the trace of one in the other). The remains of the day offers a vision in which the singularity of the present metamorphoses into a paradoxical constellation that denies the dichotomy between singularity and plurality.[19] Chamoiseau's hybrid (and impossible) term "la Trace-mé-

---

tural pluralism as its expiation. It understands all agents *in power and out of it* to face the dilemma of asserting their moral will solely to guard their particular interests." Rose, *Mourning Becomes the Law*, 62.

19. I have written about the "othering" of the singular in relation to Hélène Cixoux's "Bare feet" and Jacques Derrida's *Monolingualism of the Other: or, the Prosthesis of Origin* in "Knotted Intersections: Cixous and Derrida," *Wasafiri* 57 (Spring 2009), 9–13.

moires" captures this paradox perfectly by connecting the upper-case "T" and singular noun of "Trace" with the lower-case "m" and plural noun of "mémoires." It suggests that History and histories, and the monument and the memory-traces are both singular and plural at the same time, one always in the other. Chamoiseau states this clearly: "The memory-Traces are both collective and individual, vertical and horizontal, of one community and trans-communitarian, fixed and mobile, and fragile" (17). More recently, writing about Martinique in *Écrire en pays dominé* (1997), he describes this hybrid network once again through the metaphor of the knot: "I am announcing here a site (*un Lieu*) . . . , a sovereign Meta-Nation, mixed and tangled with all the countries in the world, haughty and interdependent, knotted and unknotted in the Stone-World (Pierre-Monde)."[20]

Reading *Guyane* as a poetico-historical meditation on memory "at the remains of the day" gives us a particular way of understanding "noeuds de mémoire" in relation to racialized violence, horror, and dehumanization. The knots of the memory-trace mean that we are never simply there where we find ourselves but split across different times and spaces. We are situated within a complex history with no possibility of escape to take the distanced view. To pretend otherwise is to indulge in the folly of hubris and mastery that leads to the erection of camps and colonies. *Guyane: Traces-mémoires du bagne* offers us hope that this folly can one day be avoided, not by offering us total liberation from a camp mentality but rather an awareness of our complicity in the very site on which that mentality is founded.

---

20. Cited in Lorna Milne, *Patrick Chamoiseau: Espaces d'une écriture antillaise*, 182. Stones appear in the quote by Victor Segalen that Chamoiseau uses as a preface to *Guyane*: "Alone, immobile against the tide, here are the memorial Stones that no order of erosion can touch or loosen. They remain." As McCusker says of stones in Chamoiseau's work, emphasizing the ambiguous temporality in his writing, "These ancient formations are at once outside time and deply imbricated in it; they suggest a connection to a time beyond memory, while they simultaneously—by virtue of their very age and physical scale—encourage reflection on the past. It is through their timelessness, indeed, that they can be made to speak to every time." (McCusker, *Patrick Chamoiseau: Recovering Memory*, 117.)

Contributors

DAVID CARON is Professor of French and Women's Studies at the University of Michigan. He is the author of *AIDS in French Culture: Social Ills, Literary Cures* (Wisconsin 2001) and *My Father and I: The Marais and the Queerness of Community* (Cornell 2009). He is currently working on a book on tact, and on a collection of essays on the work of Charlotte Delbo.

ROSS CHAMBERS retired from the University of Michigan in 2002. His critical and theoretical work—on figures like Nerval, Baudelaire, and Rimbaud; on the pragmatics of narrative; and on the genre of testimonial—arguably revolves around the concept of oppositionality (as opposed to resistance) in relation to power.

ELIZABETH EZRA is Professor of Cinema and Culture at the University of Stirling in Scotland. She is the author of *The Colonial Unconscious* (Cornell University Press, 2000), *Georges Méliès* (Manchester University Press, 2000), and *Jean-Pierre Jeunet* (University of Illinois Press, 2008). She is the editor of *European Cinema* (Oxford University Press, 2004), and co-editor (with Sue Harris) of *France in Focus* (Berg, 2000), and (with Terry Rowden) of *Transnational Cinema: The Film Reader* (Routledge, 2006).

JIM HOUSE is Senior Lecturer in French at the University of Leeds. He is the author (with Neil MacMaster) of *Paris 1961: Algerians, State Terror, and Memory* (Oxford University Press, 2006), and has published articles and chapters on colonial repression, colonial migration, memory, and antiracism. He is currently writing a social and political history of late-colonial Algiers and Casablanca.

FRANÇOISE LIONNET is Professor of French and Francophone Studies, Comparative Literature, and Women's Studies at UCLA, and co-director of the Mellon project on "Cultures in Transnational Perspective." Recent publications include two co-edited volumes, *Minor Transnationalism* (Duke University Press, 2005) and *The Creolization of Theory* (Duke University Press, 2010). She is completing *The Indies, Otherwise: Creolization, Comparison and the Dissonances of Globalization* (forthcoming, Stanford University Press).

BILL MARSHALL is Professor of Comparative Literary and Cultural Studies and Head of the School of Languages, Cultures and Religions at the University of Stirling, Scotland. He is the author of *Victor Serge: The Uses of Dissent* (1992), *Guy Hocquenghem* (1996), *Quebec National Cinema* (2001), *André Téchiné* (2007), and *The French Atlantic: Travels in Culture and History* (2009). He has also edited works on *Musicals* (2000), *Montreal-Glasgow* (2005), and a three volume encyclopedia on *France and the Americas* (2005).

MICHAEL ROTHBERG is Professor of English and Conrad Humanities Scholar at the University of Illinois at Urbana-Champaign, where he also directs the Holocaust, Genocide, and Memory Studies Initiative. He is the author of *Multidirectional Memory: Remembering the Holocaust in the Age of Decolonization* (2009) and *Traumatic Realism: The Demands of Holocaust Representation* (2000). He has also co-edited *The Holocaust: Theoretical Readings* (2003) and *Cary Nelson and the Struggle for the University: Poetry, Politics, and the Profession* (2009).

DEBARATI SANYAL is Associate Professor of French at the University of California-Berkeley. She is the author of *The Violence of Modernity: Baudelaire, Irony and the Politics of Form* (Hopkins, 2006) and has published articles on nineteenth-century poetry, World War II, the Holocaust, and postwar France. She is currently working on a book titled *Dangerous Intersections: Allegory, Complicity and Memory in Postwar France*.

LIBBY SAXTON is Senior Lecturer in French and Film at Queen Mary University of London. She is author of *Haunted Images: Film, Ethics, Testimony and the Holocaust* (Wallflower, 2008), co-author, with Lisa Downing, of *Film and Ethics: Foreclosed Encounters* (Routledge, 2009), and co-editor, with Simon Kemp, of *Seeing Things: Vision, Perception and Interpretation in French Studies* (Peter Lang, 2002).

CONTRIBUTORS 241

RONNIE SCHARFMAN is Professor Emerita of French at Purchase College and has published widely on Francophone authors from the Maghreb and the Antilles, including the Jewish writers El Maleh, André Schwarz-Bart, and Edmond Jabès, for 30 years. Her book, *Engagement and the Language of the Subject in the Poetry of Aimé Césaire* (University of Florida Press, 1987), won a Gilbert Chinard Literary Prize. She co-edited a volume of *Yale French Studies* on "Post/Colonial Conditions" with Françoise Lionnet in 1993, and an anthology of French and Francophone women writers, *Ecritures de Femmes* (Yale University Press, 1996) with Mary Ann Caws, Marianne Hirsch, and Mary Jean Green.

MAX SILVERMAN is Professor of Modern French Studies at the University of Leeds. He has written two monographs, *Deconstructing the Nation* (1992) and *Facing Postmodernity* (1999), and has edited works on *Race, Discourse and Power in France* (1991) and *Frantz Fanon's 'Black Skin, White Masks'* (2005). He is currently writing a monograph on connections between the Holocaust and colonialism in the French cultural imaginary and directing a project with Griselda Pollock on "Concentrationary memories and the politics of representation."

ESTELLE TARICA is Associate Professor of Latin American Literature and Culture at the University of California, Berkeley. She is the author of *The Inner Life of Mestizo Nationalism* (Minnesota 2008) as well as numerous articles on race and nation in Spanish America. She is currently working on a book about the presence of the Holocaust in Latin America.

FRANÇOISE VERGÈS is Consulting Professor at Goldsmiths College, London, director of the scientific and cultural team of the forthcoming museum and cultural center in Reunion Island, Maison des civilisations et de l'unité réunionnaise (www.mcur.re) and president of the Comité pour la mémoire et l'histoire de l'esclavage (www.comite-memoire-esclavage.fr). She writes on memory, slavery, the colony and postcolony, race, and citizenship.

Yale French Studies is the oldest English-language journal in the United States devoted to French and Francophone literature and culture. Each volume is conceived and organized by a guest editor or editors around a particular theme or author. Interdisciplinary approaches are particularly welcome, as are contributions from scholars and writers from around the world. Recent volumes have been devoted to a wide variety of subjects, among them: Lévinas; Perec; Paulhan; Haiti; Belgium; Crime Fiction; Surrealism; Material Culture in Medieval and Renaissance France; and French Education.

Yale French Studies is published twice yearly by Yale University Press (yalebooks.com) and may be accessed on JSTOR (jstor.org).

For information on how to submit a proposal for a volume of *Yale French Studies,* visit yale.edu/french and click "Yale French Studies."